An Historical Geography
of Scotland

D0770555

An Historical Geography of Scotland

Edited by

G. Whittington

Department of Geography
St Salvator's College
University of St Andrews
St Andrews
Fife
Scotland

I. D. Whyte

Department of Geography
University of Lancaster
Lancaster
England

ACADEMIC PRESS 1983
A Subsidiary of Harcourt Brace Jovanovich, Publishers
London   New York
Paris   San Diego   San Francisco
São Paulo   Sydney   Tokyo   Toronto

ACADEMIC PRESS INC. (LONDON) LTD
24/28 Oval Road, London NW1 7DX

United States Edition published by
ACADEMIC PRESS INC.
111 Fifth Avenue, New York, New York, 10003

British Library Cataloguing in Publication Data

An historical geography of Scotland.
1. Scotland—Geography, Historical
I. Whittington, G.   II. Whyte, I. D.
            911'.411   DA760

ISBN 0-12-747360-2 Casebound edition
ISBN 0-12-747362-9 Paperback edition

Photoset in Great Britain by
Rowland Phototypesetting Ltd, Bury St Edmunds, Suffolk
and printed by St Edmundsbury Press,
Bury St Edmunds, Suffolk

Contributors

G. Clark Department of Geography, The University, Bailrigg, Lancaster, LA1 4YR, England

R. A. Dodgshon Department of Geography, University College of Wales, Llandinam Building, Penglais, Aberystwyth, Dyfed SY23 3DB, Wales

J. Doherty Department of Geography, St Salvator's College, The University, St Andrews, Fife, KY16 9AL, Scotland

R. Fox Department of Geography, Kenyatta University College, PO Box 43844, Nairobi, Kenya

G. Gordon Department of Geography, The University of Strathclyde, Livingstone Tower, Richmond Street, Glasgow, G1 1XW, Scotland

H. Jones Department of Geography, The University, Perth Road, Dundee, DD1 4HN, Scotland

I. A. Morrison Department of Geography, The University, Drummond Sheet, Edinburgh, EH8 9XP, Scotland

A. Small Department of Geography, The University, Perth Road, Dundee, DD1 4HN, Scotland

D. Turnock Department of Geography, The University, University Road, Leicester, LE1 7RH, England

G. Whittington Department of Geography, St Salvator's College, The University, St Andrews, Fife, KY16 9AL, Scotland

I. D. Whyte Department of Geography, The University, Bailrigg, Lancaster, LA1 4YR, England

Preface

The year 1978 saw the publication of *An Historical Geography of England and Wales*, and inevitably a volume entitled *An Historical Geography of Scotland* will be seen as a sister and complementary volume to that earlier work. The needs for such a volume on Scotland have the same origins as those referred to by Dodgshon and Butlin in the preface to their book on England and Wales. However, before a direct parallel is drawn between the two volumes, it must be pointed out that Scottish historical geographers do start from a different base compared with that enjoyed by their colleagues in England. Despite the appearance of *An Historical Geography of Scotland* in 1926, there is no long tradition of historical geography in Scotland and there are no comparable milestones to those erected by H. C. Darby in England. The number of historical geographers working on Scottish topics is still too small to allow any satisfaction as to the future of Scottish historical geography. The gaps left in this volume by, for example, the lack of chapters on the development of transport or the importance of the church, along with other institutional structures, are bound to be seen as flaws. Such omissions provide one of the ills besetting Scottish historical geography and, serious though it may be, it can be cured. The oft-quoted lack of early documentation as a cause of this ill cannot really be supported; Scotland's archival resources may be lacking in some respects when compared with England's but they are also different and in some cases richer. More problematic than the gaps in our present knowledge is the lack of critical thinking which marks many of the writings on Scottish topics. There are also a lack of methodological commitment and still too unbalanced an involvement with agrarian and rural settlement features to the exclusion of most other topics, the hallmark of British historical geography in general until the 1970s. Industry, population and urbanism are topics still too little regarded. There has also been scant concern with attempts to explain the role of the general populace in the creation of Scotland's past geographies.

What then of the future for this branch of geographical study in Scotland? Its practitioners are faced with an apparent dilemma. Should they be concerned with Scottish historical geography or with historical geography in Scotland? There is so much to explain about Scotland's past that immersion in Scottish material is vital. This must not, however, be used to continue what has been an all too prevalent practice: that of concentrating on features that are felt to be singularly Scottish. There is a need to place things Scottish into a wider areal context. Advances that have been made in Scottish historical geography owe much to the references that have been made to practices elsewhere, especially those of Wales, England, Germany and Scandinavia. Our present understanding of infield–outfield origins, rural settlement evolution, and land tenure all owe much to a shedding of parochial attitudes. An involvement in all areas of Scottish historical geography with the wider European experience instead of the continuation of a narrow, myopic national view can only lead to a quicker pace of understanding. To that end, it is hoped, this present book will provide a springboard. It, along with a recent volume on *The Making of the Scottish Countryside* (Parry and Slater, 1980; see references to Chapter 1), has established a broad synthesis, mainly of a chronological nature, which should allow a more adventurous exploration of Scotland's past geographies, involving a further move away from description towards analysis based upon a greater critical and methodological awareness. Unless such progress is made it might be thought, with much justification, that Hadrian is still alive and keeping his wall in good repair.

G. Whittington   *I. Whyte*
January 1983

Contents

List of Illustrations

List of Tables

1
Prehistoric Scotland

I. A. Morrison

To start a book on 'historical' geography with a chapter on 'pre'-history may seem paradoxical. There is, however, no clear point after which all that the 'historical' geographer wishes to know about the evolution of landscape and settlement in Scotland is fully illuminated by written records. For most periods there are lacunae in the documentary cover of particular regions or whole themes. Thus although the area we now call Scotland may technically emerge from prehistory when it figures briefly in the writings of Tacitus or Cassius Dio, for long after that the techniques of archaeology for retrieving data preserved in the soil or in structures and artefacts rather than on the page can remain useful. Even those working on the nineteenth century may find themselves turning to air photographs and excavation to capture aspects of landscape evolution that have eluded historical record.

Alongside the artificiality of the distinction between document-based and other approaches, there is a more compelling reason for including a prehistoric prelude here. Each generation appraises in its own terms not some hypothetical 'natural' landscape, but whatever its forebears have left it. The writer once coined the phrase The Inherited Landscape to keep before his students the fact that in inhabited lands human groups seldom confront any landscape that has remained unaffected by the lives of their predecessors.

Much of the remainder of this book deals with a Scotland heavily reliant on subsistence agriculture and with the country's latter-day transition to an industrialized and urbanized society. The present chapter seeks to complement this by considering the much earlier transitions that form the essential foundation without which these later phases would not have developed in ways familiar to us, i.e. the local adoption of agriculture and beyond that the colonization of the country and its initial exploitation by non-agricultural societies.

Because of the relative recency of severe glaciation, the story of continuous human occupation in Scotland seems short compared to many other areas of the world. None the less a review of 'Prehistoric' Scotland covers as many millennia as some of the following chapters cover decades. It would be unprofitable to attempt a compressed narrative of the whole sequence of events, especially as recent accounts are available (notably A. and G. Ritchie, 1981; Megaw and Simpson, 1979). These give particular attention to phases from the Neolithic onwards, so here fuller treatment will be given to preceding stages.

This is also appropriate in another respect. A main aim in the present context is to use the long view given by prehistory to provide a perspective against which the evolving patterns of Scotland's later geography may be considered. Although the environmental changes of later times merit attention in their own right, the scale and nature of the events that typified the millennia prior to the Neolithic give this earlier period an especial importance. The legacy of what happened then has had a major role in shaping the problems and potential of the landscapes of Scotland for the inhabitants of later times, right through to the present day.

It is perhaps also salutary to focus on the earlier period in another respect. For at least the first half of what we suspect has been the span of man in Scotland, the people lived as hunters and gatherers. Yet Atkinson envisaged that Neolithic farmers arrived to be 'confronted with a terrain hitherto virtually uninhabited, and certainly unchanged by man from its natural condition' (1962, 7). Certainly, at the start landscape evolution was dominated by the processes of nature, but in general these were to give way increasingly to those initiated by man. Even this early natural dominance must however, be regarded as relative, rather than absolute; in considering the earliest pre-agricultural communities of which we have evidence, it is now becoming clear that one should not neglect the possibility that they were already modifying aspects of their environments that were critical for their subsistence. Equally, at the present day, in assessing which options of land use may be economic, one can not affort to discount the realities of Scotland's physiography and regional climates. Throughout, it is necessary to assume that successive landscape developments reflect not single factors but complex interactions. On the one hand are cultural aims, technological and economic capabilities; on the other, interlinked non-anthropogenic influences, involving natural processes which themselves vary markedly through time.

In what follows, especial attention is thus given to the legacy of the prehistoric past in environmental terms because of its wider relevance to the historical geography of Scotland in later times. Cultural aspects of the relationship between change and continuity are also explored, and the chapter ends by considering to what extent settlement types evident in the later stages of the fully prehistoric period were also characteristic of early historic Scotland.

THE PLEISTOCENE: THE EARLIEST POTENTIAL FOR COLONIZATION

It is not known when the area now called Scotland first acquired 'human' geography. Some of the numerous Pleistocene interglacials were longer and climatically more hospitable than the present Holocene 'post-glacial' phase, and it is by no means inconceivable that people moved into Scotland during some of these interglacials. Indeed, even during the less favourable minor interstadials some of the Palaeolithic cultures highly adapted to life in tundra environments could certainly have coped with periglacial conditions in Scotland.

Evidence has been found of the animals, including reindeer, that such groups exploited. A woolly rhinoceros bone was found at Bishopbriggs near Glasgow (Rolfe, 1966), and remains of mammoths have come to light along the Clyde, at Kilmaurs in Ayrshire (Ritchie, 1920; Shotton et al., 1970; Sissons, 1976), and at St Fort in Fife (found 1976; Dundee Museum). These all appear to date from phases in the last major glacial cycle of the Pleistocene. Unfortunately little direct evidence of the long sequence of previous cycles, well attested elsewhere, has survived the effects of the last ice sheets which engulfed Scotland.

With each successive glaciation reworking and dispersing the deposits of its predecessors, almost no organic material from full interglacials has been found. The first such deposit that has been securely identified survived because of its location in north Shetland, far from the centres of subsequent major ice activity (Birks and Ransom, 1969). With even the thousands of tons of natural organic material that must have accumulated now so poorly represented, the chance of happening upon the sparse relics of any Palaeolithic population must be very slight and the date of the initial colonization may always remain a matter of speculation.

The last full ice sheet probably reached its maximum around 15 000 b.c. Whether or not people had been in Scotland previously, at that time north Britain would have been essentially uninhabitable. An ice-free enclave in the north-east has been claimed, but doubts about it persist (Clapperton and Sugden, 1975): even if it had existed, the ice would have totally surrounded it (Synge, 1956) and possibly the whole Scottish mainland was covered.

Deglaciation appears to have occurred in irregular stages, and Sissons (1979a) has suggested that Scotland may first have become fully ice-free again between 11 000 and 10 500 b.c. It is to this period that two flint points from Jura in the Inner Hebrides have been attributed (Mercer, 1980). Both are incomplete, however, and come from secondary deposits (one being the present beach) in which large numbers of artefacts from much later periods are mixed. There is no direct chronometric or stratigraphic evidence for the proposed date for the flint points. This rests only on the excavator's view of their typology. It seems probably that out of the several thousand flint artefacts collected there, these two broken and rolled examples might bear some resemblence to earlier forms, either fortuitously or because of persistence of tradition, without necessarily being older than the Mesolithic material among which they were found. Stronger evidence would seem necessary before accepting them as the first Palaeolithic artefacts to have been recovered in Scotland. Caution is particularly advisable in light of the recent review by Jacobi (1980) of Palaeolithic resettlement on deglaciation, in Britain as a whole.

The intermission of *c*. 11 000 b.c. was a short one. Glaciers may have started to reappear in some areas by 9500 b.c. (Sissons, 1979b), and although by no means all the country was covered, in the western Highlands ice reached 600 m in thickness and major glaciers pushed into the lowlands. One emerged from the trough now occupied by Loch Lomond, and this last very cold period is usually known as the Loch Lomond Stadial. There is some divergence in the dates suggested for its end, but most would agree that the glaciers had disappeared several centuries before 8000 b.c. and that Scotland entered the Holocene ice free.

The repeated glaciations of Scotland, together with their severity and the relative recency of their latest phases, have had effects which go far beyond their bearing on the survival of evidence for possible Palaeolithic populations. The human significance of the events of the Pleistocene period for later times is undeniable.

The predominantly western distribution of the ice had reflected the interaction between the pattern of Scotland's mountains and maritime climatic influences. The contrast between the Atlantic zone and the drier, more 'continental', east-facing side of the country forms a *leitmotiv* that recurs in varying forms through much of Scotland's prehistoric and historical geography, as well as influencing the ways in which glaciation affected different parts of the country.

The interactions between the geology of Scotland and the processes of erosion and deposition associated with the ice have influenced not only the patterns of routeways that have been practicable at each technological level. They have often been an element in the basic options available for subsistence and for the location of settlements, from prehistory to modern times. Thus, the terrain has been made more rugged in some areas, smoothed in others. Extensive areas have been stripped to bedrock; others have been deeply buried in till or fluvioglacial sands and gravels, of markedly varying usefulness. Even soils of good potential were often littered with stones and boulders in great profusion, while the processes of both erosion and desposition tended to leave landscapes with disrupted drainage.

The problem of coping with this legacy, in all its regional variations, was not restricted to the prehistoric inhabitants of the country. It has remained part of the life of those who have occupied Scotland throughout historical times.

THE EARLY HOLOCENE: SCOTLAND WITHOUT FARMERS

Although the Pleistocene left a lasting legacy, this is not to say that Scotland has been characterized since then by a static fossil landscape. On the contrary, the picture in the succeeding 10000 years of the Holocene is a dynamic one, with change itself the norm. Nor is this change only a record of the increasingly pervasive influence of man. The wide perspective of prehistory brings out the potential human importance of long-term secular variations in environmental factors in Scotland, tending to support Parry's view (1978) that such changes also merit more thorough investigation in historical periods.

During the earlier parts of the Holocene, the environmental impact of human groups was clearly less than it was to become later when population grew and technological momentum increased. The relative importance of natural agencies of change also reflects the fact that these were particularly active in Scotland then.

In the opening millennia of the Holocene, not only the climate, vegetation and fauna but the whole outline of the country changed markedly. The glacio-eustatic effect of the large amounts of water remaining locked up in the ice sheets of areas such as Canada and Scandinavia meant that the oceans were still far below their present level (e.g. Morrison, 1976). What is now Scotland was then part of continental Europe. While the southern part of the present North Sea basin was still dry land, round much of the periphery of Scotland shorelines lay far to seawards of their present positions (Morrison, 1980a,b). Many of the Northern and Western Isles were then continuous blocks of land.

Although many of Scotland's early postglacial shorelines are now submerged, this is not true of all of them. The glacio-isostatic depression of the land caused by the weight of the ice was still severe after 8000 b.c. in areas near former centres of glacial loading. Thus, some areas that have since been raised by isostatic recovery to positions above present sea level were below even the depressed ocean level of that time. The progress of the ensuing upward race between rebounding land and rising ocean level was a complex one. Even in rapidly rising areas, such as the upper estuaries of the Tay and Forth, the slowing uplift of the land was usually outstripped several times by the ocean rise, before this in turn slackened as the major Scandinavian and Canadian ice sheets finally melted. The early Holocene shorelines thus tend to have an overburden of later estuarine and marine deposits, even where the persistence of land uplift has eventually left them well inland, above today's coasts.

Thus, just as the immediate effects of glaciation militate against the recovery of Palaeolithic material in Scotland, so too does the postglacial aftermath of glacio-eustasy and glacio-isostasy work against the prospect of finding many coastal Mesolithic sites from the earlier millennia of the Holocene. It seems that most Scottish shorelines dating from before c. 5000 b.c. must be sought either underwater or underground (Morrison, 1980a; Sissons, 1976). Finds have been made from such contexts, but not surprisingly they are few in number.

It used to be widely assumed that the relationship between Scottish archaeological material and sea level change could be reduced to a simple model, the concept of 'the 25 foot raised beach'. This came to be regarded by some as an 'Early Post-Glacial Raised Beach' (e.g. Lacaille, 1954, 55), with implications for the early dating of material believed to be Mesolithic. It is now clear that this view is untenable and indeed that Jamieson (whose classic work in the nineteenth century had led to the identification of glacio-isostasy) was right when as early as 1906 he dismissed the whole concept of late-glacial '100 foot' and post-glacial '25 foot' raised beaches in Scotland as mere 'articles of faith' rather than observed facts (Morrison, 1969, 1980a).

Because the need for accurate, detailed measurements of shoreline displacements was not generally appreciated, these conveniently uncomplicated concepts persisted until by the middle of the twentieth century faith in them was such that even Gordon Childe did not question that the age of the early cultures of hunters and gatherers of Scotland was 'guaranteed by geology, for they lived on the shore of the sea, when its waters stood some twenty-five feet higher than today' (1946, 3). Indeed, the '100 foot' and '25 foot raised beaches' still figure in at least one recent archaeological textbook (Morrison, A., 1980, 103).

Major geomorphological survey programmes by numerous workers (summary with references in Sissons, 1976) have confirmed that while many former shoreline features may be found along the 100 foot and 25 foot contours, these belong to complex suites of tilted shorelines of a wide range of ages. They slope through these height bands at varied gradients which reflect their histories of isostatic displacement.

Whatever their problems for archaeological chronology, the prehistoric changes in the levels of land and sea, like the more direct effects of glaciation, have a practical human significance in Scotland that extends from early times through to the present day. Elevated marine benches form the basic site for many settlements, and fossil cliff lines have influenced their layout. Late- and post-glacial raised beaches have provided extensive areas of lighter soils: better drained and quicker to warm in the spring than heavy glacial till, these have been appreciated by farmers of many periods. Blown shell sand, in part derived from areas beyond present coasts, has provided the special environment of the machair (e.g. Simpson, 1976) but has also created dune areas of low productivity. Raised estuarine deposits such as those of the Forth valley have often proved negative areas for millennia, merely accumulating peat until the major technical and economic problems of drainage could be tackled to release their potential for agriculture (and subsequently as flat-land sites for industry).

The marked coastal changes following upon deglaciation accompanied a rapid climatic amelioration. In Scotland although the warming showed up promptly in mobile insect faunas (e.g. Coope, 1977), more time elapsed before it worked through the processes of plant colonization. The re-establishment of the flora was retarded not only by distance from the main source areas but also by the unstable slopes and soil destruction brought about by recent glacial and periglacial activity. Furthermore, in the extensive upland areas the marked altitudinal deterioration of climate, characteristic of much of Highland Britain (e.g. Taylor, 1976), enhanced the delay. Smith and Pilcher (1973) have drawn attention to the diachroneity of pollen zonations, with characteristic stages in the Holocene vegetation succession being delayed by as much as a millennium or a millennium and a half in upland areas.

In Scotland it seems that the major forest patterns of prehistory were eventually established by around 4000 b.c. (Birks, 1977). These and the successions leading up to them varied across the country, reflecting the regional differentiation of climate by relief in ways that foreshadow patterns familiar in later times. Thus, in the comparatively mild area comprising the south of Scotland and much of the west coast, initial juniper scrub soon tended to be replaced by birch-hazel woodland, which was well established by 7000 b.c. When Scots pine arrived about 6000 b.c., it had little success in competing either with the existing flora or with the oak and elm which later replaced the hazel. The Lowlands and Southern Uplands, together with the western coastal strip as far north as Skye, thus came to support an oak forest with birches.

Most of Scotland north of the Highland line, however, became characterized by pine forest, with subsidiary birch and oak. There is some evidence (e.g. McVean and Radcliff, 1962) that birch did better than pine in the eastern coastal lowlands where both soils and climate were more suitable. In the Cairngorms, juniper long remained important in open woodland, and hazel was never as prolific as to the south and west. From its arrival about 5000 b.c. the Scots pine expanded at the expense of birch which had until then been important despite the poor acidic soils. Along with the severe Cairngorm climate, these had tended to minimize competition from oak and elm.

In the far north and west of the mainland and in the outlying islands birch and hazel were in general the only trees that could cope where there was exposure to the frequent gales. In sheltered localities other tree species might be found, though the birch tended to predominate. Tree species are recorded from Orkney and Shetland, but tall-herb and scrub communities seem to have been much more typical there. Several of the smaller of the Hebridean islands, e.g. Barra and Canna (Birks, 1977), show at most dwarf shrub heaths with seemingly no tree development at all during the Holocene.

A strong regional patterning is thus evident. The way this shows through the flux of detailed changes accompanying the major environmental variations of the earlier part of the Holocene helps to identify basic characteristics of Scotland's physical geography that can profitably be kept in mind when considering the more moderate variations of later times. The importance of altitude has already been noted. The pattern of forest development reinforces this but also underlines the significance of factors that qualify its effect, both locally and across the country.

Substantial areas of the upland massifs that occupy so much of Scotland afford little shelter, and this has enhanced the value of any local factors that ameliorate microclimate. The detailed pattern of the terrain can produce significant variations over short distances, not only in protection from the wind but in orographic rainfall, local cloud cover and hence insolation. Slope steepness and aspect can be critical: in these latitudes, a south-facing slope may be almost half as warm again as a north-facing one (Taylor, 1967). The Soil Survey of Scotland has attempted to map present-day bioclimatic subregions (Macaulay Institute, 1970, 1971). Although the lack of a close network of stations recording ground-level microclimate makes the documentation of these variations problematic, they are no less real for that. Farmers coping with areas of marginal agricultural potential are very aware that the upper limits of viable cultivation in Scotland can vary markedly within a very small compass. These factors leading towards local diversity are not anarchic. Because they operate in consistent and inter-related ways, they have tended to produce mosaics of landscape units in which characteristic tesserae recur as a result of the interplay between terrain, climate, and the cultural level current at a given period.

Superimposed upon the details of the mosaic are the broader country-wide trends that influence the regional combinations of the landscape units and the altitudes at which they are represented. Compared to more continental regimes, oceanic climates suffer a relatively rapid deterioration with increasing altitude. Scotland as a whole is more subject to this effect than many parts of Europe with higher mountains. Even within the country there have always been notable east–west as well as north–south differences in altitudinal limits for plant communities and subsequently for crops too. Conditions in the Northern and Western Isles and in West Highland areas fully exposed to the Atlantic weather often contrast unfavourably with those at much higher altitudes in the sunnier east.

Where the curve of annual temperature is flattened by the moderating effect of the Atlantic, the rise of temperature in spring is slow and the rate of decrease in the length of the growing season with increasing altitude is accordingly serious. Furthermore, when the temperature is only marginally above plant growth thresholds, rates of growth are low and there is greater vulnerability to minor variations in warmth and precipitation. In view of these constraints, the effectiveness of the cultural adaptations involved in supporting the populations later achieved in some of the Atlantic crofting areas should not be under-rated. Equally, the early vegetation of such bioclimatically marginal areas must be presumed to have been vulnerable to the impact (inadvertent or deliberate) of even quite sparse prehistoric populations at low levels of technology.

However, it is not yet clear when human groups first began to modify the early Holocene landscapes of Scotland. The difficulty of detection has been enhanced by the submergence and burial of the shorelines from this phase, when the coastal zone often figured prominently in Mesolithic economies. The rate of natural change in the millennia immediately following glaciation makes it difficult to discern whether or not the pollen record may include some of the subtle and indirect ecological effects to be expected from a limited population of hunters and gatherers. Certainly, in the Kintyre peninsula Nicholls (1966 –67) has reported an early shift away from tree species to open grassland with bracken, while in Ross-shire and elsewhere in the Highlands and Islands (Durno and McVean, 1959; McVean, 1964) charcoal horizons indicate major forest and moor fires. Nevertheless, it remains difficult to decide whether natural or human agencies were responsible in such cases.

Even if human involvement is accepted, there remains the intriguing question of whether the motive in fire-raising were merely immediate expediency in driving game or whether there was a considered policy of long-term landscape modification. Studies of deer populations in Europe and North America (some reviewed by Mellars, 1975) show that removal of forest cover produced notable increases in carrying capacity. Herbaceous species that had been shaded out proliferate again, alongside shrubs and young trees with succulent sprouts. The increase in the numbers and individual weight of the deer population can augment the local biomass available to hunters by a factor of five or even ten. After forest fires areas would also exhibit enhanced grazing potential due to regenerating vegetation, and possibly our forebears realized this and themselves set fires. That the results observed elsewhere on the correlation between burning and the improved reproductive rates and body weight of red deer herds can be replicated in specifically Scottish conditions has been demonstrated by experiments on Rhum in the Hebrides (Lowe, 1971).

For gathering vegetable foods as well as hunting, the expanses of close canopied forest, with their limited ground cover and restricted ranges of species of plants as well as of animals and birds, are likely to have been less attractive than the more varied woodland-edge situations. It seems likely that ecotones, the transition zones between major ecosystems, would have been particularly attractive. Not only were they characterized by a diversity of resources, but groups locating there could set out to exploit the contrasting possibilities on either side of the divide, whether this was between upland and lowland, moor and forest, forest and lake, or land and sea.

A traditional image of the Mesolithic populace was of 'strand loopers' gathering shellfish and depositing their debris in great 'kitchen middens'. The massiveness of such shell mounds early attracted archaeological interest (e.g. review in Lacaille, 1954) and somewhat distracted attention from research inland. Recent studies, however, have confirmed the importance of the ecological interface at the seashore to many Mesolithic communities (e.g. Clark, 1980), and this has been borne out in Scotland in both Atlantic and North Sea Provinces (e.g. Mellars, 1979; Coles, 1971).

The exploitation of seas and estuaries was by no means confined to shellfish picked up at low tide. Modern standards of excavation are disclosing increasing evidence of sea fishing. Many of the species represented, including cod, could have been taken from the shore but some competence with boats is to be suspected. Steward (1975) has emphasized that few pre-farming societies have lacked some kind of water transportation. He points out that even very simple craft can give enormous advantages, not only in moving the group about and in fishing, but in other forms of hunting and gathering aquatic foods. In a landscape so scattered with lochs and so deeply penetrated by estuaries as that of Scotland, the canoe has added value in extended foraging range by making it easier to bring back to a central camp the products of on-shore food collecting and hunting.

What appears to have been a fishing coracle has been excavated at a site overlooking the Forth at Dalgety Bay (Watkins, 1980). This example dates from around three and a half millennia ago, but skin-covered craft may well have been in use very much earlier (e.g. Piggott, 1974; Ellmers, 1980). Many of the more durable log boats have been found in Scotland. Some, encountered deep in the estuarine deposits of the Clyde when docks were being excavated, are likely to be of early date. One dugout that certainly seems Mesolithic was found at Friarton by Perth, lying on a forest bed buried by early Holocene carse clays of the Tay estuary (Geikie, 1894).

Equivalent carse clays also occur in the Forth estuary. There too, as the initial glacio-isostatic rebound of the land slackened, it was overtaken by the continuing rise in ocean level. Forests were flooded, and the estuary was so extended that many whales (some almost 30 m long) ventured inland of the site of Stirling. Although there is no evidence that they were hunted from boats, some of their stranded carcasses were certainly exploited by the Mesolithic inhabitants of the area, as marks on the bones and finds of several antler implements show (e.g. Turner, 1889; Clark, 1952).

With the progressive development of the country's vegetation cover super-imposed on large-scale changes in its physiography, Scotland in the first half of the Holocene thus presented a rich variety of environments. In the barer mountain areas, relict arctic and sub-arctic species persisted. The ptarmigan and variable hare have survived there to the present day, although reindeer eventually died out. The thickets and forests of the lowlands and much of the rest of the hill country, besides providing vegetable foods of many kinds, supported numerous bird species and animals, including elk and wild cattle. Boar, beaver and bear survived into medieval times, red and roe deer up to the present. The seas, rivers and lakes offered wide ranges of plant and animal resources and wildfowl in plenty came to the saltmarshes.

A marked seasonality characterized many of these resources. Some birds and animals were long distance migrants, disappearing entirely for part of the year. Others had a more local regime but followed the annual changes in the distribution of their food. This must have influenced hunting patterns, while the yearly rhythms of abundance and dearth in nuts, berries and other vegetable foods would have varied the reliance placed on shellfish, say, even where these were always readily available.

With the mosaic of juxtaposed habitats represented in Scotland's broken terrain, it would seem not unlikely that the inhabitants would find it profitable not only to exploit ecotone sites but also to conform to the seasonal rhythms of their resources by adopting some degree of transhumance or nomadism. The economic effectiveness of strategies of multiple-habitat exploitation is clear from ethnographic studies (e.g. Ingold, 1980; Johnson, 1969; Lee and Devore, 1975), and the view that they were adopted in prehistoric Britain is now finding considerable support (e.g. Mellars, 1975; Simmons, 1975; Taylor, 1980; Woodman, 1978).

Until relatively recently, Mesolithic sites in Scotland have usually been considered individually rather than as potential components in networks of co-ordinated annual activity. Population estimates on the former basis tended to suggest very restricted numbers indeed. Thus in 1962, when attention was still focused primarily on shell middens, Atkinson noted 'one is forced to the conclusion that until the neolithic colonization the population at any one time can hardly have exceeded two people for each of the modern counties' (1962, 7). The ethnographic studies cited confirm that transhumant subsistence strategies exploiting several complementary ecosystems can support consider-ably higher population levels than those relying on one alone, particularly if it has seasonal limitations. Although the Mesolithic population was certainly sparse, older estimates like that of Atkinson thus now seem decidedly on the low side.

THE LATER HOLOCENE: SCOTLAND WITH FARMERS

The coming of the 'Neolithic Revolution', as it was once known, was long regarded as representing a decisive break in the relationship between people and their environment, not least in Scotland. There is still a measure of truth in this. Some at least of the attitudes and techniques involved in farming were certainly imports from elsewhere, as were the main domestic animals and crop strains. However, in Scotland, too, it is becoming evident that the change is likely to have been much less of a 'revolution' than was once thought.

It is now clearly simplistic to envisage an absolute contrast between a few impoverished shellfish collectors and an incoming farming peasantry equipped for organized settlement. The level of organization of Mesolithic groups may well have been such that some used settlements with permanent buildings. What appears to be a large hut was excavated in 1980 on a Mesolithic site near Banchory in north-east Scotland (James Kenworthy, pers. comm.). It is probably 7000 years old. Such houses may have been used during only part of the year or they may represent the permanent base camp from which parts of the group would move out temporarily to satellite specialist settlements (located to take advantage of particular raw materials or seasonal food resources). Many parallels may be found in later times for either of these types of settlement use. Both are familiar among historical pastoral and farming communities certainly eligible for classification as "Neolithic" (see e.g.: for settlements involved in transhumance, Braudel (1973) and Johnson (1969); for central steadings with out-stations for various functions, Borchgrevink (1980), cf. the Scottish sheiling system).

The blurring of what was formerly regarded as a hard line between Mesolithic and Neolithic extends also to the question of the relationship between 'resource management' and 'domestication'. Mellars (1975), noting that deliberate forest destruction by Mesolithic communities would not only have increased deer productivity but controlled annual herd movements, has concluded that whether this is described as a simple form of 'domestication' is largely a question of definition of terms. Indeed Ingold (1980) finds it profitable to consider hunting, pastoral and ranching economies together, being critical of both the 'Neolithic Revolution' and the form of 'Palaeoeconomy' counter-concept propounded by Higgs and Jarman (1975). That 'the Mesolithic, so far from being a dead end, was in fact an essential prelude to fundamental advances in the development of culture' has recently been underlined by Clark (1980, 7).

The capabilities of the advanced hunters and foragers and their potential importance in Scotland's early geography should not be under-rated. Nevertheless, the current reassessments ought not to distract from the fact that it was after farming in the usual sense started to be practised in Scotland that the main modifications of the developed mid-Holocene forest cover took place.

This is not to say, however, that the reduction of the forests was a straightforward reflection of the impact of the activities of the farmers and their beasts. By the time that Neolithic cultural material becomes evident around the middle of the fourth millennium b.c., the greater part of the postglacial Climatic Optimum was over. Tree lines in Scotland were higher then than before or since, with pine and birch being found up to 790 m altitude in the Cairngorms (Pears, 1968). Thus (as Taylor (1980) has also suggested for Wales) in Scotland, for natural as well as human reasons, the period which saw the establishment of Neolithic culture was a watershed in environmental relations. Until then the Mesolithic colonization and development of population had been accompanied by a generally benign trend in temperatures, with limited reversals. Afterwards, despite some remissions, the opposite was the case. Thus a general trend towards climatic deterioration coincided with the part of the prehistoric period during which the impact of man was increasing notably.

From about 3000 b.c. onwards, major reductions of forest cover start to occur in many areas (Birks, 1977) and through later prehistory the overall tendency was towards progressive deforestation (see, *inter alios*: O'Sullivan, 1974; Turner, 1965; Durno, 1957; overviews: Birks, 1977; Whittington, 1980). This seems to have been greater in the 'Bronze Age' than in the 'Neolithic' and very much greater in the 'Iron Age' than previously. It would, however, be too simplistic to assume neat stages that correspond to these nineteenth-century typological divisions, with the type of axe available as a prime determinant, and as Burgess has emphasized, among prehistorians 'the recent trend has been to stress the concept of continuity, both from Neolithic to Bronze Age, and Bronze to Iron' (1980, 244).

Although the introduction of the new materials does not appear to have coincided with radical social or economic transformations, the relationship between people and their environments did not necessarily follow a smooth curve of increasing human dominance. Evidence accumulating from diverse parts of Britain seems to imply that in prehistoric as in historic times agricultural crises occurred that were serious enough to have major social, economic and demographic repercussions. For instance, one may have developed in the first half of the third millennium b.c. (e.g. Whittle, 1978), another in the final centuries of the second millennium (e.g. Bradley, 1978).

If this reading of the archaeological material proves correct, it would imply that even four and a half thousand years ago populations in substantial areas of Britain were reaching levels that could threaten to deplete the environmental resources available to them at the level of technical and economic organization then current. Probably rightly, workers in Scotland have been rather reticent in drawing conclusions about population figures. It is notable, however, that while Atkinson (1972) proposed an Early Bronze Age population for England and Wales as small as 2000 persons, many would consider this far too low: Green (1974) would favour a figure 50 to 100 times larger then, and Stanford (1972) has gone as far as to suggest that by the end of the traditional Bronze Age, populations may have matched those of the time of the Domesday Book.

Particularly during the last decade, research making considerable use of air photography (e.g. Riley, 1980) has revealed traces of extensive and highly organized Neolithic and Bronze Age field systems in parts of Britain ranging from the west of Ireland to Dartmoor and the English Midlands. In Scotland, it is becoming clear not only that prehistoric field boundaries may be preserved under peat cover (e.g. Ritchie *et al.*, 1974) but that such evidence occurs widely (Whittington, 1977–78).

Work on sites of this kind is just beginning, and it remains difficult to follow the evolution of the rural landscape. During the last millennium b.c. there was a further major depletion of forest, and in some cases there seems good evidence that the clearance reflected direct human action. Even at this late stage in Scotland's prehistory, however, it is not easy to evaluate the relative roles of human and natural processes because the middle of that millennium was marked by a climatic deterioration inimical to forest cover. This has been widely recognized not only in Scotland but elsewhere (e.g. Piggott, 1972; Simmons and Tooley, 1981). The podsolization of soils and the development of peat at that time produced substantial areas of moorland, some of which have remained intractable ever since.

Whatever the combination of causes, this last millennium before the coming of the Romans 'saw novel and far reaching changes in the prehistoric lifestyle of Scotland' (Ritchie, 1981, 89). Social turbulence of the kind attributed traditionally to the Celts becomes apparent in the archaeological record. The earliest known substantial sets of fortifications in Scotland, timber-laced forts, appeared in the sixth or seventh centuries , as did homesteads enclosed by timber palisades. The earliest of the crannogs so far dated were also being constructed around this time (Morrison, 1981). These were wholly or partially artificial islands, built in lochs to provide secure dwellings for people and in some cases their animals. A range of other types of defensive settlement emerged during the remainder of the pre-Roman period. Like most of the forts, the majority of these are small, implying groups of only a few families. From this it has been suggested (for example by Megaw and Simpson, 1979) that particularly in the west, pre-Roman Iron Age society in Scotland was more fragmented than in southern England or on the Continent.

Nevertheless, there is a possibility that some of Scotland's towns may be based on settlements of more substantial Iron Age communities. Many interesting sites such as the Castle Rocks of Edinburgh and Stirling are irremediably overlaid by later structures, but their potential is perhaps indicated by the scale of the forts on Traprain Law and Eildon Hill North. It would be misleading to equate these sites with the highly developed *oppida* encountered by the Romans in Gaul, but during their most developed phase each enclosed around 16 hectares. Although these two forts have not been definitively excavated, 296 house sites have been identified within the latter, and it is accepted that around 200 more were destroyed by forestry operations. This would seem to imply dense permanent occupation, rather than occasional refuge, and Feachem (1966) suggested a population of 2000–3000. It is to be hoped that sufficient excavation will be carried out to throw more light on the chronology, organization and functions of a settlement that has some claim to be the earliest known precursor of the towns of Scotland.

CONTINUITY AND CHANGE

Whether there was any true continuity between major Iron Age settlements and later town development is likely to remain a moot point. Defensible sites were liable to be re-used at any perilous period, prehistoric or historic, and the problems of excavation in built-up areas tend to militate against the chances of extracting the complete story from well-used urban sites. The destruction or inaccessibility of remains due to repeated re-use of favourable locations is also a serious problem in the interpretation of rural evidence. None the less, before turning to an appraisal of 'Dark Age' Scotland in the next chapter, the extent of the legacy of late prehistoric to early historic Scotland requires further consideration. What was the balance between change and continuity in settlement forms, for example, across the traditional Iron Age, Roman and Dark Age divisions?

The broch was one notable innovation in settlement style. This form of elegant hollow-walled dry-stone tower had evolved by about 100 b.c. Around five hundred of them were built, mostly in the Northern and Western Isles and on the northernmost part of the Scottish mainland, and all it seems within a span of a few centuries. Although a spectacular development, broch building was thus a brief and passing fashion, and although some use was made of what remained of them during later times, they hardly form a significant legacy from pre-Roman to historical Scotland.

Although in formal terms the country leaves 'pre'-history when it begins to figure in contemporary written accounts at the time of the Romans, as indicated in the introduction, the transition to a fully documented society was a protracted and uneven one (cf. Crawford, 1967; Whittington, 1980). Scotland was not unique in this. For some parts of continental Europe and indeed of England, one might argue that emergence into the light of Latin literature did coincide with extensive and lasting changes in settlement and landscape organization. For most of Scotland, however, such a view would be much harder to sustain.

This is not to deny that the Romans had an impact; in political terms their activities had wide ramifications. These probably began even before their first major incursions into Scotland in the Agricolan campaigns of the 80s AD (Hartley, 1972), and in considering their final phase Mann (1974) has gone so far as to suggest that the rise of the Pictish Kingdom in the fourth century AD was a by-product of Roman pressure. Furthermore, there are indications that contact with Rome brought native communities within a wider trading network than hitherto, while land use patterns in parts of the Lowlands may temporarily have been geared to providing a surplus for the Roman authorities. The garrisons must at any rate have required local supplies of perishable foods. In a few instances, such as Inveresk, there is evidence of a satellite native settlement outside a Roman fort.

One must, however, agree with the conclusion of the Ritchies (1981, 140/1) that such contacts were at best comparatively superficial and that there is little evidence of Roman civilian life beyond the forts. The occupation of north Britain was essentially military and intermittent (Breeze and Dobson 1976; Kenworthy, 1981), and in Scotland, in contrast to some parts of England, it can often be difficult or indeed impossible to detect Roman influence in the archaeological record of the native societies. This is particularly true in the extensive highland areas, where even their military presence was fleeting.

If the effect of the Roman incursion was in many respects evanescent, this is not to say that the native forms of settlement continued unchanged through this period, although the extent to which the changes may relate directly or indirectly to the Roman presence must be a matter for speculation. Thus there appears to have been a tendency between the first and fifth centuries AD towards smaller examples of some types of fortifications, with few of the latter-day duns, for instance, suggesting a capacity for more than a few dozen people. In a recent reappraisal of hill-forts, Alcock (1981) suggested that post-Roman establishments tend to differ in both size and location from those built earlier.

The situation was thus far from static. Overall, however, it is the degree of continuity in settlement types that emerges as a salient feature of the transition from 'prehistoric' to 'historic' Scotland. Although sizes and distributions might be modified, as Laing (1975, 33), puts it, 'The settlement types of Early Christian Scotland are those of the Iron Age, and there is no category of late Iron Age settlement (i.e. one occupied in the first to second centuries AD) that does not appear to have been occupied at least sporadically in the period from the fifth century onwards'. It was not just a matter of casual re-use or refurbishing of old structures. In each category, there are at least a few examples which appear to be of entirely post-Roman construction.

Until the Norse long-house and the Anglo-Norman contributions were added, it would seem that the landscape of early historic Scotland was typified by forms of settlement either rooted directly in the indigenous Iron Age or springing from closely related traditions. Although many of these forms ceased to be built in the course of the first millennium AD, this was not so of all of them. The longevity of the crannog is particularly notable. In Scotland's relatively freshly glaciated and hence loch-strewn landscape, these purpose-built islands offered a form of security that remained popular from at least the end of the Bronze Age to the seventeenth century AD. They appear to have been constructed through a period of some two thousand years, making them surely one of the longest-favoured styles of dwelling in Scotland.

Even after new settlement forms came in during the medieval and post-medieval periods, some use continued to be made of surviving settlements of prehistoric type. Besides crannogs, a range of hillforts, duns, wheelhouses, souterrains and other Iron Age settlement types were all re-occupied on occasions, and some were modified to suit medieval requirements.

Although the degree of continuity in settlement types goes some way to help us envisage the cultural landscape of early historic times, it also presents problems. As Megaw and Simpson put it (1979, 494), in Scotland 'as elsewhere in the British Isles the period when British prehistory merges into history is paradoxically still very much the Dark Age of archaeology'. Not only has more archaeological effort been invested in earlier phases, but throughout much of the period for which a document-based history may first be sketched, both the archaeological and the documentary evidence tends to be sparse and problematic; notable difficulties in equating them also occur.

The chapter that follows introduces some of the groupings of people who can be named from documentary sources referring to the first millennium AD. Although they may be recognized as political entities from these sources, it is often difficult to identify them unambiguously in archaeological terms. This is exacerbated by the way that several settlement forms common in Scotland have minimal diagnostic value because the continuity they exhibit runs not only across the regional boundaries that place-names and documents suggest for these named groups but also extends far beyond their chronological limits. Thus, although the presence of highly characteristic symbol stones identifies certain general areas with the Picts, it remains difficult to be sure which individual settlements are theirs or what their distribution pattern was in detail. The other leading groups of the time, including the incoming Scots themselves, can be just as elusive in archaeological terms. As the Ritchies state (1981, 158), 'the political distinctions that have been made between Britons, Angles and Scots have not been mirrored in their cultural assemblages . . . and some types of sites (for example "nuclear" forts and crannogs) have distributions which cut across such political "boundaries".'

CONCLUSION

It would have formed a neat ending to this chapter if the geographical patterns of archaeological evidence on Scotland's emergence from prehistory could have been shown to correspond directly with the territories of the first peoples who can be named from historical sources. This is not the case, but there is a compensation for the lack of tidyness. The disparity between the two types of evidence, archaeological and documentary, brings out the way in which remains of everyday artefacts and settlements often reflect not merely short-term predilections of particular groups but rather adaptations to characteristic exigencies of life in Scottish environments (social as well as physical). The material culture that is the subject of archaeological study formed the intermediate term between the inhabitants and the landscapes and neighbours they had to cope with. Basic elements of economy and settlement type often proved viable for peoples of different associations and thus might remain in use through periods running across several of the divisions traditionally adopted to categorize the past.

The situation at the end of the fully prehistoric phase is thus consistent with one of the main conclusions arising from any overall perspective of the prehistoric prelude to the country's historical geography. This is simply that much of Scotland has always been a relatively difficult place to inhabit. Whether amelioration or deterioration of climate was in progress, negative areas large and small have offset those of more obvious potential, and even the latter have seldom been devoid of problems.

Those who have sought to make their living from the landscapes of Scotland have thus had to make shrewd environmental evaluations and develop subtle strategies for deploying the means available to them. This is still true today of those confronting the economic pressures of modern farming, and the more that we learn of our forebears, even in the further reaches of prehistory, the more we come to suspect that it was as true of them also.

Note

In accordance with convention, dates stated in uncalibrated radiocarbon 'years' have been distinguished by lower case (b.c.) from calendar dates shown in capitals (BC, AD).

REFERENCES

Two overall reviews of the prehistoric archaeology of Scotland that may be particularly recommended are those by A. and G. Ritchie (1981) and by V. Megaw and D. Simpson (1979).

Alcock, L. (1981). Early historic fortifications in Scotland. *In* 'Hillfort Studies: Essays for A. H. A. Hogg'' (G. Guilbert ed.) pp. 150–80. Leicester University Press, Leicester.

Atkinson, R. J. (1962). Fishermen and farmers. *In* 'The Prehistoric Peoples of Scotland.' (S. Piggott, ed.), pp. 1–38, Routledge and Kegan Paul, London.

Atkinson, R. J. (1972). Burial and population in the British Bronze Age. *In* 'Prehistoric man in Wales and the West: Essays in honour of Lily F. Chitty.' (F. Lynch and C. Burgess, ed.), pp. 107–16. Adams and Dart, Bath.

Birks, H. J. (1972). 'The Present and Past Vegetation of the Isle of Skye: a Palaeoecological Study.' Cambridge University Press, Cambridge.

Birks, H. J. (1977). The Flandrian forest history of Scotland: a preliminary synthesis. *In* 'British Quaternary Studies: Recent Advances.' (F. W. Shotton, ed.), pp. 119–35. Clarendon, Oxford.

Birks, H. J. and Ransom, M. (1969). An interglacial peat deposit at Fugla Ness, Shetland. *New Phytologist* **68**, 777–96.

Bishop, W. and Coope, R. (1977). Stratigraphical and faunal evidence for late glacial and early Flandrian environments in south-west Scotland. *In* 'Studies in the Scottish Late-glacial Environment.' (J. M. Gray and J. J. Lowe, ed.), pp. 61–88. Pergamon, Oxford.

Borchgrevinck, A.-B. (1980). The houses of the Norwegian seters, part 1. *Northern Studies* **16**, 53–69.

Bradley, R. (1978). 'The Prehistoric Settlement of Britain.' Routledge and Kegan Paul, London.

Braudel, F. (1973). 'The Mediterranean and the Mediterranean Worlds in the Age of Philip II.' Vol. 1. Collins, London.

Breeze, D. D. and Dobson, B. (1976). 'Hadrian's Wall.' Allen Lane, London.

Burgess, C. (1980). The Bronze Age in Wales. *In* 'Culture and Environment in prehistoric Wales.' (J. Taylor, ed.), pp. 243–86. British Archaeological Reports (76), Oxford.

Burgess, C. and Miket, R. (ed.) (1976). 'Settlement and economy in the 3rd and 2nd millennium B.C.' British Archaeological Reports (33), Oxford.

Burnett J. (ed.) (1964). 'The Vegetation of Scotland.' Oliver and Boyd, Edinburgh.

Chandler, T. and Gregory, S. (ed.) (1976). 'The Climate of the British Isles.' Longman, London.

Childe, V. G. (1946). 'Scotland before the Scots.' Methuen, London.

Clapperton, C. and Sugden, D. (1975). The glaciation of Buchan—a reappraisal. *In* 'Quaternary studies in North-East Scotland.' (A. Gemmell, ed.), pp. 19–22. Aberdeen.

Clark, G. (1952). 'Prehistoric Europe—the Economic Basis.' Methuen, London.

Clark, G. (1980). 'Mesolithic Prelude.' Edinburgh University Press, Edinburgh.

Coles, J. (1971). The early settlement of Scotland: excavations at Morton, Fife. *Proceedings of the Prehistoric Society* 37 (2), 284–336.

Coope, R. (1977). Fossil coleopteran assemblages as sensitive indicators of climatic change during the Devensian (last) cold stage. *Philosophical Transactions of the Royal Society of London*, Series B, 280, 313–40.

Crawford, I. (1967). The divide between medieval and post-medieval in Scotland. *Post Medieval Archaeology*. 1, 87–96.

Davidson, D. and Shackley, M. (ed.) (1976). 'Geoarchaeology.' Duckworth, London.

Duffey, E. and Watt, A. (ed.) (1971). 'The Scientific Management of Animal and Plant Communities.' Blackwell, Oxford.

Durno, S. (1957). Certain aspects of vegetational history in north-east Scotland. *Scottish Geographical Magazine* 73, 176–84.

Durno, S. and McVean, D. (1959). Forest history of the Beinn Eighe nature reserve. *New Phytologist* 58, 228–36.

Ellmers, D. (1980). Ein fellbot-fragment de Ahrensburger Kultur aus Husum, Schleswig-Holstein? *Offa* 37, 19–24.

Evans, J., Limbrey, S. and Cleere, H. (ed.) (1975). The effect of man on the landscape: the Highland zone. CBA Research Rep. 11, London.

Feachem, R. (1966). The hill-forts of northern Britain. *In* 'The Iron Age in Northern Britain.' (A. L. F. Rivet, ed.), pp. 59–85. Edinburgh University Press, Edinburgh.

Geikie, J. (1894). 'The Great Ice Age.' Stanford, London.

Gemmell, A. (ed.) (1975). 'Quaternary Studies in North-east Scotland.' Department of Geography, University of Aberdeen, Aberdeen.

Goudie, A. (1977). 'Environmental Change.' Clarendon, Oxford.

Gray, M. and Lowe, J. (ed.) (1977). 'Studies in the Scottish Late-glacial Environment.' Pergamon, Oxford.

Green, H. (1974). Early Bronze Age burial, territories and population in Milton Keynes, Buckinghamshire, and the Great Ouse Valley. *Archaeological Journal* 131, 75–139.

Hartley, B. (1972). The Roman occupation of Scotland. *Britannia* 3, 1–55.

Higgs, E. S. and Jarman, M. (1975). 'Palaeoeconomy.' Cambridge University Press, Cambridge.

Ingold, T. (1980). 'Hunters, Pastoralists and Ranchers.' Cambridge University Press, Cambridge.

Jacobi, R. (1980). The Upper Palaeolithic in Britain. *In* 'Culture and Environment in Prehistoric Wales.' (J. Taylor, ed.), pp. 15–99. British Archaeological Reports (76) Oxford.

Johnson, D. (1969). The Nature of Nomadism. University of Chicago, Geographical Research Paper 118.

Kenworthy, J. (ed.) (1981). Agricola's campaigns in post-Roman Scotland. *Scottish Archaeological Forum* 12.

Lacaille, A. (1954). 'The Stone Age in Scotland.' Oxford University Press, Oxford.

Laing, L. (1975). Settlement types in post-Roman Scotland. British Archaeological Reports, 13, Oxford.

Lee, R. and Devore, I. (ed.) (1975). 'Man the Hunter.' Aldine Press, Chicago.

Lowe, V. (1971). Some effects of a change in estate management on a deer population.

In 'The Scientific Management of Animal and Plant Communities for Conservation.' (E. Duffey and A. Watt, ed.), pp. 437–56. Blackwell, Oxford.

Macaulay Institute for Soil Research (1970) Vols 1 and 2, (1971) Vol 3. 'Assessment of Climatic Conditions in Scotland.' Aberdeen.

McVean, D. (1964). Prehistory and ecological history. *In* 'The Vegetation of Scotland.' (J. H. Burnett, ed.), pp. 561–7. Oliver and Boyd, Edinburgh.

McVean, D. and Ratcliffe, D. (1962). 'Plant Communities in the Scottish Highlands.' HMSO, Edinburgh.

Mann, J. (1974). The northern frontier after A.D. 369. *Glasgow Archaeological Journal* **3**, 34–42.

Megaw, V. and Simpson, D. (ed.) (1979). 'Introduction to British Prehistory.' Leicester University Press, Leicester.

Mellars, P. (1975). Ungulate populations, economic patterns and the Mesolithic landscape. *In* 'The Effect of Man on the Landscape: the Highland Zone.' (J. Evans, S. Limbrey and H. Cleere, ed.), pp. 49–56. Council for British Archaeology, Research Report 11, London.

Mellars, P. (1979). Excavation and economic analysis of Mesolithic shell middens on the island of Oronsay. *Scottish Archaeological Forum* **9**, 43–61.

Mercer, J. (1980). 'The Palaeolithic and Mesolithic occupation of the Isle of Jura, Argyll, Scotland.' Jahrbuch Institut Canarium und GISAF, Hallein, Austria ix–x, 347–67.

Morrison, A. (1980). 'Early Man in Britain and Ireland.' Croom Helm, London.

Morrison, I. A. (1969). Some problems in correlating archaeological material and old shorelines. *Scottish Archaeological Forum* **1**, 1–7.

Morrison, I. A. (1976). Comparative stratigraphy and radiocarbon chronology of Holocene marine changes on the western seaboard of Europe. *In* 'Geoarchaeology.' (D. Davidson and M. Shackley, ed.), pp. 159–74. Duckworth, London.

Morrison, I. A. (1980a). Holocene water level changes and Scottish archaeology. Proceedings of the Sixth Scientific Symposium, CMAS.

Morrison, I. A. (1980b). (i) Changing levels of land and sea. *and* (ii) Land and sea in northwest Europe. *In* 'Archaeology Underwater: an Atlas of the World's Submerged Sites.' (K. Muckelroy, ed.), pp. 132–7. McGraw-Hill, London and New York.

Morrison, I. A. (1981). The extension of the chronology of the crannogs of Scotland. *International Journal of Nautical Archaeology* **10**(4), 344–6.

Nicholls, H. (1967). Vegetation change, shoreline development and the human factor in the late Quaternary history of southwest Scotland. *Transactions of the Royal Society of Edinburgh* **67**, 145–84.

O'Sullivan, P. (1974). Radiocarbon dating and prehistoric forest clearance on Speyside. *Proceedings of the Prehistoric Society* **40**, 206–8.

Parry, M. L. (1978). 'Climatic Change, Agriculture and Settlement.' Dawson, Folkestone.

Parry, M. L. and Slater, T. R. (ed.) (1980). 'The Making of the Scottish Countryside.' Croom Helm, London.

Pears, N. (1968). Postglacial tree-lines of the Cairngorm Mountains, Scotland. *Transactions and Proceedings of the Royal Botanical Society of Edinburgh* **40**, 361–94.

Piggott, S. (1962). 'The Prehistoric Peoples of Scotland.' Routledge and Kegan Paul, London.

Piggott, S. (1972). A note on climatic deterioration in the first millennium B.C. in Britain. *Scottish Archaeological Forum* 4, 109–13.

Piggott, S. (1974). Innovation and tradition in British prehistory. *Transactions of the Architectural and Archaeological Society of Durham and Northumberland* 3, 1–12.

Riley, D. (1980). 'Early Landscape from the Air.' University of Sheffield, Sheffield.

Ritchie, A. and G. (1981). 'Scotland: Archaeology and Early History.' Thames and Hudson, London.

Ritchie, A., Ritchie, G., Whittington, G. and Soulsby, J. (1974). A prehistoric field boundary from the Black Crofts, North Connel, Argyll. *Glasgow Archaeological Journal* 3, 66–70.

Ritchie, J. (1920). 'The Influence of Man on Animal Life in Scotland.' Cambridge University Press, Cambridge.

Rivet, A. L. F. (ed.) (1966). 'The Iron Age in Northern Britain.' Edinburgh University Press, Edinburgh.

Rolfe, W. (1966). Woolly rhinoceros from the Scottish Pleistocene. *Scottish Journal of Geology* 2, 253–8.

Scottish Archaeological Forum (1980). '10: Settlements in Scotland, 1000 B.C.–1000 A.D.'

Shotton, F., Blundell, P. and Williams, R. (1970). Birmingham University radiocarbon dates: IV. *Radiocarbon* 12, 385–99.

Simmons, I. (1975). The ecological setting of Mesolithic man in the Highland Zone. *In* 'The Effect of Man on the Landscape: the Highland Zone.' (J. Evans, S. Limbrey and H. Cleere, ed.), Council for British Archaeology Research Report 11, 57–64, London.

Simmons, I. and Tooley, M. (1981). 'The Environment on British Prehistory.' Duckworth, London.

Simpson, D. (ed.) (1971). 'Economy and Settlement in Neolithic and Early Bronze Age Britain and Europe.' Leicester University Press, Leicester.

Simpson, D. (1976). The later Neolithic and Beaker settlement site at Northton, Isle of Harris. *In* 'Settlement and Economy in the Third and Second millennium B.C.' (C. Burgess and R. Miket, ed.), British Archaeological Reports, Oxfords, 33, 221–31.

Sissons, J. B. (1976). 'The Geomorphology of the British Isles: Scotland.' Methuen, London.

Sissons, J. B. (1979a). Palaeoclimatic inferences from former glaciers in Scotland and the Lake District. *Nature* 278, 518–21.

Sissons, J. B. (1979b). The Loch Lomond stadial in the British Isles. *Nature* 280, 199–203.

Smith, A., and Pilcher, J. (1973). Radiocarbon dates and vegetational history of the British Isles. *New Phytologist* 72, 903–14.

Stanford, S. (1972). The function and population of hill forts in the Central Marches. *In* Prehistoric Man in Wales and the West: Essays in Honour of Lily F. Chitty.' (F. Lynch and C. Burgess, ed.), pp. 307–20. Adams and Dart, Bath.

Steward, J. (1975). Causal factors and processes in the evolution of pre-farming societies. *In* 'Man the Hunter.' (R. Lee and I. DeVore, ed.), pp. 321–3, Aldine Press, Chicago.

Synge, F. (1956). The glaciation of North East Scotland. *Scottish Geographical Magazine* 72, 129–43.

Taylor, J. (1967). 'Weather and Agriculture.' Pergamon, Oxford.

Taylor, J. (1976). Upland climates. *In* 'The climate of the British Isles.' (T. Chandler and S. Gregory, ed.), pp. 264–87. Longman, London.

Taylor, J. A. (1980a). Environmental changes in Wales during the Holocene period. *In* 'Culture and environment in prehistoric Wales.' (J. A. Taylor, ed.), pp. 101–30. British Archaeological Reports 76, Oxford.

Taylor, J. A. (ed.) (1980b). Culture and Environment in prehistoric Wales. British Archaeological Reports 76, Oxford.

Thoms, L. (ed.) (1980). Settlements in Scotland, 1000 B.C.–1000 A.D. *Scottish Archaeological Forum* 10.

Turner, J. (1965). A contribution to the history of forest clearance. *Proceedings of the Royal Society of London*, Series B. 161, 343–53.

Turner, W. (1889). On some implements of stag's horn associated with whales' skeletons found in the Carse of Stirling. *Reports of the British Association.* 789–91.

Watkins, T. (1980). A prehistoric coracle in Fife. *International Journal of Nautical Archaeology* 9(4), 277–86.

Whittington, G. (1979). A sub-peat dyke on Shurton Hill, Mainland, Shetland. *Proceedings of the Society of Antiquaries of Scotland* 109, 30–35.

Whittington, G. (1980). Prehistoric activity and its effect on the Scottish landscape. *In* 'The making of the Scottish Countryside.' (M. L. Parry and T. R. Slater, ed.) pp. 23–44. Croom Helm, London and Montreal.

Whittle, A. (1978). Resources and population in the British Neolithic. *Antiquity* 52, 34–42.

Woodman, P. (1978). The Mesolithic in Ireland: hunter gatherers in an insular environment. British Archaeological Reports 58, Oxford.

2
Dark Age Scotland

A. Small

Broadly based accounts of post-Roman Scotland until 1100 are hampered by the relative paucity of reliable data compared to the period immediately preceding and following the Dark Ages. Literary sources consist mainly of Irish annals, genealogies, and law books written long after the events they purport to describe. Church records and other literature are also of dubious value. The archaeological record is limited, and before modern dating technologies became available many sites which may well have post-Roman material were consigned to the pre-Roman Iron Age. Place names have received much less systematic attention than those of England, largely owing to the lack of documentary evidence of their early forms.

In the period following the Roman abandonment of Hadrian's Wall it is possible to identify three, and in later times four, political units which make up what is now Scotland. North of the Forth–Clyde line, including the Northern and Western Isles, lay Pictland, although Argyll and its islands became a separate unit under Scottish control. To the south lay the territory of the Britons, a region where the older British tribal groupings – the Damnonii in the Clyde Area, the Novantae and Selgovae of the south west, and the Votadini in the south east – were gradually emerging into primitive states such as Strathclyde, Rheged and Gododdin. In the fifth and sixth centuries this south eastern part of Scotland came under Anglian control and this is therefore considered as a fourth political unit.

SOUTH-EAST SCOTLAND

The Votadinian way of life seems to have continued in south-east Scotland for some time after the Romans left. Their major centre on Traprain Law continued to be used until at least the mid-fifth century, after which Din Eidyn (Edinburgh) and possibly Stirling became the key centres, perhaps reflecting a fluctuating frontier with the Picts to the north. That Pictish power seems to have on occasion advanced south of the Forth is evidenced by early symbol stones being found at Edinburgh and Borthwick. The fortifications on Dalmahoy Hill, near Edinburgh, and Rubers Law, Roxburghshire, can also be attributed to this period (Stevenson, 1949).

Few settlement sites can be securely dated to the immediate post-Roman period, but the typology seems to be similar to that of the Roman Iron Age in north-east England with enclosed groups of circular stone dwellings such as those at Crock Cleugh (Steer and Keeney, 1947) and Hownam (Piggott, 1948) in Roxburghshire. At Traprain, in the latest levels several groups of interconnected sub-rectangular rooms have been identified. Each group may represent a single entity.

From the sixth century onwards the Tyne–Forth province gradually came under Anglian domination, partly as a result of military conquest and the establishment of the Kingdom of Bernicia (later to become part of Northumbria). Archaeology has to date produced little to indicate extensive Anglian settlement. At Doon Hill near Dunbar a seventh-century rectangular hall some 23 m in length, of similar construction to the Anglian palace of Yeavering in Northumberland, has been excavated and shown to overlie a large British hall (Hope-Taylor, 1966). Air photography suggests that one or two similar sites may exist in the Roxburgh and Peebles districts. Other archaeological evidence of settlement is extremely sparse, being limited to a pagan grave from Dalmeny and a scatter of small finds. In artistic terms the most important remains are the sculptured stones including a superb seventh-century panel from Jedburgh and a fine cross from Aberlady. Another group is associated with the monastic settlement at Abercorn on the Forth.

The place-name evidence for Anglian settlement is also very slight. The greatest concentration is in the Tweed Valley. The earliest phases of settlement are probably represented by the -*ham* and -*ingham* names (meaning a settlement), a few of which reach as far north as the Lothians; -*worth* (enclosure) occurs only in the Tweed Valley as do most -*ham* names. Other Anglian elements such as -*ingtun* (*tun*, enclosure) and -*botl* (dwelling) extend from East Lothian to Ayrshire. From present evidence it can be suggested that the most intensive area of Anglian settlement was in the lower Tweed Valley, whereas British landowners maintained their power in the higher areas and in the frontier region of the Lothians. From the mid-seventh century Anglian power seems to have weakened and the straggle of Anglian place names across the Southern Uplands and into Ayrshire (e.g. Crawford, Maybole, Prestwick) may well represent an infilling of the British settlement pattern rather than the take-over of occupied land.

SOUTH-WEST SCOTLAND

The post-Roman period in south-west Scotland saw the gradual emergence of the historical kingdoms of Rheged and Strathclyde. Although the early boundaries of these kingdoms are impossible to define it seems that Strathclyde was a descendant of the former tribal area of the Damnonii while Rheged rose to its height in the sixth century from the former territories of the Selgovae and Novantae in Dumfries and Galloway. Archaeological evidence suggests a remarkably high density of population and also indicates considerable wealth.

The relatively unstable political conditions are reflected by the numerous defended settlements and the evidence of the re-occupation of several hill forts along with the development of nuclear defended sites similar to those in other parts of post-Roman Britain. Of the excavated sites to date, Mote of Mark in Kirkcudbrightshire (Laing, 1975) is by far the most informative, revealing occupation from the late fifth to the seventh century. An open hilltop settlement was later protected by a partially timber-laced earth and stone rampart which was ultimately fired and vitrified. A later phase of occupation includes Anglian material. The small finds from Mote of Mark clearly demonstrate extensive manufacturing ability with raw materials and finished goods drawn from the local area and imported from abroad. Iron- and bronze-working are confirmed and, less certainly, that of gold and silver. Shale or lignite, probably from Ayrshire, and bone and antler were also worked on the site and a glass-making industry used raw materials from Ireland and the Rhineland. Clearly, therefore, this was a rich centre in Rheged with extensive external contacts, and future excavations may well prove that this site is by no means unique.

In Strathclyde, to the north, a similar settlement pattern appears to have existed. Alt Clut or Castle Rock, Dumbarton (Alcock, 1976) is historically described as the major stronghold of the Britons of Strathclyde, its significance in part arising from its geographical features and location. Archaeological finds from the site, including evidence of metal-working, indicate fifth- to eighth-century occupation. Surface indications also suggest that several of the hillforts in Ayrshire and Renfrewshire may have been re-occupied during this period.

The defended aspect of many of the homesteads of the period is well demonstrated by the crannogs of south-west Scotland. These artificial islands are mostly of uncertain age. Milton Loch, near Crocketford, Kircudbrightshire (Piggott, 1953) although probably constructed in the pre-Roman period (Guido, 1974), has a demonstrable second-century occupation (Wild, 1970), while Buiston, formerly Buston, (Munro, 1882) near Kilmaurs, Ayrshire, has produced sixth- to eighth-century pottery, suggesting that crannogs may have been built as well as re-occupied in the post-Roman period.

As has been suggested above, historical, place-name and archaeological evidence all indicate a significant period of Anglian domination in at least a substantial part of the south west. While there may have been some Anglian influence as early as the sixth century, it is certain that by the end of the seventh century large areas of Dumfriesshire, Ayshire and the Clyde Valley were subject to Northumbrian colonization. Most of the archaeological evidence is of an ecclesiastical nature and reveals little of the settlement pattern. The well-known Talnotrie hoard of hack silver from Kircudbrightshire, buried *c.* 910, contains Anglian material and was allegedly found close to a group of hut circles and a rectangular building, but the nature of these structures is unknown (Maxwell, 1913).

In the extensive evidence for early Christianity in south-west Scotland, Irish contacts have been clearly demonstrated and in the past archaeological and place-name evidence has been used in attempts to show Irish settlement on a significant scale in Galloway. Current interpretation of the evidence, however, tends to deny settlement and to limit Irish influence to the ecclesiastical field.

It has long been held that the post-Roman inhabitants of Southern Scotland practised a pastoral economy, counting their wealth in cattle. This fitted well with the evidence of the climatic deterioration of the sub-Atlantic phase and the extension of peat cover. More recent palynological work, however, indicates that fairly extensive land clearance was going on. Turner (1970) suggests clearance around Bloak Moss in Ayrshire in the fifth century. This could imply an increasing concentration on farming in parallel with similar developments in England and possibly in Pictland. Turner's evidence does not give any clear indication as to whether the farming was of an arable or pastoral nature, but the extent of the clearance would seem to favour the former.

Cultivation terraces are widely distributed in south-eastern Scotland with a remarkable concentration in the Tweed Valley and eastern Roxburghshire. Their distribution correlates more closely with areas of Anglian influence, as demonstrated by literary sources, place names and crosses, rather than with any pre- or post-Anglian feature (RCAHMS, Peeblesshire Volume I), which points to Northumbria as a likely place of origin. However, as Graham (1939) shows, the dating evidence for these cultivation terraces is extremely limited, and a range of dates between the seventh and seventeenth centuries is possible. The correlation with Anglian evidence may be nothing more than areal co-incidence; there is no evidence to suggest population pressure or other factors to justify the not inconsiderable labour required in the construction of the terraces.

THE SCOTS

According to the literary sources the Scots' colonization of Argyll and the adjacent islands, an area known as Daldriada, began in the period 490-510.

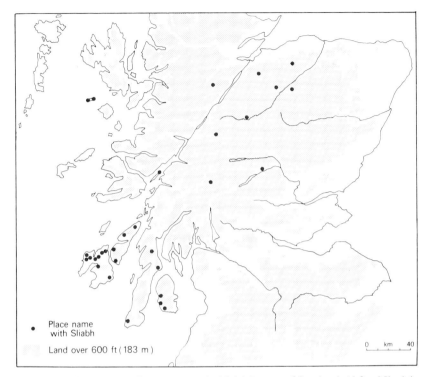

Fig. 2.1   Distribution of place-names in Sliabh in part of Scotland. (After Nicolaisen, 1965)

Some authorities would argue, however, that intermittent colonization by Irish settlers had been taking place since the Roman period. From the scanty historical evidence it is possible to suggest that the colonization process was relatively peaceful, perhaps because the existing population density in Argyll was relatively low and some land, although of relatively poor quality, was available for settlement. However, their expansion was limited by the Picts to the north and east and the British kingdoms to the south and this soon created conflict.

For a people who were ultimately to dominate Scotland there is, to date, surprisingly little place-name or archaeological evidence for their early settle-ment. Nicolaisen (1965) considered the element *sliabh* (a hill) to be of Dalriadic origin, although its distribution extends far into the Central Highlands (Fig. 2.1). This is the element which has been used to suggest early Irish settlement in south-western Galloway. Not enough excavation has been completed to generalize about settlement patterns, but certain points are clear. Dunadd and Dunolli are both mentioned as family strongholds in contemporary annals.

Dunadd on a substantial knoll rising above the Moss of Crinan, which in former days before drainage would have given excellent protection, lies astride one of the main portages across the Argyll peninsula. Excavation (Christison, 1905; Craw, 1930) suggests that this complex stone-built nuclear fort may have contained stone buildings of a rectangular nature. Some pre-Roman finds are recorded, but the bulk of the pottery and metal work confirms a sixth- to eighth-century date. Dunolli, north west of Oban, is on a precipitous headland site controlling the seaward approaches, and recent excavation has confirmed Dark Age occupation and metal-working similar to that of Dunadd.

Settlement sites are similar to those found south of the Forth–Clyde line, and the same need for defence is also reflected in the use of crannogs, of which that in Loch Glashan is an appropriate example (Scott, 1961; Laing, 1975). Two phases of building on the artificial island were noted, the first associated with a long, rectangular building some eight metres by five while the second saw its replacement with a circular house some four metres in diameter. On the basis of pottery finds and a penannular brooch, a date between the sixth and ninth centuries has been suggested. This site is also important as it demonstrates the importance of timber for the manufacture of many articles.

As the Scots came from Ireland, it is surprising that raths do not feature among Dalriadic settlement types. Their equivalent in Scotland would appear to be duns, small and often irregularly shaped single-family fortlets with disproportionately massive walls. Only a few of the many duns have been satisfactorily excavated, and these demonstrate that although many were built during the Iron Age, occupation in the Dark Age, although not necessarily continuous from the earlier period, is well attested. The dun at Kildonan Bay (Fairhurst, 1939) was apparently constructed in the first or second century and extensively used during the seventh and eighth centuries. Dark Age finds are also recorded from sites such as Kildalliog and Ugadale in Kintyre and Little Dunagoil (Bute). Until it is possible to be more certain of the nature and role of a much larger number of duns it is unwise to generalize about the settlement pattern. However, the intermittent use of caves such as Keil Cave at the south end of the Kintyre peninsula (Ritchie, 1967), which was used from the third or fourth century onwards, suggests that less substantial structures are also to be expected.

Some further evidence of the extent and types of areas settled can be gained from the evidence of the Early Christian Church. The monastic settlements are the best documented, particularly that of Iona, founded by Columba in 567, and Lismore, traditionally founded by Moluag in the latter third of the sixth century. Kingarth in Bute may also be part of this group. Geographically the Irish monasteries founded on Eigg and at Applecross in Wester Ross are significant: they were sited in Pictland and may be a clue to one of the methods of diffusion of Scottish ideas and language among the Picts. It may have been through the church that the Picts acquired the ogham alphabet from the Scots in the sixth or seventh century. The Celtic Church was also an evangelizing church, and the distribution of *Kil-* place names and Early Christian carved stones may well reflect significant pockets of Dark Age settlement of sufficient size to attract the attention of the church.

The Scots settlers in Dalriada brought the Common Gaelic language from Ireland, and partly through the activities of the church this spread into Pictland. Some authorities argue that there may well have been some Scots settlement in Pictland long before the union of the Picts and Scots *c*. 849. Scots Gaelic seems to have been diverging significantly from the Irish Gaelic by the tenth century, and ultimately it became the language of the whole of Scotland except for a strip along the border and the Norse-speaking areas to the north and west.

Little is known of agricultural practices in Dalriada, and although the traditional view would favour a predominantly pastoral economy, the location of sites indicated by the settlement evidence outlined above suggests a potential for arable cultivation as well; indeed, grain growing is well-attested by the number of querns recorded from excavated sites. Columba is claimed to have encouraged land drainage and promoted the culture of bees, so the church may well have had a role in the improvement of agricultural practices as it did in later times. Perhaps therefore it would be better to suggest a mixed economy in accord with the environmental limitations of Dalriada.

PICTLAND

The first historical mention of the Picts occurs in the writings of Eumenius in 297, the term *Picti* being applied to the peoples living north of the Antonine Wall. No clue is given to the origin or meaning of the term, and since there is no evidence for population movements in the area it must be assumed that the Picts are the direct descendants of the Early Iron Age population. Their place names, their symbolism on standing stones, and the almost total dearth of settlement sites until recent years have led to a vast literature of varying quality on many aspects of Pictish society. Recent work, well summarized by Alcock (1980), is beginning to solve some of the problems of the Picts.

Stone monuments bearing incised and sculptured symbols are usually taken to give a reasonable indication of the distribution of Pictish activity, despite the fact that many stones have obviously been lost and the destruction of these monuments during the Reformation was of unequal intensity through the area. These monuments can also be used in an admittedly overlapping chronological sequence in three classes:

Class I   Rough undressed boulders bearing incised geometric or zoomorphic symbols only.

Class II Dressed stones with the symbols standing out in relief and frequently incorporating a cross on one side.

Class III Stones which do not include any pre-Christian symbols

The sequence is thus in three stages with a pre-Christian phase (Class I), a period associated with early Christianity (Class II), and a later phase (Class III) which covers a very broad group of many monuments through to the twelfth century. The interpretation of the symbols remains a matter of intense debate as does the dating of the Class I stones, which relies on artistic parallels. Some authorities argue that Class I stones could begin as early as the fifth century; others favour the second half of the seventh century. The distribution of Class I and II stones (Fig. 2.2) suggests that the heartland of Pictish territory was in Eastern Scotland with the major concentrations in Angus, Aberdeenshire, particularly in Donside, and the Moray Firth area from Speyside to Sutherland. A scatter of stones extends northwards to Shetland with a very few on the west coast, notably in Skye, and a single example in North Uist, suggesting that these areas were, at least for part of the time, an integral part of Pictish territory.

While there can be no doubt that these stones represent points of human activity, solid archaeological evidence of actual Pictish settlements has been limited until recent years. However, certain similarities to what was taking place in other parts of Scotland are now beginning to emerge. The re-use and sometimes refortification of pre-Pictish hilltop and promontory forts has been demonstrated at a number of sites including Craig Phadrig, Inverness, (Small and Cottam, 1972) Cullykhan, Banffshire (Greig, 1971, 1972) and Clatchard Craig, Fife (Feachem, 1963), while others were constructed by the Picts themselves using techniques including timber lacing, which on occasion led to vitrification, as had been common in the pre-Roman Iron Age. Of this group Dundurn in Strathearn is the most well known, guarding the approaches to Pictish royal centres at Forteviot and Scone. Recent work by Alcock (1980) has confirmed its construction in the seventh century. Burghead in Morayshire appears to have been built in the fourth century and continued in occupation until the ninth century (Small, 1969; Edwards and Ralston, 1980). The scale of this fortress, which has sometimes been described as of *oppidum* proportions suggests a substantial population in the area. Other forts, such as Green Castle near Portnockie, Castle Urquhart and Dunottar, have either historical or archaeological evidence of Pictish occupation. It may well be that a great number of hill and promontory forts which in the past have been regarded as Iron Age could have been re-used or even built by the Picts, particularly as

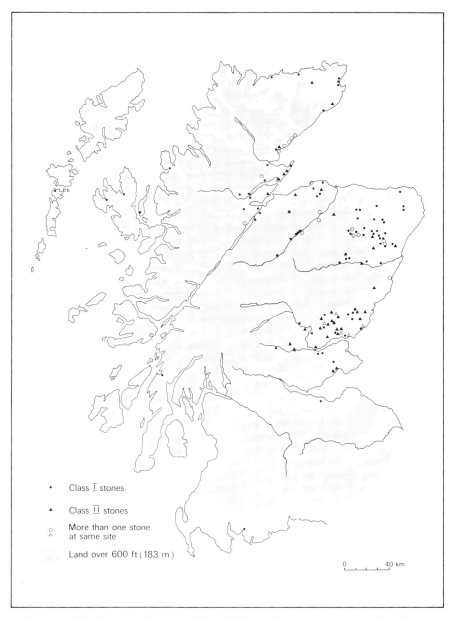

Fig. 2.2   Distribution of Class I and Class II Pictish Symbol Stones, excluding Orkney and Shetland. (After Whittington, 1977 and others)

Within the figure:

Class I̅ stones

Class I̅I̅ stones

More than one stone at same site

Land over 600 ft (183 m)

0   40 km

there is a degree of correlation between Class I Pictish symbol stones and forts (Cottam and Small, 1974).

Domestic settlements of the Picts are more or less unknown from their heartland areas. The souterrains and their associated surface huts such as those at Carlungie and Ardestie in Angus (Wainwright, 1963) have been assigned to the first or second century and therefore belong to the proto-Picts. However, a very wide range of dates has been obtained for earth houses in other parts of Britain, and it may well be that small groups of oval or circular surface huts with attached underground storage facilities continued in use into the Pictish period. Recent work, as yet unpublished, has produced sixth and ninth century dates for souterrains in eastern Scotland. Indeed it has been claimed that the pottery evidence from the Gress Lodge souterrain near Stornoway indicates a fourth- to fifth-century date (MacKie, 1966). The bulk of the evidence for Pictish house types comes from the Northern and Western Isles, in other words from the periphery of Pictland rather than the core, and there must always be some doubt whether examples taken only from the peripheral areas are typical. This is most certainly true of the west coast where the respective influences of Scots and Picts are unclear. Brochs, one of the outstanding monuments of the proto-Picts, appear to have gone out of use in the first half of the second century to be succeeded on some sites by wheel-houses and aisled round houses. At other broch sites the dereliction of the tower appears to have been followed by a reversion to a complex of irregular cellular structures around the base of the tower. A lack of datable small finds makes it impossible to say to what extent these types of structures extended into the period of the historical Picts.

Certainly within the Pictish time period are houses at Coileagean an Udail in North Uist and Buckquoy in Orkney, although the former may be Scottish. In the pre-Norse period Udail was a nucleated village consisting of houses with one main room about 6 m long by 3·5 m across with one or more substantial roughly circular cells leading off (Crawford, 1974). At Buckquoy (Ritchie, 1977) cellular houses of a free-standing type with a central chamber surrounded by a series of cells are recorded, as well as a fine example of the more sophisticated *figure-of-eight* houses where the main chamber and small cells are arranged in linear fashion (Fig. 2.3). Although the evidence is still sparse, it is gradually becoming clear that Pictish settlement typology has certain parallels in broad terms to that evolving among the Scots and Britons. A number of structures, apparently large timber halls, have been located by air photo-graphy, and while it is tempting to see these as the centres of Pictish estates, excavation is essential to prove their date as one example has been shown to be Neolithic (Anon., 1980).

When the known settlement evidence is combined with that of the stones, it is clear that there was a substantial population occupying both coastal and

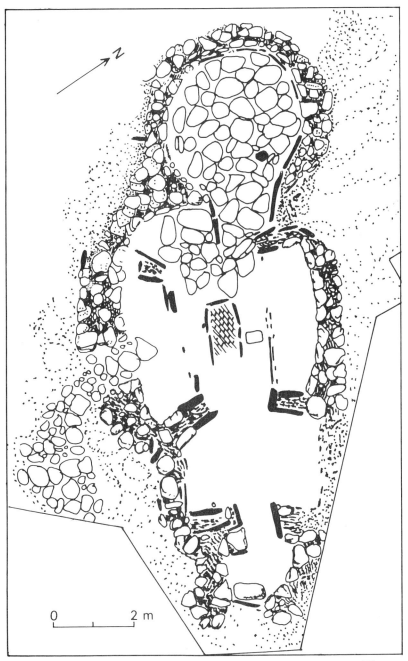

Fig. 2.3 Pictish house from Buckquoy, Orkney. (After Ritchie, 1977)

inland sites, and a number of attempts have been made to relate the archaeological evidence to the environment. From this it can be shown that agriculture played an increasingly important role as Pictish society evolved. The cool, wet, sub-Atlantic climatic phase was well established. The extension of blanket bog would have limited settlement possibilities in upland areas, and in lowland areas increased podsolization and gleying of soils would have occurred. If Class I stones can be used to give some indication of the distribution of settlement in the earlier part of the historical Pictish period, it would seem that cultivation at this time was of much less importance than it was in the ninth and tenth centuries. Over 60% of the Class I stones in Aberdeenshire are on podsols, one of the poorest soils, and a similar proportion is located on poor soils in Angus and Fife. Class II and and Class III stones on the other hand show a greater affinity with Brown Forest soils, which are much more suited to cultivation. In general terms the mean altitude of Class II and Class III stones is also slightly lower than that of Class I stones, suggesting a downhill movement of settlements which may be associated with agricultural expansion. This pattern would appear to be borne out by the distribution of the controversial place-name element *pit*.

Pit is one of a number of place-name elements, including *aber* (confluence), *carden* (thicket), *lanerc* (clearing), and *pert* (copse), which come from the spoken language of the Picts—a P-Celtic tongue related to that of Wales and Cornwall and distinct from the Q-Celtic of the Irish and Scots. There is still considerable debate as to the period when *pit* was a place-name forming prefix. It has been shown (Nicolaisen, 1975) that it does not occur in areas of Scotland where the Norse language became dominant in the ninth and tenth centuries and that the suffix element is usually Gaelic in origin, suggesting that the name-forming period was after the political union of the Picts and the Scots and that a bilingual situation existed in eastern Scotland (Fig. 2.4). Whittington (1977), however, suggests possible processes by which the *pit* element may have survived in some areas but not in others and re-opens the possibility of at least some of the names being early. Although there is no doubt that the world *pit* itself means a portion or a share, there is considerable controversy as to its significance in its place-name context. Barrow (1973) hypothesized its use as a land division with the shire superimposed upon a series of *pit* divisions; others have argued that it simply means farm or settlement. Small and Cottam (1974) draw attention to the fact that most of the Angus *pit* names are in areas known to have been forested in slightly later times and, following the argument for a late dating, suggest that they are associated with forest clearance and the extension of settlement with a growth of population, possibly contributed to by immigration after the political union with the Scots.

Whatever the original context of these names there is general agreement that they are related to land in use and as such may give a more accurate indication

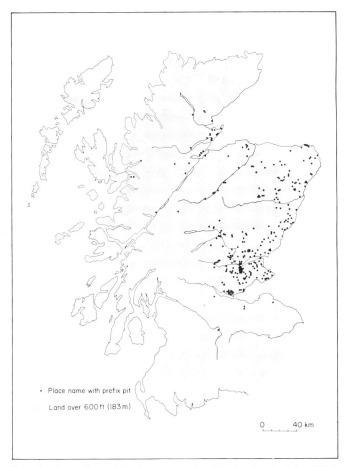

Fig. 2.4   Distribution of locatable place-names in *pit* in Scotland. (After Whittington, 1977)

of types of sites which were settled than do the sculptured stones, some of which may have been transported in post-Pictish times (it is possible that a number of the *pit* names may also have migrated). Whittington and Soulsby (1968) draw attention to the relationship of *pit* place names to the better soils, particularly Brown Forest soils in sheltered well-drained areas, and Whittington (1977) has extended this work showing that the *pit* names most frequently occur on Class I and Class II land as defined on the Land Use Capability maps of the Soil Survey of Scotland. As Class II land includes some of the better-drained podsols, it would seem that soil potential is more important than soil type, assuming that the modern classification is applicable to a period one thousand years earlier. The current view, therefore, is that by the ninth and tenth centuries, if not earlier, arable agriculture had become the mainstay of Pictish society.

As in the south of Scotland, there are tantalizing pointers to the existence of some sort of hierarchical structure in both the land organization and settlement patterns. The many questions about the Picts will not be answered until archaeology has revealed much more about open settlements and investigated problems such as the extent of dispersed as opposed to nucleated settlements and whether hamlet clusters or indeed villages evolved. Does the fact that there is an increasing clustering of Class II and Class III stones indicate a growth of larger settlements in the later Pictish period? Thus although there are still very many unanswered questions about the Picts, knowledge of them has increased substantially since Wainwright published *The Problem of the Picts* (1955).

THE VIKINGS

The Viking Settlement of Scotland started sometime between 790 and 810 and seems to have transformed the geographical patterns of much of northern and western Scotland.

Raiding and plundering activities by the Vikings are recorded in the church records, but current archaeological research suggests that many of their Scottish raiding activities took place after settlements had already been established. From the place-name evidence it is clear that there was substantial migration in the ninth and tenth centuries to Scotland from Norway, particularly the fiord areas of Western Norway. This outward movement appears to have been largely stimulated by the poverty of the natural environment and the shortage of land, although other factors such as the legal system and the unreliability of harvests may well have maintained the flow of emigrants.

Nicolaisen (1969) has shown that the earliest Norse Settlement names in Scotland, e.g. *stadr*, are concentrated in Orkney and Shetland with a thin scatter in the Western Isles. The distribution of *setr* and *saetr*, a slightly later name, shows the extension of settlement into Caithness as the concentration on the Northern and Western Isles increases. The latest settlement element *bolstadr* may well show the maximum extension of Norse settlement in northern Scotland. The *bolstadr* element reaches as far south as the Black Isle on the east coast. On the west coast it extends all along the islands from Lewis to Islay, and although a few examples exist on the western mainland of Scotland that area seems to have been less attractive to the settlers than the outer islands. A concentration of Scandinavian place names is also found in Galloway but this is believed to represent later, probably tenth-century, settlement of that area by Norse-Irish migrants from Ireland and/or the Isle of Man.

This essentially northern and western distribution can be explained most obviously in terms of the proximity of Orkney and Shetland to Norway. The extension of settlement into the Western Isles is probably related to the richness of Ireland at this time, a feature which quickly attracted the Vikings' attention. It is worth stressing also that the Scottish Viking settlements are in those parts of Scotland with environmental similarities to western Norway, although the milder climate and the more extensive areas of good soil available must have been a great attraction to the peasant farmer. Extensive raiding took place along the east coast, but there is no evidence for Viking settlement south of Inverness. This may reflect the military power of the Picts and later of the Scots in repulsing settlement attempts but may also be the result of higher population densities in eastern Scotland with less land available for colonization. Much of the success of Viking raiding, and perhaps also colonization, depended on their ships and seamanship, and the distribution of Norse settlement names reflects this sea mobility. Their failure to colonize the north-east knuckle of Scotland may have been due to the land-based military strength of the native population.

Turning to the settlement process, ideas such as the belief that the Vikings settled virtually empty islands in the North must be rejected. Discoveries such as the St Ninian's Isle treasure (Small et al., 1973) suggest that there was a wealthy and probably substantial Pictish population in the Northern Isles immediately prior to the Viking migrations. This is supported by the plethora of secondary structures around brochs which may well represent the continuity of settlement through the Early Christian period. Nor does the evidence suggest that newcomers drove out the existing population.

Marwick (1952), in his study of Orkney farm names, drew attention to the lack of primary Norse names on the areas of best soils, which is surprising if the Vikings were essentially land grabbers. Most recently Small (1981) has shown that in Shetland the distribution of broch sites and their related postbroch structures (usually associated with the areas of highest agricultural potential) and primary Norse settlement names are virtually mutually exclusive. Similar studies, as yet unpublished, show the same pattern emerging in Skye and Caithness. Thus it seems clear that Viking settlers did not push the natives off the good land but rather infilled the settlement pattern, taking up land which was uncultivated or only used as rough grazing.

Since the place-name evidence points to the migration of thousands of settlers in the period 800–1000 it is at first sight surprising that only a handful of Norse settlement sites have been discovered. By far the most well-known is Jarlshof (Hamilton, 1956) near the southern tip of the Shetland mainland where a sequence of Viking farmsteads overlies prehistoric structures going back to the Bronze Age. As at other sites, there seems to be a break between the pre-Viking and the Norse settlement rather than continuous sequent occupation. The scale of settlement at Jarlshof is almost certainly atypical, being the result of a combination of special environmental circumstances, which allowed a whole series of farmsteads to form a township-like structure utilising extensive (in Shetland terms) arable possibilities, and the location of the site which made it the natural contact point with the Viking settlements in Orkney to the south. More typical are likely to be the dispersed farmsteads such as Underhoull, in Unst (Small, 1967) and Buckquoy, in Orkney (Ritchie, 1977).

There is a tendency to regard the traditional Norse farmstead as being represented by the longhouse on the Icelandic or Scandinavian model, strictly defined as an extended structure incorporating a linear arrangement of dwelling house, byre and, on occasion, barns, stores and other units under one roof. Both Jarlshof and Underhoull, however, show that both separate outhouses and annexes to the long side of buildings were not uncommon and that the detail of farm layout reflected the individual whims of the farmer, building to meet his operational needs, either real or perceived (Fig. 2.5). What is more important is that a rectangular concept of building of various sizes seems to have replaced the somewhat amorphous cellular structures associated with pre-Norse sites and it may be that many of the features of the plan and building styles introduced by the Vikings continued through to the nineteenth-century croft (Roussell, 1934; Small, 1981).

Settlements are usually sited close to the shore or at a break of slope just clear of the best soils nearby and are constructed of local stone. Archaeological and historical evidence suggests an agricultural pattern similar to that which was to continue far into the mediaeval period, with a limited quantity of grain being grown in field strips close to the farm while the main emphasis was placed on stock rearing and providing sufficient fodder for winter feed. Each farm had a few cattle and some sheep, which even in Shetland could be outwintered—a major advantage over Norway, where this was only possible in the most favoured areas. From the examination of the midden deposits at Buckquoy in Orkney, Ritchie (1977) has shown that cattle provided by far the most important source of food supply, the proportion of animals on the site being approximately 50% cattle, 30% sheep and 20% pig, which is perhaps surprising in the light of the nature of the landscape and what is known of later times. None of the excavated Norse sites has produced convincing evidence of a seasonal autumnal slaughter, but the Buckquoy evidence suggests that about one-third of the animals died during the first year of life, indicating that their main function was the provision of meat and hides. Saga evidence suggests that seabirds, in particular their eggs, were an important source of food supply, providing a welcome variation in the diet. At present there is little archaeological evidence to support this or to suggest that domestic poultry was of any significance on the Norse farmstead.

Clear evidence of fishing, in the form of hooks, sinkers and bones, is

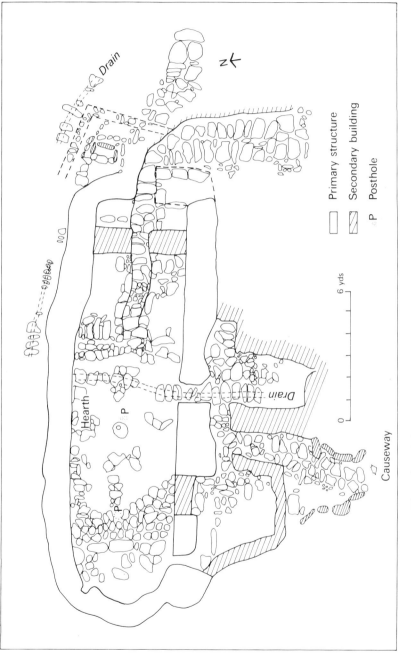

Fig. 2.5 Viking house, Underhoull, Unst, Shetland. (After Small, 1967)

Drain

N

Hearth

P

P

P

Drain

6 yds

0

Causeway

Primary structure

Secondary building

P Posthole

recorded from most Norse sites. At both Jarlshof and Underhoull it has been suggested that fishing was unimportant in the primary phase of the settlement and tended to become more significant as time went on, perhaps as a response to the limitations of the agricultural environment as the population increased. Bones and fishing tackle confirm that net and line techniques including deep water fishing from boats were used. Shellfish, mainly limpets and winkles, are recorded from a number of sites, but do not seem to have been as integral a part of the diet as they were at some prehistoric sites.

The paucity of Norse sites so far discovered can be best explained in the light of the house types and agricultural system outlined above. Their similarity to later settlements, both in form and function, suggests continuity of occupation until the recent past. Furthermore, as the Jarlshof and Underhoull sites clearly demonstrate, drystone construction facilitates modification and rebuilding at frequent intervals on the same site rather than moving to a new one.

The growth of towns in the Viking period in Ireland is well-known, but at present there is little evidence to support such developments in Scotland. It is doubtful whether northern and western Scotland could have generated the wealth to justify the evolution of large trading settlements, and although a case can be made for one or two small settlements, for example Kirkwall, it is doubtful whether even it was a sizeable community before the Later Norse period and the ultimate building of St Magnus cathedral.

The bulk of the Norsemen who settled in Scotland were simple peasant families who made maximum use of the local resources within the limits of the technology of the time. Their food supply was local, their fuel came from the peat bogs of the hillsides, their clothing was home-made, and their raw materials for household goods were also essentially local. Steatite, a soft rock which can be carved with a knife or simple chisel, provided cooking pots, gaming boards, children's toys, and numerous other household objects. Many areas of Norse settlement, for example Orkney, do not have outcrops of steatite, so some trade even at the peasant farmer level must have developed; most probably this was organized through the higher levels of society. The sagas record the import of timber to the Northern Isles from both Norway and the Western Isles. This would have been essential for constructional and boat-building purposes, as even despite the Little Climatic Optimum there was no growth of any substantial timber in the Northern Isles. Salt, pottery, and luxury goods also appear to have entered the trade patterns from time to time. The archaeological and place-name evidence thus presents an entirely different view of the Vikings from the bloodthirsty, boorish warriors presented in the literary sources. Raiding and plundering did occur, but so it did frequently in later times. Why then have the Vikings achieved such notoriety? The answer may well be that they were particularly efficient at it and also that they were pagans to whom a church was no more than a likely source of treasure to be treated in the same way as a defended homestead. The church records are one of the main sources of information about these events, and had they not attacked the churches the Vikings might not have been seen as any more brutal than any other contemporaneous people.

Although the Vikings' political control was gained by a small number of astute and powerful leaders and there is no evidence that the Picts were driven out, enslaved or exterminated, there can be little doubt that it was ultimately the large numbers of new settlers which submerged Pictish society and culture in the Norse settlement areas. It is tempting to believe that most Pictish peasant farmers continued to extract a living from their old homesteads, ultimately intermarrying with the newcomers and adapting to their ways and learning their language. This raises all kinds of new questions which at present have no satisfactory answer. Was the Norse agricultural system very similar to that of the Picts? Did Norse building styles offer features which the Picts found advantageous and superior to their own? Only further excavation can answer such questions.

CONCLUSION

The past decade has seen considerable advances in archaeological and place-name studies of the Dark Age period, but there is still an inadequate data base on which to build an adequate geographical synthesis. Palynological work is needed to confirm the extent of forest clearance now suspected as being a significant feature of change in the Dark Age landscape with considerable implications for the development of agriculture. Such studies may also lead towards an understanding of the effects of the amelioration in weather conditions leading up to the Little Climatic Optimum towards the end of the period. It will not be until many more excavations of domestic sites have been undertaken, particularly in the core areas of the various groups, that it will be possible to judge whether the settlements known today are typical of a much wider area. The small finds from new sites, particularly from the midden deposits, are essential before it will be possible to speculate on the nature of the economy in Dark Age Scotland. Similarly, place names need much detailed philological study before geographers can make maximum use of them.

From the material which is available it is clear that the process of landscape evolution continued through the Dark Ages, and it is interesting to speculate whether in geographical terms the differences between Picts and Scots and Britons were as great as the historical divisions appear to make them. In the same way it may be asked whether the arrival of the Vikings, although introducing new settlement forms, had a great deal of effect on the everyday life of the peasant farmer who made up the bulk of the population. If landscape evolution is a slow, continuing process affected only to a limited degree by political change, how many of the patterns of the post 1100 Scottish landscape have their origins in the Dark Ages or even earlier?

REFERENCES

Alcock, L. (1976). A multi-disciplinary chronology for Alt Clut, Castle Rock, Dumbarton. *Proc. Soc. Antiquaries Scot.* **107**, 103–13.

Alcock, L. (1980). Populi bestiales pictorum feroci animo: A survey of Pictish settlement archaeology. *In* 'Roman Frontier Studies 1979'. (W. S. Hanson, and J. Keppie, ed.) *Brit. Archaeol. Rep. Internat. Ser.* **71**, 61–95.

Anon. (1980). Balbridie. *Curr. Archaeol.* **70**, 326–8.

Barrow, G. W. S. (1973). 'The Kingdom of the Scots'. Arnold, London.

Christison, D. (1905). Excavations of forts on the Poltalloch estate. *Proc. Soc. Antiquaries Scot.* **39**, 259–322.

Cottam, M. B. and Small, A. (1974). The distribution of settlement in southern Pictland. *Med. Arch.* **18**, 43–65.

Craw, J. H. (1930). Excavations at Dunadd. *Proc. Soc. Antiquaries Scot.* **64**, 111–46.

Crawford, I. A. (1974). Scot (?) Norseman and Gael. *Scot. Archaeol. Forum.* **6**, 1–16.

Edwards, K. J. and Ralston, I. (1980). New dating and environmental evidence from Burghead fort, Moray. *Proc. Soc. Antiquaries Scot.* **109**, 202–210.

Fairhurst, H. (1939). The galleried dun at Kildonan Bay, Kintyre. *Proc. Soc. Antiquaries Scot.* **73**, 185–228.

Feachem, R. W. (1963). 'A Guide to Prehistoric Scotland'. Batsford, London.

Graham, A. (1939). Cultivation terraces in south-eastern Scotland. *Proc. Soc. Antiquaries Scot.* **73**, 289–315.

Greig, J. C. (1971). Excavations at Cullykhan, Castle Point, Troup, Banffshire. *Scot. Archaeol. Forum* **3**, 15–21.

Greig, J. C. (1972). Cullykhan. *Curr. Archaeol.* **32**, 227–31.

Guido, M. (1974). A Scottish crannog re-dated. *Antiquity* **68**, 54–6.

Hamilton, J. R. C. (1956). 'Excavations at Jarlshof, Shetland'. HMSO, London.

Hope-Taylor, B. (1966). Doon Hill. *Med. Arch.* **10**, 176–7.

Laing, L. (1975). 'The Archaeology of Late Celtic Britain and Ireland c. 400–1200 A.D.'. Methuen, London.

MacKie, E. W. (1966). Iron Age pottery from the Gress Lodge earth-house, Stornoway, Lewis. *Proc. Soc. Antiquaries Scot.* **98**, 199–203.

Marwick, H. (1952). 'Orkney Farm Names.' W. R. Mackintosh, Kirkwall.

Maxwell, H. (1913). Note on a hoard of personal ornaments from Talnotrie, Kirkcudbright. *Proc. Soc. Antiquaries Scot.* **47**, 12–16.

Munro, R. (1882). 'Ancient Scottish Lake-Dwellings or Crannogs.' David Douglas, Edinburgh.

Nicolaisen, W. F. H. (1965). Scottish place names: 24 slew and sliabh. *Scottish Studies* **9**, 91–106.

Nicolaisen, W. F. H. (1968). Place names of the Dundee Region' In "Dundee and District.' (S. J. Jones, ed.). Dundee Local Executive Committee of the British Association for the Advancement of Science, Dundee, 144–52.

Piggott, C. M. (1948). The Excavations at Hownam Rings, Roxburghshire, 1948. *Proc. Soc. Antiquaries Scot.* **82**, 193–224.

Piggott, C. M. (1953), Milton Loch Crannog I. A native house of the 2nd century A.D. in Kirkcudbrightshire. *Proc. Soc. Antiquaries Scot.* **87**, 134–152.

Ritchie, A. (1977). Excavation of Pictish and Viking-Age farmsteads at Buckquoy, Orkney. *Proc. Soc. Antiquaries Scot.* **108**, 174–227.

Ritchie, J. N. G. (1967). Keil Cave, Southend, Argyll: A Late Iron Age cave occupation in Kintyre. *Proc. Soc. Antiquaries Scot.* **99**, 104–110.

Roussell, A. (1934). 'Norse Building Customs in the Scottish Isles,' Williams and Norgate, London.

Scott, J. (1961). Loch Glashan Crannog. *Med. Arch.* **5**, 310.

Small, A. (1967). Excavations at Underhoull, Unst, Shetland. *Proc. Soc. Antiquaries Scot.* **98**, 225–48.

Small, A. (1969). Burghead. *Scot. Archaeol. Forum* **1**, 61–8.

Small, A. (1981). 'The Norse Building Tradition in Shetland.' Stavanger Museum.

Small, A., and Cottam, M. B. (1972). Craig Phadrig. *University of Dundee, Department of Geography, Occ. Paper. 1.*

Small, A., Thomas, C., and Wilson, D. M. (1973). 'St Ninian's Isle and Its Treasure.' Oxford University Press, Oxford.

Steer, K. A., and Keeney, G. S. (1974). Excavations in two homesteads at Crock Cleugh, Roxburghs. *Proc. Soc. Antiquaries Scot.* **81**, 138–57.

Stevenson, R. B. K. (1949). The nuclear fort of Dalmahoy, Midlothian, and other dark age capitals. *Proc. Soc. Antiquaries Scot.* **83**. 186–98.

Turner, J. (1970). Post-Neolithic disturbance of British vegetation. *In* 'Studies in the Vegetational History of the British Isles.' (D. Walker and R. G. West, ed.). Cambridge University Press, Cambridge.

Wainwright, F. T. (ed.) (1955). 'The Problem of the Picts.' Nelson, Edinburgh.

Wainwright, F. T. (1963). 'The Souterrains of Southern Pictland.' Routledge and Kegan Paul, London.

Whittington, G. and Soulsby, J. A. (1968). A preliminary report of an investigation into *pit* placenames. *Scot. Geogr. Mag.* **84**, 117–25.

Whittington, G. (1977). Placenames and the settlement pattern of dark-age Scotland. *Proc. Soc. Antiquaries Scot.* **106**, 99–110.

Wild, J. P. (1970). Button-and-loop fasteners in the Roman provinces. *Britannia* **1**, 137–55.

3

Medieval Rural Scotland

R. A. Dodgshon

The face of rural Scotland during the six or seven centuries that followed the unification of the kingdom in the eleventh century can hardly be classed as familiar. Except for the shafts of light that have been brought to play on a few select issues or localities, our appreciation of its general forms and processes remains seriously incomplete. Exploring the general theme of society's relationship to the land soon exposes these weaknesses in our understanding, with large swathes of the countryside cast in shadow for much of the period and some of its key problems barely capable of definition let alone solution. Altogether, four main areas of discussion stand out. First, there is the extent to which the increasingly feudal character of Scottish rural society after unification produced a distinct phase in the development of the countryside, a medieval landscape *sui generis*. Secondly, there is the extent to which the period witnessed the colonization of fresh land, either through the expansion of established settlements or the creation of new ones. Thirdly, there is the problem of how farming townships were constituted in tenurial terms and how this constitution affected the layout of their constituent holdings. Included under this heading is runrig, or the subdivision and intermixture of land belonging to different landholders. Fourthly, there is the debate that surrounds the field economy of townships, or the way in which their various sectors and resources were exploited, a debate that centres around the infield–outfield system of husbandry.

MEDIEVAL SETTLEMENT AND COLONIZATION: ITS TENURIAL CONTEXT

The human landscape is an adjustment between man and the land which takes account not just of environmental opportunities but equally the social context in which these opportunities were exploited. In medieval and early-modern Scotland, the social context of land exploitation can be reduced to the problem of land tenure. Although admittedly only a part of the problem, land tenure has the merit of focusing all the relationships, conflicting interests and pressures within rural society on to a single plane. Moreover, if the landscape of this period has any claim to distinction, then it is to the persuasive and formative influence of tenure that we must turn. Obviously, in a countryside possessed of so much physical and social diversity, it would be unrealistic to expect a single, uniform tenure to have prevailed over the length and breadth of the country during the medieval period. In fact, significant variations can be detected over both space and time. However, some unity of theme can be devised by concentrating on the way feudal ideas fashioned a distinct form of land tenure.

In essence, feudal tenures were dependent and service-bearing, with land being held of a superior (the crown or a lord) in return for services and dues of one kind or another. Initially, some probably involved a degree of unfreedom or bondage for the ordinary peasant, but this had disappeared by the four- teenth century, though instruments of lordly authority, like the courts of barony and regality, gave landowners until the eighteenth century a close and often oppressive control over those who actually tilled the land. As a concept that transformed Scottish rural society and landscape through its impact on tenures, feudalism is usually linked with the spread of Anglo-Norman ideas and landholders under David I (1124–1153) and subsequent Scottish kings. Whatever its character prior to the eleventh century, it now emerged as a hierarchy of tenurial relationships extending downwards from the king, via the great territorial barons, knights and lesser landowners to the common hus- bandman and bondman. Its diffusion on these terms was a gradual affair, with successive kings granting land by charter in return for allegiance and service, often to landholders who had previously held the same land allodially or without a superior. Naturally, the task of converting the possession of land to feudal tenure under the Scottish king was easier in royal demesne areas, like Fife, than in areas like the south-west or the Western Isles where independent celtic earls and chiefs resisted royal authority in preference to their own. Broadly speaking, the feudalization of tenures made rapid progress in the Borders and in the central and eastern Lowlands over the twelfth and thirteenth centuries. It was accompanied by the implantation of Anglo- Norman landholders and the creation of large territorial lordships (e.g. Annandale, Lauderdale), lordships which 'profoundly affected, indeed may be said to have determined, the feudal landscape of Scotland' (Barrow, 1980, 64). By the late thirteenth century, it had already started to make deep inroads into the Highlands, with the establishment of Anglo-Norman families like the de Meyners (Menzies) and Fleming Freskin (Moray) along the southern and eastern fringes, but with other native landholders (e.g. the earls of Lennox and Atholl) acknowledging the Scottish king as their superior and thereafter holding their land from him by charter. However, its subsequent diffusion through the rest of the Highlands was prolonged. Areas like the southern Hebrides remained beyond the Crown's authority until the collapse of the Lordship of the Isles in the late fifteenth century. Even here, it is likely that some feudalization of tenures had taken place by the time local chiefs acknowledged the Scottish kings as their superior. Certainly, it is difficult to find positive reference in early sources to the small, independent freeholds—perhaps based on four-generation kin-groups—which are thought by some to have been the basis of early Highland tenures (Levie, 1927). By the time documents shed light on the area, property rights appear to have been concentrated in the hands of clan chiefs and land was let to their kinsmen on a nominally short-term rather than hereditary basis. Admittedly, kin groups occupied specific localities and townships, but they did so through the affectations of the clan system and the warmth and consideration which it introduced into the tenurial contract, not through any basis of absolute or hereditary right (Macpherson, 1966; Cregeen, 1969). The acquisition of the Northern Isles by the Scottish Crown in the fifteenth century paved the way for a more self-evident process of feudalization with many odal lands (independent freeholds held on an allodial basis) being grasped by the bishop and earl during the fifteenth and sixteenth centuries and re-set as rented or tenant land.

It has been argued that whilst the spread of Anglo-Norman feudalism created new lordships and introduced new tenants, it did not necessarily alter the disposition of holdings on the ground even in areas like the south-east. The changes involved were rooted more in tenure and possession. Whether the process was sudden or phased, early or late, connected directly to the spread of Crown feudalism or merely symbolized by it, the feudalization of tenure had profound implications for the terms on which land was possessed. In particular, once holdings were held for rent and service, it became necessary to scale the amount of land held in return. As a response, feudalism developed what might be termed a quantum theory of landholding—the notion that within each estate or district, fixed amounts of land should bear a fixed and equal proportion of rent, dues and services. Linking these two sides of the tenurial contract together were the customary land units used to compute the extent of both townships and their constituent holdings: the davach, ounceland (or tirunga), pennyland, merkland, ploughgate, oxgate, and husbandland. Rentals for the medieval and early-modern period are dominated by these customary land measures. Their strength of usage is best demonstrated by their persistence, with many estates still making use of them to set land during the seventeenth and early eighteenth centuries. For example, a late seventeenth-century rental for the Breadalbane estate, which included districts like Glenorchy and Strathfillan (SRO, GD50/15) as well as a rental of 1718 for South Uist (SRO, GD201/1257/5), both assessed townships in terms of merklands; a list of townships in Ardnamurchan and Sunart drawn up in 1727 gave them each a pennyland assessment (Murray, 1740); while a mid eighteenth century rental for Strathspey still saw townships as equalling a davach or fractions of a davach, organizing its entries under such headings as the 'Dauch of Ballintomb' or the 'Dauch of Rothemure' (SRO, GD248/248/32). Nor do we have to probe too far back in time to find rentals which still preserved the set relationship between each land measure and the different forms of rent levied on it, either within a particular locality or throughout the entire estate. Thus, a rental of 1600 for the parish of Kingussie burdened each plough share (of which four equalled a davach) with an annual rent of £1 1s. 1d. in silver mail, two bolls of grain, one firlot of ferme, one boll of multure, two pecks of teind, a small number of sheep and poultry and 'areadge and careadge and due service' (Macpherson, 1893, 505). All large estates, however, had one or two townships rented exclusively for services that could not be tied to land measures in this standardized way, such as Sterigerly in South Uist which was held by Donald McMoury in 1718 'from the family of Clanranald for Registring the Deeds & Genealogie of the family & makeing paneyricks when Desyred' (SRO, GD201/1257/5).

All the different types of land measure used in medieval Scotland represented definite—not abstract—amounts of land, with those making up a particular township (or its assessment) being anchored by marked or known boundaries. Equally important, when set down in the landscape, township assessments did not form a continuous cover but had the character of islands of assessment in a sea of non assessed land. The feudal landscape, then, had not only a measured basis but also a chequerboard appearance, with rights of occupation being firmly tied to particular squares or blocks of countryside. From his fermtoun or clachan, the medieval peasant looked out not on a world of boundless opportunity but towards an horizon that was carefully prescribed by his township's assessment in land units. The limits of his township, however, added up to more than geographically defined space. It focused all the rights and obligations that gave meaning to feudal tenure. Even use-rights over non-assessed land (i.e. grazing, peat-cutting, timber) were proportioned through a township's or person's assessed land. What is more, rural society could only colonize new land and create new settlements when it was legitimized by a new block of assessed land, since this was the means whereby feudal superiority over land imposed itself on the countryside—and the husbandman. When communities eventually came to cultivate land *outside* their assessed framework and even to create new settlement on non-assessed land, it heralded—and was labelled—a fundamental shift in lordly attitudes to land and its tenure. Only with these various points grasped can we begin to make sense of the medieval landscape and its trends.

SETTLEMENT AND COLONIZATION 1100–1700

Although its exact phasing cannot yet be determined, the overall trend of the period 1100–1700 appears to have been one of expansion, both as regards the number of settlements created and the amount of arable taken in from the waste. The one major counter-trend was the Black Death of the mid-fourteenth century, which probably induced a sharp reversal, with communities contracting. However, caution is needed before applying the so-called 'Postan-model' in a blanket-like fashion to Scottish rural society, assuming that the thirteenth and early fourteenth centuries must have been the phase of *maximum* land pressure in the countryside and that the Black Death precipitated a long phase of contraction and stagnation (Postan, 1966). The Black Death unquestionably reduced demand for land, but whether the high-point of rural colonization in Scotland was reached on the eve of the Black Death or later, after population growth had recovered its momentum (sixteenth and seventeenth centuries?), is a problem that still has to be resolved.

The overall trend towards expansion was expressed in three ways. First, there was the straightforward creation of new settlements. Secondly, there occured a splitting of townships into two or more separate units as they grew larger and more complex. Thirdly, and by no means least, townships expanded into their non-assessed land, an overflow that acquired the distinct and special status of outfield.

(1) The Creation of New Settlements 1100–1700

Rural settlements created after *c*. 1100 divided themselves into two categories: those that pioneered the occupation of whole new areas and those that infilled established patterns of settlement, taking up the more marginal or interstitial sites.

Given the extent of settlement by *c*. 1100, it is doubtful whether the pioneering of whole new areas played a substantial role in post-1100 colonization. Most areas had some population, however thin, at the outset. Only where settlement was pushed more deeply into an upland valley or where a hunting forest was disafforested is this category of new settlement likely to have been important. The Southern Uplands offer quite a number of examples. Thus, when David I granted Eskdale to Robert Avenel (*c*. 1185), he used the higher parts as a hunting forest. However, by the time the area can be glimpsed through a rental of *c*. 1376, farms like Eskdalemuir, Lyneholm and Effgill were already to be found in its more remote or wilder corners. The same rental records farms in upper Liddesdale and along Hermitage Water as having been carved out of forest land, presumably during the thirteenth or early fourteenth centuries (*Registrum Honoris de Morton*, Vol. 1, 1853). Just a few miles to the south, a charter drawn up 1153 x 1157 documents the advance of settlement up Dodburn with the grant of 'that clearing called Kershope' (Barrow, 1960, 200). Apart from the forester's stedes, the vast royal hunting forest of Ettrick did not experience settlement on any scale until it was extensively feued over the early sixteenth century and the sheep farming economy which had been established during the fifteenth century was extended. By comparison, the higher parts of both Ettrick and Yarrow Waters were granted in free forest to Melrose abbey in 1235 and thereafter used as sheep grazings. Settlements like Chapelhope and Over Kirkhope probably emerged soon after 1235. Place names are also helpful in dating settlement in the middle and upper reaches of Clydesdale. There, the implantation of Anglo-Norman knights during the twelfth century led to a series of settlements that combine an Anglo-Norman personal name with the element -*ton* (i.e. Lamington, Roberton). However, it is not entirely clear whether these settlements pioneered the area or simply provided new foci for established patterns of landholding.

Ettrick apart, the hunting forests of the Southern Uplands were dis-afforested by the early fourteenth century, having lasted for barely two or three centuries. By contrast, the life-cycle of the forests in the Highlands followed a different chronology. Some of the larger forests, such as Cluny, Alyth and Birse, were being exposed to settlement by the fifteenth and sixteenth centuries, but others, like Mamlorn and Glenfalloch, were only just being formally established. The map of opportunities—if these largely barren areas can be described as such—was being constantly redrawn. Where former forest land contained reserves of colonizable land, their legal disafforestation triggered off small waves of pioneering. This was especially true of forest land around the southern and eastern edges of the Highlands. For instance, when the Forest of Affraick lost its status as a hunting forest, its lower ground slowly filled with new settlements over the fifteenth and sixteenth centuries (Mather, 1970). A charter conveying Cabrach to the earl of Huntly in 1508 captures a similar moment in its history, for it gave the earl the 'power either to turn the lands into arable ground or to keep it as Forrest according to the Forrest Law' (SRO, GD44, Vol. 1, part 1, no. 47). The former option was chosen, and even its higher ground had farms such as Elrick and Geauche by 1600. Generally speaking, forests established on the more difficult ground, such as the royal forest of Carrick in Argyll, preserved their status for longer, but their high, mountainous ground can hardly be classed as a loss to the husbandman.

In the Lowlands, settlement established after 1100 tended to have the character of infill, with lightly occupied landscapes becoming more densely settled. Only occasionally can the formation of such settlements be traced through their foundation charters, such as the ploughgate that was 'lawfully measured' in a clearing at Burgin on the coastal lowlands of Moray and granted to Kinross abbey, 1153 x 1165 (Barrow, 1960, 278), or the grant of Carroc near Lesmahagow in 1236 which gave the holder the freedom to assart anywhere within its bounds (*Liber S. Marie de Calchou 1113–1567*, Vol. 1, 278). One useful suggestion is that the early occurrence of ploughgates north of the Tay, such as the 'two measured ploughgates' at Kennethmont in Aberdeenshire which were conveyed 1189 x 1195 (Barrow, 1971, 315), may mark the spread of Anglian influence—and new settlement—from the twelfth century onwards. But there is a chance that such ploughgates were old davach assessments re-expressed in terms of a now more favoured measure: this may well have been the case with ploughgates given to Dunfermline abbey, 1189 x 1195, and which had overtly Pictish names like *Pet*malduith and *Pet*macduuegile (Barrow, 1971, 315).

A notable feature of Scottish settlement history is the extent to which new settlement continued to be formed as late as the sixteenth and seventeenth centuries. This is apparent from rental series which become widely available from the sixteenth century onwards. Many of those formed at this late date occupied marginal sites, both physically and locationally. Their marginality is further underlined by the fact that many were small, filial settlements, attached by rentals to a parent settlement. Even more revealing is the fact that some were clearly developed on non-assessed land, being carved out of commonty, measured in acres and held for a cash rent. Examples of such outsets abound, such as the toun of Whitestane in Birse parish (Aberdeenshire) which is noted in a rental of 1511 as having been established on uncultivated land taken out of the touns of Ennochty and Tillygarmouth (Browne, 1923, 192), the tenement or outset reported as 'in communi mora de Eyemouth' (Berwickshire) by a charter of 1584 (Thomson, 1888, 236) or the Perthshire toun of Crottis which, by 1585, was conveyed 'cum *lye outsettis* appellat Cauldcottis' (Thomson, 1888, 283). Often these outsets betray their marginal condition through place-names, with topographical elements like Muirton and Woodset being especially commonplace. In the Northern Isles, the term quoy was used instead of outset, as with Angusquoy and Quoy Ingybister which are entered in a rental of 1612 for Paplay and Greenwall parish in Orkney (Peterkin, 1862, appendix 11, 10). Surviving rentals for the western Highlands and Islands, such as those for Islay (Smith, 1895, appendices) and Kintyre (Innes, 1854, Vol. 2, part 1, 3; McNeill, 1897, 625–30; Macphail, 1920, 72–88) suggest that there, too, new settlement continued to be formed in the sixteenth and seventeenth centuries. Coming so late in the colonizing process, these new settlements were again on the more marginal, less favoured sites.

(2) Township Splitting

Inextricably bound up with the appearance of new settlements after 1100 was the splitting of townships into two or more separate units. Some examples are referred to in the style of 'the 2 Boturchys' or 'the three Lanarkynris' (SRO, GD198/59). However, owing to the use of standardized procedures for carrying out the process, most examples are distinguished by the place name prefixes *East*, *West*, *Nether* and *Upper* or by the affixes *Mor* and *Beg* (Dodgshon, 1975a). The large number of these elements to be found on the modern map is a measure of how widespread and important township splitting was to the long-term history of the rural landscape. Still other examples are hidden behind personalized forms of place-name, townships having substituted more distinctive titles for the dreary sameness imparted by prefixes like *East*, *West*, etc.

The reasons why townships were split are varied. In the Northern Isles, the custom of partible inheritance practised by odallers was an important cause, with co-heirs dividing their family patrimony into split settlements by a process known as an 'airff and division'. Its potency as a cause of splitting in Orkney was recognized by J. Storer Clouston. Among the examples which he researched was that of Grimbister in Firth parish, which was divided between co-heirs into Over-, Mid- and Nether-bigging (Storer Clouston, 1932, 347–9). On the mainland, primogeniture was the normal rule of inheritance, at least in the areas which came under the sway of Anglo-Norman ideas on property descent. However, where landowners were succeeded only by daughters, it is clear that partible inheritance operated and that the resultant division could produce split settlements. Thus, when John Dickson died in the late fifteenth century, his holding of Denys (Peebles-shire) was split between his two daughters and their husbands. By 1532, it had become Easter and Wester Denys (Buchan and Paton, 1927, Vol. 1, 67–8). Similarly, when Sir John Fraser died *c.* 1400, his land of Menzies (Peebles-shire) was divided into Over and Nether portions between his two daughters (Buchan and Paton, 1927, Vol. 1, 407). Allied to those townships split between co-heirs were those that underwent fission after being set or granted to more than one landholder. Thus, Lumsden (Berwickshire) appears to have become Great or East and Little or West Lumsden when it was set to two different landholders in the twelfth century (Thomson, 1908, 242–3). The alternative for landholders brought together in this way was to divide their holdings into runrig, or sub-divided fields. Those who did so sometimes had second thoughts, for the desire to remove runrig is occasionally stated as the reason for splitting. This was the case when Old Flinders was divided into an Over and Nether Plough in 1641 (SRO, GD225/269). In other instances, such as when Grenane (Dumfries-shire) was split into two separate holdings in 1485, it was simply declared that the two landholders concerned had previously held their land 'ryndale' but that now it was to be 'ewinly dividyt betuix the saidis parteis be equale portionis' and then each portion allocated to the landholder whose dwelling was closest (Murray, 1958, 53–4).

The forementioned causes of splitting were probably at work from as early as the twelfth century onwards. In time, however, the most general cause became the problems associated with the increasing scale and complexity of townships. To some extent, this cause cannot easily be disentangled from the problems posed by runrig, for the organizational demands of the latter accentuated any problems posed by the increasing size and complexity of townships. However, it does stand as a separate explanation accounting for the many townships that were shared between tenants and then split, yet whose fission re-created smaller but still runrig townships. The estate of Coupar Angus abbey provides a number of well-documented examples of this sort of splitting which date from the mid-fifteenth century. Many other large estates, both in the High-lands and Lowlands, afford more circumstantial proof for this sort of splitting over the sixteenth and seventeenth centuries (Dodgshon, 1977). That a preference for smaller townships was a root cause is given confirmation by Gordon of Straloch, the seventeenth-century topographer. After observing how townships in Banffshire had earlier been much larger, he went on to explain how husbandmen had found the problems of cultivating distant grounds and negotiating with so many fellow tenants irksome and had opted for smaller—albeit runrig—townships (Macfarlane, 1907, 463–4). The numerous split townships along the Livet and Speyside bear out this claim.

(3) The Formation of Outfield

A major component of colonization over the late-medieval and early-modern period was the outward expansion of established townships into their sur-rounding waste. At first, we might reasonably expect such expansion to have used up the slack within the bounds of a township's assessed land and then to have made more intensive use of such land, before turning to the prospect of cultivating their non-assessed land. Of course, it would make nonsense of having an assessed territory if early communities could breach its bounds as soon as need arose. Initially at least, assessments imposed definite limits on the extent of a township. When their rigidity was eventually relaxed, it was probably accomplished in one of three ways. First, growth beyond the existing framework of assessed land could have been underwritten by the creation of extra land units. Since customary land units focused all the rights and obligations of feudal tenure, this addition could only be sanctioned by lords, not by the farming community. Although it would seem a logical solution, there is not much support for it. The new blocks of assessed land that were being laid out over the twelfth and thirteenth centuries have the appearance of new townships, not of appendages for the expansion of old ones.

A second possibility would have been for townships to have had the size of land units re-defined. Outwardly a township's assessment would remain a fixed number of land units, but inwardly each land unit—and consequently the total extent of the township—would be increased. At first, this would seem a forced, contrived interpretation, but it would circumvent the particularly strong conservatism that surrounded the number of land units to be found in a township or even a district. The acreage of individual land units, meanwhile, shows signs of having had more flexibility—so much so that there are quite a number of sources which remind husbandmen (and perhaps the estate also) of what their acreage was meant to be. However, there are also interesting discrepancies of size between the land units of different areas, discrepancies which might be explained by envisaging an expansion of some from one level of acreage to another. For example, the davachs of the western Highlands and those of the north-east appear to have been different in size, radically so, with the former seemingly based on a sub-unit of eight acres and the latter on the Anglian (and therefore, later) oxgate of 13 acres. A comparable problem is raised by land measures in the extreme south-east. There, the majority of townships appear to have been based by the late medieval period on a land unit of around 13 acres (the husbandland), but there were some townships based on an eight-acre unit (the merkland), like Horndean and Paxton (Dodgshon, 1973, 7; Raine, 1841, lxxxv *et seq.*). To see them as denoting different layers of settlement would be one explanation, but they could also signify an incomplete attempt to re-value the land units of the district. Such a re-valuation (from 'eight-aiker cavills' to 13-acre husbandlands) seems to have occurred at Newstead in the Tweed valley (Dodgshon, 1981). If the experience of New-stead has a general bearing on the problem, it would be in the context of the thirteenth or fourteenth centuries and before. Perhaps when Sim Sawand was commanded by the earl of March to lay out the Merse into husbandlands in the thirteenth century (*APS*, 1, Notices of MSS, xxiv), it conceals a local re-definition of land measures into larger units. After all, given the antiquity of settlement in this area, we can hardly believe that Sim Sawand was faced with a wilderness still to be pioneered.

A third possibility was for townships to expand beyond the bounds of their assessed land and, in the process, beyond the customary framework of their tenure. In fact, this was a form of overflow that was eventually forced on most Scottish townships. Given what has already been said about township assess-ment, it follows that this involved more than simply pressure for renewed growth. It presupposed that any changes had finally ceased and that any legal barriers to the cultivation of non-assessed land had been eroded. Assisting the latter was a growing tendency from the thirteenth and fourteenth centuries onwards for estates to exercise a more exclusive control over their common grazings. All blocks of assessed land had rights of common-grazing over their surrounding waste, like the grant of Loherwet (Peebles-shire), 1198 x 1202, which carried with it 'common pasturage without the cornfield and meadow' (Harvey and Macleod, 1930, 4). At first, such common pasture was generally shared by the livestock of different estates and townships. Progressively, however, many common grazings were legally divided between them, each estate or township with an interest being awarded a separately defined share (Harvey and Macleod, 1930, 230; Anderson, 1899, 130–1; SRO, GD4/262). Although it must be stressed that these pre-1695 divisions of commonty did not in themselves legitimize the cultivation of non-assessed land, they did provide the conditions under which the customary and legal restraints on its cultivation could be more easily dismantled under pressure from a growing population and changing attitudes towards tenure.

The first signs of non-assessed land being cultivated are provided by the earliest references to the term outsets, whose derivation as land outside that which was set captures all the character of this new direction in township growth. The term first appeared during the fifteenth century as something appendaged to a township's assessed land and became widespread over the sixteenth century, being mentioned in charters and rentals from the Borders to the Northern Isles. By the late sixteenth century, however, a change in usage was afoot. From being the term used of all the cultivated patches in the non-assessed land surrounding townships, the term outsets became more and more confined to those on which new, filial settlements were established (see p. 53). Where non-assessed land continued to be cultivated by townships as a projection of their existing arable (or their assessed land), outfield appears to have taken over from outsets as the preferred term of description. The shift from one to the other possibly manifests the emergence of the distinct cropping system commonly associated with outfield. It is a shift that can be read from charter sets, such as those in the published volumes of the *Register of the Great Seal of Scotland*. It can also be read from the experience of the individual townships. Thus, charters for Ballone (Inverness-shire) talk of insets and outsets in 1635 but of infield and outfield of 1673 (Mackenzie, 1941, 115–6 and 123–7). Outfield, then, represents the expansion of townships into their non-assessed land, an expansion which seems to have begun during the fifteenth and sixteenth centuries.

By way of a check on this proposed relationship between outfields and the cultivation of non-assessed land, the problem can be reversed and couched in terms of a link between infields and assessed land. Work on townships in south-east Scotland yielded two kinds of support for this side of the problem (Dodgshon, 1973). First, there were those townships like Gattonside and

Paxton whose infield acreage alone (based on eighteenth-century surveys) equalled the expected acreage of their assessed land (their total number of land units × the presumed acreage of each individual land unit). Secondly, there were townships like Nether Ancrum and Newstead whose listing of the land units held by husbandmen in their infield exhausted the total number supposedly in the entire township, with outfield 'acres' and common pasture being treated as appendages whose possession was necessarily subsumed under that of infield. Qualified support for a linkage between infield and assessed land has also been provided by work on estates in Lothian (Whyte, 1979) and Angus (Whittington and Brett, 1979). A difficulty with this approach, however, is that by the time surveyor's reports give information on infield acreages— or the mid-eighteenth century—the gerrymandering of infield layouts may have started to destroy any former meaning it had as assessed land. After all, many infields were soon to disappear entirely over the following few decades.

THE LANDHOLDING STRUCTURE OF TOWNSHIPS

Among orthodox ideas on the nature of early farming townships none is more entrenched than the assumption that they were invariably held by small groups of landholders. In fact, analysis of rentals and tacks for the extreme south-east (Dodgshon, 1972, 126), as well as more general surveys of the Lowlands as a whole (Whyte 1979b, 141–4), have revealed that barely a half of all townships were in the hands of multiple tenants by the late seventeenth and early eighteenth centuries. On some estates, the percentage was much higher, but on others it was much lower. Nor is there any consistent pattern to this variation. Using the poll tax of 1696, Whyte found that single-tenancy townships in Aberdeenshire were to be found mainly on the lower, more fertile ground (Whyte, 1979b, 151–2), whereas a study of rentals for the Roxburghe and Buccleuch ducal estates in Roxburghshire found that single tenancy there was more prevalent on the large commercial sheep farms in the Cheviots and upper Teviotdale area (Dodgshon, 1972, 126–7).

By comparison, the level of multiple tenancy in the Highlands and Islands was undoubtedly higher. However, the number of tenants carried by townships in the region is not easily researched from early rentals, owing to the prevalence of the tacksmen system, whereby one person would be held responsible for the tack but would in turn sublet most or all of it to those who actually worked the land. Some tacksmen were responsible for whole disticts. This sort were usually close kinsmen of a clan chief, responsible not just for collecting rent but for the allegiance of under-tenants. Rental entries that treat solely with such tacksmen are patently inadequate for any full analysis of landholding. We learn little, for instance, about the landholders carried by townships on both Jura and Colonsay from a rental of 1541, for the 12 townships on the former were set to Alistair Maclean whilst the 14 townships on the latter were set to Archibald McFee (McNeill, 1897, 620–1). Fortunately, there are rentals which specify whether townships were set to a tacksman and some even go on to list other 'occupiers', or those holding of the tacksman. Such lists overcome some of the interpretative problems created by the tacksmen system. A few record only a small proportion of multiple-tenant townships, such as a 1735 list of 'Tennents and Possessors' in Aboyne which suggests that less than a half of its 72 townships were held by more than one tenant (SRO, GD312/3). Most, however, tend to show a much higher proportion than in the Lowlands. For instance, lists of occupiers and tenants for the Breadalbane estate in 1682 (SRO, GD50/15), Rannoch in 1695 (SRO, GD50/156), Menzies in 1706 (SRO, GD50/135), South Uist in 1718 (SRO, GD201/1257/5) and Ardnamurchan in 1727 (Murray, 1740) all show two-thirds of their townships or more in the hands of multiple tenants.

Inevitably, the fact that the foregoing conclusions are based on rentals and lists for the late seventeenth and early eighteenth centuries begs the question of whether earlier sources would display a still greater preponderance of multiple tenancy, particularly in the Lowlands. In fact, one or two studies of Lowland estates have detected signs of a slight but perceptible shift into single tenancy by the late seventeenth century (Dodgshon, 1972, 123–5; Whyte, 1979b, 151–2). However, if rentals for, say, the sixteenth century are examined, it soon becomes apparent that single tenancy had long been a significant, if not dominant, element in the landholding structure of Scottish townships (Robertson, 1862, Vol. 3, 116 and Vol. 4, 144–5).

Multiple-tenant townships faced problems of resource allocation that did not exist in single-tenant townships. How these problems were tackled reflected conditions of tenure, and two broad types can be recognized. First, there were those multiple-tenant townships in which landholders were held responsible, individually as well as collectively, for the rent and management of the entire farm, a type defined here as joint tenure. Early rentals and tacks refer to such tenants as holding 'jointly', 'conjointly' or 'conjointly and severally', as when Alexander and Charles Farquharson leased part of Ballindory on the Huntly estate 'conjointly and severally' in 1745 (SRO, GD312/30/15). Only in the Highlands and Islands is this likely to have been an important type of tenure, with estates like that of Assynt making quite extensive use of it (Adam, 1960, 66–7). Certainly, it is only in the Highlands and Islands that topographers such as Dr Samuel Johnson (Johnson, 1775, 1971 ed., 89) and Thomas Pennant (Pennant, 1774, 176) thought it worth noting. Logically, townships held in this way can be aligned alongside those townships in which only the produce was divided, not the land. According to

Pennant, the tenants of Canna arranged their affairs in this way (Pennant, 1774, 274).

The second type of tenure assigned to each landholder a separate share of both the township and its rent. This was unquestionably the commonest form of arrangement in multiple-tenant townships, one evident in virtually all early rentals. There are differences, however, over how such shares were designated. Some estates, such as those studied by the writer in the extreme south-east, made use of explicitly stated shares (halves, thirds, etc.) at least by the late seventeenth century (Dodgshon, 1975b, 16–17). Others continued to use customary land units right down to the eighteenth century. Rentals for the Western and Northern Isles, for example, can still be found using pennylands in the eighteenth century (Macleod, 1939, Vol. 2, 79–83), while estates in the north-east continued to use davachs and ploughs (SRO, RHP2487). In some cases, estates devised their own system: the Bishopric of Moray estate made use of a system of *pars* during the sixteenth century (*Registrum Episcopatus Moraviensis*, Vol. 1, 433 *et seq.*), while the Strathspey estate employed a system of 'auchten parts', with each landholder having so-many 'auchten parts' out of each davach (SRO, GD248/248/32).

Where tenants were set a township in shares, it follows that the varied resources of the township had to be arranged among them accordingly. Broadly speaking, these are the townships that can be associated with the runrig layout of property, or the sub-division and intermixture of holdings in the form of scattered strips and parcels. Indeed, the nature of share-holding as a tenure provides an explanatory context for runrig. This context becomes clearer when we look at the practical difficulties posed by the reification of shares, or their conversion to actual holdings on the ground. By the nature of its exploitation, this was less of a problem in respect of pasture than arable. The former was divided simply by allowing each landholder to contribute to the common herd a proportion of stock (his soums) that was equal to his share of the township: the total number of stock generally being fixed according to how many could be wintered or roumed in the township. In some townships, such as those in the Barony of Menzies (Perthshire), stock seem to have been herded by their individual owners (SRO, GD50/135), the common herd earning its title by the strict rules laid down via the barony or birlay court over precisely when and where the collective stock of the township could graze. In other cases, the entire stock were constituted as a single herd. This again was sometimes reinforced by barony or birlay courts, such as at Newtyle, Keillours and Cowty in Fife where landholders were cautioned in 1725 about maintaining private herds (HMC, *Fifth Report*, 1876, Report and Appendix, 623).

The problems posed by the division of arable were more acute. The main difficulty was that shareholding was open-ended as a title to land. It conveyed a share in arable or assessed land, but said nothing about exactly where this share should be in terms of strips and parcels. As a result, landholders had to devise guidelines over how to lay out their shares into what legal sources called *known* property, or holdings that were meithed and marched on the ground. Like any customary system of tenure, there were accepted ways of carrying out this task, ways that were occasionally made explicit. A fair body of evidence suggests that the prime criterion used to reify shares was that they should be equal, land unit for land unit, portion for portion. Work in south-east Scotland uncovered references to township shares having to be 'just and equal', not only among tenants but also among those landowners and feuars who shared townships (Dodgshon, 1975b, 28). Similar sentiments were expressed elsewhere in Scotland. For example, a 1756 tack set 'the just and equall third part of the whole Town & lands of Achlay' (Angus), a share which the tenant held in return for 'the just and equall third part of the haill Rents duties ferms casualities services & others' (SRO, GD24/1/32). To the north-east, a James Findlay was set the 'Just & Equall half of Little Formestoun' (Aberdeenshire) in 1736 (SRO, GD312/30/11). At North Wideford (Orkney), a James Ennson claimed a 'just fourth part' in 1686 (Storer Clouston, 1932, 353), and earlier in the century, another landholder held 'the just and equall half of the lands of Over Auchintiber . . . the houses, yards, kiln & barn' (Anon., 1895, 211–3). Where sources are more detailed, they make it clear that it was this principle of equality that produced the runrig intermixture of holdings. In particular, stress was placed on shares being equal in terms of both extent and value, a strictness of definition that could not fail to produce intermixture in an environment as varied as that of Scotland. Although runrig plans for the mid-eighteenth century suggest that runrig layouts were not always so tidy or systematic—with strips and parcels that were irregular in shape and holdings that were unevenly distributed across the township— earlier sources confirm that formalized division procedures were originally employed to spread a person's holding systematically over the different arable shots or parcels of the township. These procedures were responsible for imparting a great deal of character to the medieval landscape. Some concentrated on establishing the order in which landholders were to receive their strips in each sequence of allocation. For instance, the portioner who claimed a 'just fourth part' of North Wideford (Orkney) in 1686 was said to have 'the fourth rig or foot of the townesland' (Storer Clouston, 1932, 353). When part of Lamington in Lanarkshire was sold by Sir William Baillie to a John Donaldson in 1611, the latter received a share comprising 'every ninth step and tree, hill and dale of the lands and barony of Lamingtoune' (NSA, *Lanarkshire*, 1845, 815). An alternative procedure was for the land to be divided into the required number of shares by a panel of arbiters and then for landholders to draw lots to decide who was to have which share. For example, when James Findlay was given the 'Just & Equall half of Little Formestoun' (Aberdeenshire) in 1736, his share was to 'be

Equally Divided, att the Sight of Four Judicious Men Chosen for that Effect &
when Divided, the Sd James Findlay, & any other Tennant who Shall take the
Same are to cast Lotts for the Different Shares with the Houses Biggings Yards
Tofts Crofts & Kail pertinents yrto belonging' (SRO, GD312/30/11).

A procedure widely used in eastern Scotland was that known as sun-division
(Dodgshon, 1975a). In a sense, a sun-division combined elements of both the
aforementioned techniques: it could be used both as an ordering principle or as
a means of giving identity to shares already divided out on the ground. Briefly,
if a landholder was given—via a lottery—the sunny portion of a township, he
received the strips or holding that lay to the east or south in each sequence of
allocation. If given the shadow portion, he received the strips or holding to the
west and north. The obvious shortcoming with a sun-division was that it had
definite limitations when confronted with complex divisions. A charter like
that wadsetting 'the shadow half of the sunny half of the mains of Balrownie'
(Angus) in 1607 demonstrates these limitations (Anderson, 1899, 368). Nevertheless, it was widely used over the medieval period. Moreover, early law
books relate the use of the prefixes sunny/shadow in share designation to the
terms east/west and upper/nether. References to tenants having the easter/
wester half or plough, therefore, probably had the same meaning. The
complexities of language and layout produced by such a system are typified by
the seventeenth-century reference to 'the third part, being the wester third
rigg, of the Easter Half Town and Lands of Easter Moniack' (Mackenzie,
1796, 9).

The origin of runrig has always been explained by assumptions about its
innate character. A persistent argument has been that its regular changes of
layout, with strips and parcels being re-allocated between landholders almost
on an annual basis, reflected an archaic system. For some, it did so because the
slavish renewal of equality between husbandmen was what might be expected
under a tribal system with its emphasis on common welfare. For others, it did
so because the constant give and take of holding-layout suggested a stage before
the emergence of private property, when land was doled out to individuals for
part of the year before being returned to a common pool. Such interpretations
overlook the shareholding context of runrig and its practical need for converting shares into holdings on the ground at the start of each new set of tenures.
Re-allocation was not a condition of tenure but part of the necessary shift
between tenures. In fact, by the late seventeenth century, many Lowland
townships did not even bother to re-cast share layouts between tacks, but
simply identified the share being set through its previous occupier. As regards
the question of whether runrig was a common or several property, the very
essence of its meaning was that of shares converted to *known* or several
property. Once these points are grasped, the question of the origin of runrig
can be posed again. Arguably, it needs to be seen in relation to the wider debate

on how subdivided fields were formed elsewhere in Britain, a debate that has stressed the interaction of piecemeal colonization, shareholding, and partible inheritance as a cause. As regards chronology, the earliest documentary references to the term date only from the mid-fifteenth century, but there is support for its existence as early as the twelfth century, including references to land being 'iacentes per diuisas' in Border townships like Auchencraw, Old Cambus and Coldingham (Raine, 1852, 43–5) and to a landholder who was granted the fifth rig of the township of Ballebotlia in Fife (Barrow, 1971, 432–3). Whether its history can be pushed back much further than this date remains an open question.

THE FIELD ECONOMY OF TOWNSHIPS

The field economy of early townships was generally organized around three sectors: infield, outfield, and common grazings, the latter being supplemented in some areas by shielings (Dodgshon, 1980, 69–92; Dodgshon, 1981, chaps. 5, 7 and 8; Whittington, 1973, 550–71; Whittington and Brett, 1979, 33–43). Infield appears from contemporary surveys and estimates to have accounted for between a quarter and a third of all the land accessible to townships, with outfield and commonty land making up the rest. In terms of acreage, the largest townships were those of the south-eastern and eastern Lowlands, whose infields ranged up to 250 acres (101 ha) and whose total extent—by the early eighteenth century—was as much as 1000 acres (404 ha) on the fertile ground. Townships in the north-east and in the south-west were noticeably smaller, with ceilings of around 80–100 acres (32–40 ha) on infields and 300–400 (121–161 ha) for the total extent of townships. The infields of Highland townships were smaller still, with few containing more than 50 acres (20 ha). However, eighteenth-century surveys, such as those for Assynt (Adam, 1960, 1–59), Ardnamurchan (Murray, 1740, plate VI) and Breadal-bane (McArthur, 1936, 1–207), show that many also had access to vast quantities of hill grazing. The same was true of *gerss* farms in the Southern Uplands. Yet despite these variations in size, townships everywhere developed remarkably similar patterns of husbandry around their different sectors (infield, outfield and common grazings). This is not to deny the differences of detail which help the geographer to distinguish the practice of one region from another, but only to stress that what impresses most about the field economy of early townships is its basic comparability from one part of the country to another.

Turning first to infield, this was an intensively cropped sector lying close to the farmsteads of the township. Given its status as assessed land, it must have been the first sector to have been settled and cropped, a background which does much to explain its intensive, almost garden-like treatment. Paucity of data precludes any historical view of how its cropping may have evolved over the medieval and early-modern period. Only during the late seventeenth century can details of its cropping be pieced together (Dodgshon, 1981, chap. 5; see also, Whittington, 1973, 571–9). The most basic systems were the many Highland examples that were divided into two breaks and cropped with a simple rotation of oats and bere (barley). Other Highland townships, however, had devised a three-break system, the extra break being given over to a second crop of oats. This continuous, heavy cropping of infield was sustained by the addition of all the dung which accumulated in the byre or kailyard over winter together with that added by the direct dunging of stock when they grazed the harvest stubble. A feature of Highland infields was the extensive use made of manurial supplements like old thatch, seaweed, peat and turf. In effect, this was a case of the Highlanders making resourceful use of their vast non-arable sector to extend and sustain the fertility of their limited arable sector. In the Lowlands, a three-break system appears to have been standard, at least in areas like the north-east or western Lowlands. It was again based on oats and bere, with oats being cropped for two years, although some townships preferred a break of peas or beans to a second crop of oats. However, by the late seventeenth century, the more fertile districts like the Merse and Lothian were starting to arrange their infields into four- and even five-break systems. These were based on a varied course of oats, bere, peas and wheat with, in the case of a five-course scheme, the addition of a fallow break. Like their Highland counterparts, these Lowland infields received all the manure that had accumulated from the byre and stockyard over winter as well as that provided by the grazing of harvest stubble.

In the mind of the husbandman, outfield's distinction derived not only from its special tenurial status as the cultivated sections of non-assessed land but also from the distinct course of husbandry to which it was subjected. It was exploited by being cropped for a few years and then left under grass for a few years, its extensive character standing in marked contrast to the intensive character of infield. A handful of sources confirm that outfield had acquired its system of alternate husbandry by the sixteenth century, soon after townships had first started to cultivate their non-assessed land. However, like infield, the details of its organization are not visible until the late seventeenth century. What emerges is a system that possessed a fair degree of regional variation, but one that was always a controlled rather than a casual affair. At one extreme were those townships that cultivated a half of their outfield each year using a simple two-break system, with each break being cropped by turns for four or five years. These were mainly to be found in the Highlands, but there were reports of even Lowland townships being cultivated on this basis. At the other extreme were townships that followed a more restrained but elaborate scheme of outfield cropping. The 'best-practice' townships of the Lowlands divided their outfield into nine breaks, three of which were cultivated during any one year, with one being under its first crop, another its second and another, its third and final crop. In between, lay a variety of arrangements that are documented in early tacks and surveys. In Aberdeenshire, some outfields were arranged into ten breaks. Each year, a fresh break was brought into cultivation and cropped for five years, so that a total of five breaks were in cultivation during any one year. In Netherlorn, outfields were cast into a simpler three-break system, each of which was cropped for two or three years at a time. In Perthshire, meanwhile, we learn from a tack of 1769 for Bellnollo township that its outfield was expected to 'regularly enjoy five Year's Rest, and after proper Tathing be then ploughed up, and bear four Cropts' (SRO, GD24/1/32).

The system of tathing referred to in the aforementioned tack was of crucial importance for outfield cultivation. It involved the nightly penning and folding of stock during the summer on that part of outfield chosen to be brought into cultivation the following spring. The manure so produced was the only source of manure for outfield, except where communities also added the turf walls used to pen stock in the tathfold. The practice of tathing appears with the earliest references to outfield back in the sixteenth century. Its use became widespread. Tacks, such as mid-eighteenth century tacks issued for the Abercairny estate in Perthshire (SRO, GD24/1/32) or the Lothian estate in Roxburghshire (SRO, GD237/66), insisted on it as a preparation for outfield cultivation. Barony court records were equally explicit. The barony court book for Menzies and Rannoch, for instance, contains a 1660 entry which required 'the tennentis in everie towne sett out their fauldis in order conform to use and want to putt their goods therin for tatheing their ley land' (SRO, GD50/135). Estate surveys recorded it, like that drawn up for the Strathyre estate in the 1750s, the surveyor explaining how the tenants folded their stock during summer on a part of outfield and 'then next spring sowe oates upon it' (Wills, 1973, 27). Published sources likewise document its details, such as the *Old Statistical Account* report for Methven parish in Perthshire which related how 'the cattle were folded in summer on that part of the outfield which was to be broken up the ensuing season, after which three crops of oats were taken' (*OSA*, X, 611), The fact that tathing could only be applied to outfield land prior to its cultivation helps to explain why cropping was of a temporary and shifting character. Tathing, outfield's prime source of manure, could only be used to prepare land for cultivation not to sustain it when in cultivation. There is no need, as past writers have done, to explain outfield's character by seeing it as a survival of some primitive system of shifting cultivation that dates from the earliest phases of agriculture's history. Tathing contains all that is needed for an historically validated explanation. Furthermore, it fits in with the argument outlined above that outfield was a late overflow by townships into their non-assessed land. At the point when communities confronted this prospect, the use—via the tathfold—of the manure that was otherwise wasted when stock grazed the common grazings over summer must have seemed an obvious step to take.

When not cultivated, outfield provided common pasture. Usually, such pasture was supplemented by meadow land and by grazings that were never cropped, while in some areas there were also the more distant shieling grounds. By the early eighteenth century, most townships in the Lowlands had only limited resources of pasture for their own exclusive use. Centuries of expansion and settlement infilling had ensured this. Some local areas were still fortunate enough to have inter-township commonties to fall back on. A well-settled area like the Merse, for example, still had inter-township commonties like Colding-ham, Fogo and Hassendean. Other Merse townships, like Chirnside, had detached blocks of grazings that stretched high on to the Lammermuirs. In all probability, such detached grazings were vestiges of a former shieling system. In fact, one of the earliest land charters for the Lammermuirs was a grant by Earl Cospatric of shielings at Bothwell (Spott parish, E. Lothian) to Kelso abbey, 1161 x 1164 (Barrow, 1960, 245). The combined pressures of baronial hunting and the concern of the abbeys for securing a private control over their pasture must have seriously undermined any shieling system in this area at a fairly early date. Understandably, Highland townships faced fewer problems over pasture provision. Surveys for the eighteenth century show most still possessed large reserves. Although much of it was close at hand, many townships continued to use their distant hill ground via the shieling system. Glimpses of the system in operation frequently surface in barony court records, through the necessity of fixing a date when stock had to be moved to the shielings. Thus, in Menzies and Rannoch, it was fixed as May 10th in 1660 (SRO, GD50/135), whereas in the Lude area, stock were sent 'on or about the first day of June yearly And that none be either behind their nightbours in going or before them in coming from the sheallings under the penalty of a good wedder' (SRO, GD50/159). Where such sources fail us, field work can supply traces of the system. For example, in Argyll, the tenants of Edenonich in Glen Strae had shielings at Airidh nan Sileag whilst those of Ardnahua and Duachy in Kilninver parish had shielings in Glen Risdale (RCAM, *Argyll*, Vol. 2, 1974, 267–8 and 271–2).

The operation of the early township economy clearly depended on a measure of cooperation between landholders. This cooperation was regulated through barony or birlay courts. All the regulations and agreements needed for the smooth working of the system were enacted by such courts. They established the rules and dates governing major tasks like ploughing, harvesting, and the building of the fold dykes and also administered the complex rules surrounding stocking. Apart from fixing the soums for each landholder, they decided on the bylaws controlling the common herd and its movements through the different sectors of the township: this movement was vital to the integration of a township's field economy. Beginning in autumn, stock were to be found grazing the harvest stubble. This naturally involved rights of common grazing over arable, a practice sufficiently widespread to be the subject of a special act of parliament in 1685, the Act anent Winter Herding. As at Chirnside in the Merse, it was seen as a right of landholders to graze their stock from 'the time the Corns are led off the Ground, To the time the Oats are Sprung up again' (Berwickshire County Library, Duns, Decreet of Division of the Runrigg Lands of Chirnside, 1740). Its history can be extended back as far as the earliest direct references to subdivided fields, most notably to a dispute in Colding-ham-shire during the fifteenth century which focused on the rights of com-mon pasture over Coldingham Mains during Winter (Raine, 1852, 63). It was this right of stubble grazing, more than any other feature, that ensured the open character of early townships. When Fynes Moryson wrote of Fife in 1598 that it was 'a pleasant little Territory of Open Fields, without inclosures' (Brown, 1891, 86), his words must have been applicable to many areas. After being herded over the arable stubble and its associated grass baulks during autumn and winter, or after being kept in the byre if the weather was bad, stock were moved on to the common pasture in spring. This too, needed control. At Selkirk, the local court fixed a day when all stock had to be out of the infield (Imrie *et al.*, 1960, 61), while at Lude, landholders were simply 'obleiged to herd their beasts whenever they or their nyghtbours begins to sow' (SRO, GD50/159). What happened over summer is summarized for us by an extract from the court book for Menzies and Rannoch which 'inactit that betuixt the first of May and the first of November that they keepe ther guids in the Tathing in the town quherein they dwell till the forsaid tyme And that their hirds stay nightly at the Sheall and Fold' (SRO, GD50/135). Obviously, not all townships would have rules over shieling ground, but most would have had bylaws over the herding of stock on the common pastures and at the tathfold. With harvest, the cycle of stock movements completed its annual cycle.

Helping to bring order to stock movements were not only bylaws, but a series of dykes that separated infield from outfield (the inner dyke) and, in some instances, outfield from common pasture (the outer dyke). The prime purpose of these dykes was to regulate stock, segregating their movement and grazing from one sector of the township to another. Their existence can be traced through acts over their maintenance in local court records, as in the case of Menzies and Rannoch (SRO, GD50/135) or from their surviving traces in the landscape itself, as on Rhum.

CONCLUSIONS

The period from the unification of Scotland to the mid-eighteenth century has generally been underplayed in discussions of how the Scottish rural landscape has evolved. For some, this low key approach was enforced by the inadequacy of data. For others, it sprang from a positive belief that some of the most basic and formative institutions of the early Scottish countryside (i.e. infield–outfield, multiple tenancy and runrig) were archaic, dating back to long before 1100. Backed by this sort of assumption, it was a logical step to suppose that any changes or developments after 1100 could only have made a modest contribution to the unfolding character of the rural landscape. This chapter has tried to dispel these misconceptions and to argue instead that—whatever the legacy in terms of settlement and colonization from the pre-1100 period—further changes can be documented, ranging from the widespread splitting of townships to the formation of outfield cropping systems. Much remains to be done in focusing such themes more precisely. In particular, future work must concentrate on proportioning their contribution to the evolution of the countryside in more exact terms, both as regards their geography and chronology. Nor is it assumed that the themes reviewed in the foregoing discussion exhaust all the possibilities. They are simply those about which early sources are more forthcoming. As the analysis of early land charters and rentals becomes more comprehensive and, above all, more systematic, other themes will undoubtedly take shape.

REFERENCES

Adam, R. J. (1960). 'John Home's Survey of Assynt.' Scottish History Society, 3rd series, LII, Edinburgh.
Anderson, J. (1899). 'Calendar of the Laing Charters A.D. 854–1837.' University of Edinburgh, Edinburgh.
Anon. (1895). 'Archaeological and Historical Collections of Ayrshire and Galloway.'
A.P.S. (1814–75). 'Acts of the Parliament of Scotland.' 12 vols. Record Society, Edinburgh.
Barrow, G. W. S. (1960). 'The Acts of Malcolm IV. King of Scots 1163–1165. Regesta Regum Scottorum.' Edinburgh University Press, Edinburgh.
Barrow, G. W. S. with the collaboration of Scott, W. W. (1971). 'The Acts of William I. King of Scots 1165–1214. Regesta Regum Scottorum.' Edinburgh University Press, Edinburgh.
Barrow, G. W. S. (1980). 'The Anglo-Norman Era in Scottish History.' Oxford University Press, Oxford.
Brown, P. H. (1891). 'Early Travellers in Scotland.' David Douglas, Edinburgh.

Browne, G. F. (1923). 'Echt-Forbes Family Charters 1345–1727: Records of the Forest of Birse 926–1781.' Printed privately, Aberdeen.

Buchan, J. W. and Paton, H. (1927). 'A History of Peebles-shire.' 2 vols. Jackson, Wylie, Glasgow.

Cregeen, E. (1968). The changing role of the House of Argyll in the Scottish Highlands. *In* 'History and Social Anthropology.' (I. M. Lewis, ed.), pp. 153–92, Tavistock, London.

Dodgshon, R. A. (1972). 'The removal of runrig in Roxburghshire and Berwickshire 1680–1766.' *Scottish Studies* **16**, 121–37.

Dodgshon, R. A. (1973). The nature and development of infield–outfield in Scotland. *Transactions of the Institute of British Geographers* **59**, 1–23.

Dodgshon, R. A. (1975a). Scandinavian solskifte and the sunwise division of land in eastern Scotland. *Scottish Studies* **19**, 1–14.

Dodgshon, R. A. (1975b). Towards an understanding and definition of runrig: the evidence for Roxburghshire and Berwickshire. *Transactions of the Institute of British Geographers* **64**, 15–33.

Dodgshon, R. A. (1977). Changes in Scottish township organization during the medieval and early modern periods. *Geografiska Annaler* **58B**, 51–65.

Dodgshon, R. A. (1980). The origins of traditional field systems. *In* 'The Making of the Scottish Countryside.' (M. L. Parry and T. R. Slater, ed.), pp. 69–92. Croom Helm, London.

Dodgshon, R. A. (1981). 'Land and Society in Early Scotland.' Oxford University Press, Oxford.

Harvey, C. C. H. and Macleod, J. (1930). 'Calendar of Writs Preserved at Yester House 1166–1625.' Scottish Record Office, Edinburgh.

HMC (1876). 'Fifth Report of the Royal Commission on Historical Manuscripts, Part 1, Report and Appendix.' HMC, London.

Imrie, J., Rae, T. I. and Ritchie, W. D. (1960). 'The Burgh Court Book of Selkirk 1503–1545, Part 1, 1503–31.' Scottish Record Society, Edinburgh.

Innes, C. (1854). 'Origines Parochiales Scotiae.' Bannatyne club, Edinburgh.

Johnson, S. (1775). 'A Journey to the Western Islands of Scotland' (M. Lascelles, ed., 1971). Yale University Press, New Haven and London.

Kelso (1846). 'Liber S. Marie de Calchou 1113–1547.' 2 vols. Bannatyne Club, Edinburgh.

Levie, W. Elder (1927). Celtic tribal law and custom in Scotland. *Juridical Review* **39**, 191–208.

McArthur, M. M. (1936). 'Survey of Lochtayside 1769.' Scottish History Society, 3rd series, XXVII, Edinburgh.

Macfarlane, W. (1907). 'Geographical Collections Relating to Scotland Made by W. Macfarlane, Vol. 2.' Scottish History Society, LII, Edinburgh.

Mackenzie, A. (1796). 'Inventory of the Title Deeds of the Estate of Easter Moniack Belonging to Edward Satchwell Fraser.' Scottish Record Office, Edinburgh.

Mackenzie, H. H. (1941). 'The Mackenzie of Ballone.' Northern Chronicle Office, Inverness.

Macleod, R. C. (1939). 'The Book of Dunvegan, Vol. 2, 1700–1920.' Spalding Club, Aberdeen.

McNeill, G. P. (1897). 'The Exchequer Rolls of Scotland, Vol. XVII, A.D. 1537–1542.' H.M. Register House, Edinburgh.

Macphail, J. R. N. (1920). 'Highland Papers, Vol. 3.' Scottish History Society, 2nd series, XX, Edinburgh.

Macpherson, A. (1893). 'Glimpses of Church and Social Life in the Highlands in Olden Times.' W. Blackwood & Sons, Edinburgh.

Macpherson, A. G. (1966). An old highland genealogy and the evolution of a scottish clan. *Scottish Studies* **10**, 1–43.

Mather, A. S. (1970). Pre-1745 land use and conservation in a highland glen: an example from Glen Strathfarrar, north Inverness-shire. *Scottish Geographical Magazine* **86**, 159–69.

Murray, Sir Alexander (1740). 'The True Interest of Great Britain, Ireland and Our Plantations.' Privately printed, London.

Murray, A. L. (1958). 'Calendar of Lag Charters 1400–1720.' Scottish Record Society, Edinburgh.

New Statistical Account of Scotland (1845). 'Lanarkshire.' W. Blackwood & Sons, Edinburgh.

Pennant, T. (1774). 'Tour in Scotland and Voyage to the Hebrides 1772.' J. Monk, Chester.

Peterkin, A. (1820). 'Rental of the Ancient Earldom and Bishopric of Orkney.' Privately printed, Edinburgh.

Postan, M. M. (1966). Medieval agrarian society in its prime: England. *In* 'The Cambridge Economic History of Europe, Vol. 1, The Agrarian Life of the Middle Ages.' (M. M. Postan, ed.), pp. 548–632. Cambridge University Press, Cambridge.

Raine, T. (1841). 'The Priory of Coldingham.' Surtees Society, Newcastle.

Raine, T. (1852). 'The History and Antiquities of North Durham.' J. B. Nichols, London.

'Registrum Episcopatus Moraviensis.' (1837). 2 vols. Bannatyne Club, Edinburgh.

'Registrum Honoris de Morton.' (1853). 2 vols. Bannatyne Club, Edinburgh.

Robertson, J. (1862). 'Illustrations of the Topography and Antiquities of the Shires of Aberdeen and Banff.' 4 vols. Spalding Club, Aberdeen.

Royal Commission on Ancient and Historic Monuments (1974). 'Argyll, Vol. 2, Lorn.' HMSO, Edinburgh.

Smith, G. G. (1895). 'The Book of Islay.' Privately printed, Edinburgh.

Storer Clouston, J. (1932). 'A History of Orkney.' W. R. Mackintosh, Kirkwall.

Thomson, A. (1908). 'Coldingham Parish and Priory.' Craighead Bros., Galashiels.

Thomson, J. M. (1888). 'The Register of the Great Seal of Scotland.' H.M. Register House, Edinburgh.

Whittington, G. (1973). Field systems of Scotland. *In* 'Studies of Field Systems in the British Isles.' (A. R. H. Baker and R. A. Butlin, ed.), pp. 530–79. Cambridge University Press, Cambridge.

Whittington, G. and Brett, D. U. (1979). Locational decision-making on a Scottish estate prior to enclosure. *Journal of Historical Geography* **5**, 33–43.

Whyte, I. (1979). 'Agriculture and Society in Seventeenth-Century Scotland.' J. Donald, Edinburgh.

Whyte, I. (1979). 'Infield–Outfield on a Seventeenth-Century Scottish Estate.' *Journal of Historical Geography* 5, 391–401.

Wills, V. (1973). 'Reports of the Annexed Estates 1753–1769.' Scottish Record Office, Edinburgh.

Urban Development, 1100–1700

R. Fox

The early twelfth century makes a convenient starting point for this chapter because it provides the first documentary evidence of the Scottish burgh as an historical and institutional entity. This period also witnessed the first diffusion of urban centres in the lowlands; any earlier towns were isolated phenomena found at particularly favoured sites. The twelfth century thus appears as an era of burgh foundation in which the basic features of medieval urban geography can be ascertained. Tracing these features is the concern of the first section of this chapter. The medieval period up to 1400 is the second historical subdivision. This period has a variety of evidence available which makes it possible to examine burgh management and the urban townscape. It can be distinguished from the third subdivision, the pre-industrial, as the number of burghs was still small and their composition (royal, ecclesiastical, baronial) was distinctive. This pre-industrial period witnessed both the founding of a large number of new burghs, mainly baronial, and the establishment of non-burghal urban centres. This was an innovation peculiar to this period. New morphological features also evolved in the town plans of the older burghs.

Various aspects of urban development are examined in each period. These may be grouped under three headings: burgh creation and diffusion, the evolution of an urban hierarchy, and the town plan.

SOURCES

At the outset it is important to establish that the documentary evidence on which this chapter depends varies in quantity, quality and time from burgh to burgh. This alone seriously hampers any attempt at an overview of urban development. In addition, the cartographical record contains no systematic surveys, so the researcher is forced to generalize nationwide trends from the few burghs that have been examined. There is also the equally difficult task of establishing the relative importance and state of development of the burghs because there is no complete or reasonably reliable set of data until the last half of the seventeenth century. The principal documentary sources can be listed as follows: in the early medieval period the Royal Charters, Chartularies of Religious Houses and Scotland's Exchequer Rolls which date back to 1200 or earlier; the medieval period introduces the Records of the Convention of Royal Burghs of Scotland, some Council Records, Sasine Registers, Protocol Books and Guildry Records; the sixteenth and seventeenth centuries have detailed information from an assortment of Burgh records and the first semi-systematic surveys such as the Poll Tax, Hearth Tax, and Tucker's Report on the State and Condition of Burghs in Scotland.

BURGH FOUNDATION IN THE TWELFTH CENTURY

Historical evidence shows us that small urban centres, burghs, existed on the Scottish mainland from the twelfth century onwards. At a national scale the distribution of the burghs was largely influenced by the physical environment. Agricultural development was favoured in the lowland areas of Scotland—the Tweed basin, the Lothians, Fife, Angus, and Moray—and Dawson (1975) correlates these low-lying agricultural areas of free draining soils and moderate rainfall with the early sites of burghs, churches and sheriffdoms. Figure 4.1a shows burghs founded by 1200 and they were predominantly in the eastern lowlands. The burghs acted as collecting, distributing and small-scale manufacturing centres and so physical factors favouring trade and defence affected their location. River mouths and estuary sites, such as at Perth and Aberdeen, were an asset, as bulk trade was water borne. Bridging or fording points exerted a strong influence. Outstanding defensive sites, for example at Stirling or Edinburgh, were clearly favoured, and the attraction of a natural harbour was another obvious factor. Where these features were combined and backed by a rich agricultural hinterland the result was a thriving burgh; Berwick perhaps provides the best example.

Small urban centres almost certainly functioned on several sites before historical records provide the first glimpse of burgh life. Brooks (1977) shows that although the archaeological evidence is very limited, it does point to the existence of earlier dwellings on twelfth-century burgh sites. Duncan (1975) maintains that it is important not to discount the possibility of genetic growth from a small pre-burghal origin, and Brooks and Whittington (1977) produce evidence from St Andrews showing the existence of 'Kinrimund' prior to the formal laying out of the burgh 1124 x 1144. It was, however, in the reign of

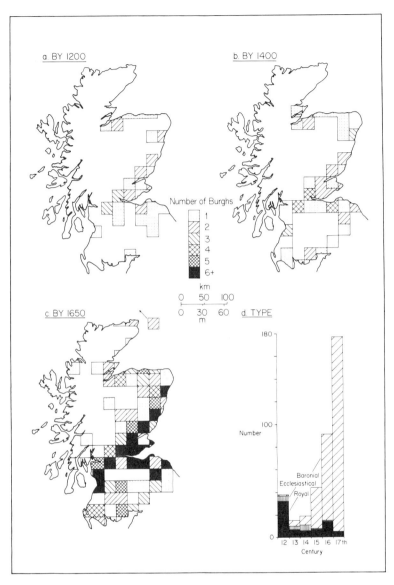

Fig. 4.1   The foundation of burghs

David I that the formal recognition and promotion of burghs was adopted as a royal policy. This had a great impact upon pre-existing settlement and was a stimulus to the foundation of urban centres throughout the realm. Regrettably, few of the original foundation charters have survived, and it is possible that the first granting of burghal rights was, in any case, verbal and undertaken before witnesses. Fortunately, charters of ratification were commonly given by the king's successors and these relate the nature of the privileges bestowed upon the burghs. Pryde (1963, 1965) has produced the best critical assessment of these charters, which are reproduced in Lawrie (1905) and Barrow (1960, 1971).

The burgesses were granted property in the burgh and for this a rental payment was due to their superior. In the majority of twelfth-century burghs, the feudal superior was the crown, but in a few cases ecclesiastical burghs were founded, for example at Glasgow and St Andrews. The distinction between the two types of burgh was one mainly of political function (Pryde, 1963); burghal commerce and constitutions were much the same. The feudal superior was either the king, a bishop, or latterly a baron, and all burghs enjoyed monopolistic trading privileges in the sheriffdom, regality or barony. However, the royal burghs were also the basis of the national administration and commonly acted as the caputs of sheriffdoms, for example Aberdeen, Inverness, Perth and Peebles. In addition to property the burgesses were also granted a market which was protected by the king's peace. Burgesses and their agents were obliged to buy and sell in the burghs and their hinterlands. Foreign trade was also their privilege. The burgesses gained freedom from tolls throughout the kingdom, the right to hold fairs, a limited amount of municipal jurisdiction, and the right to form a merchants' guild. These privileges were not all bestowed in one charter but acquired in the course of time.

By 1200 there were 38 burghs in Scotland (Fig. 4.1d), and several theories have been proposed to explain this rapid development. The most commonly accepted theory, which has been introduced above, is MacKenzie's (1949) creation theory. This emphasizes the importance of the royal creative act in bestowing a set of privileges upon a burgh which might or might not have been in existence as a small settlement at the time of foundation. Pryde (1949) stresses that this act of creation was 'a deliberate measure of planning policy, the burgh was "made" by royal *fiat*, much as "new towns" are called into being today'. The validity of this view is further argued by Dodd (1972) in his study of the burgh of Ayr. Earlier attempts to arrive at a theory of burgh growth were rather simplistic in relating growth to the presence of the royal castle (Neilson, 1902), the granting of commercial monopoly (Ballard, 1915), or of communal rights (Murray, 1924). The creation theory does not attempt to isolate any one function but stresses that burgh foundation was fundamentally an act of settlement. Newcomers, often Flemings or Englishmen, were deliberately encouraged to settle in the Scottish burghs through the freedom of kirset—the period of one to five years in which the burgess was allowed to build his dwelling before rent was due to the king.

The creation of burghs needs to be seen in the perspective of the other reforms being undertaken by David I and his successors. Three features—the church, the castle and the burgh—were interlinked in an ambitious scheme of national development. Under David the religious orders were granted sites for their abbeys with lands and properties throughout the kingdom; they provided a cultural and agricultural stimulus and links to their mother orders on the Continent. The castle was the royal residence and the seat of government for a king constantly touring the country dispensing justice. The royal castles were the basis of the king's feudal power and thus the means whereby political stability was maintained, a necessary condition for successful urban life. The burghs fostered economic development through the stimulation of trade and manufacture and provided the king with money revenue derived from rent, tolls and customs. It is also pertinent that the first Scottish coinage, silver pennies, can be attributed to David's reign.

Figure 4.2 gives an indication of the degree to which the burghs and churches were interlinked. Charter evidence shows that Cambuskenneth Abbey held land or property in Stirling and many other burghs; it also shows which religious houses held property or rights in Stirling. The strongest links were clearly in the local area, the estuaries of the Forth and Tay, where Cambuskenneth Abbey owned churches, land, crofts and building plots in the fledgling burghs. The major foundations of Dunfermline Abbey, Holyrood, Scone and Cambuskenneth were the chief recipients of tithes, rights and property in Stirling itself.

There is good evidence to suggest that the Scottish kings were emulating a system which the Normans had introduced to England from the continent (Ritchie, 1954). Dickinson (1957) points out that David's marriage to Matilda de Senis gave him vast properties in England where he could see both the old boroughs and the newer towns. It would be logical for such an enlightened monarch to imitate this successful system, as Adams (1978) maintains, firstly in his Border earldom with the founding of towns such as Roxburgh and later as king throughout his realm. There is also a notable similarity between the Scottish 'Laws of the Four Burghs' and the customs of Newcastle-upon-Tyne, Winchester, Nottingham and Northampton (the latter two being in David's English estates). Bateson (1900, 1901) has shown that the laws of Breteuil served as a common model for many English and Welsh boroughs, and it seems reasonable to propose that these laws diffused further north into Scotland.

Although the twelfth century burghs were formal foundations, there does not appear to have been a common town plan. Pryde (1949) describes one type as being a single, axial, market street with a widening for a market place, for

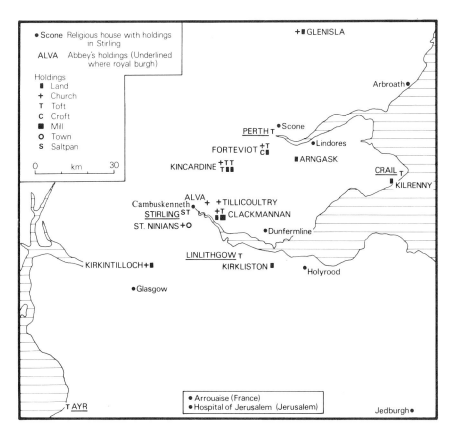

Fig. 4.2   Stirling and Cambuskenneth Abbey: rights and property

example Edinburgh or Stirling. The parallel-street plan, for example St Andrews, Perth, Crail, was a more ambitous variation of this. Whitehand and Alauddin (1969) agree with this basic distinction and furthermore show that the parallel-street system was found primarily on the east coast, especially around the Firths of Forth and Tay, perhaps reflecting the greater prospects and prosperity of this region. Studies of Ayr (Dodd, 1972), St Andrews (Brooks and Whittington, 1977) and Berwick (Ellison, 1976) show that the basic pattern was modified by the local topography, pre-existing routeways and settlement.

The reconstruction of early medieval burghs can be undertaken from evidence in royal charters, the earliest cartographic sources (as late as 1745 for Stirling), and the first 1:500 scale Ordnance Survey maps of the late 1850s, which give very accurate information on plot boundaries. From these sources we can infer a great deal. Figure 4.3 indicates that the burgh of Stirling developed in two stages, with a pre-twelfth-century nucleus at the head of the ridge and burgage plots being subsequently laid out to the south-east. The burgesses' arable land (burgh roods) was located to the north-east, pasture land (burgh meadows) lay beyond the burgh mill to the east, and the burgh's saltpans were probably adjacent to the Forth in this area. Common land at the Gowan Hills provided rough grazing, timber and stone. The King's Park was the other major land holding to the west of the burgh. The burgh was probably surrounded by a wooden palisade, later refashioned in stone, with entry restricted by gates or ports. The parish church was typically located at the market.

The population of the new burghs was very small and included a high proportion of foreign elements. Dickinson (1957) refers to an early record of the size of two of the country's leading burghs, Perth and Berwick. In 1219 Perth had three *prepositi* and 20 other burgesses; by 1291 70 burgesses were listed and at the same time 80 burgesses of Berwick were swearing fealty to Edward I. After allowing for large numbers of servants, dependants, apprentices and craftsmen not admitted to burgess-ship, this gives a limit of around 500 persons some 150 years after these important burghs were founded. Many of the first craftsmen came from England and Flanders, and there was a particularly strong influx of Flemings after 1155 when they were expelled from England. We can trace the activity of one Fleming, Mainard of Berwick, from the early charter of St Andrews, 1144 x 1153 (Dickinson, 1953): Mainard, who was the king's burgess of Berwick, was made provost of the ecclesiastical burgh of St Andrews and was given three tofts (building plots) of land in the burgh 'because Mainardus was one of the first to build and stock the burgh'.

Throughout the twelfth century, therefore, burghs were being founded in Scotland. There were political motives behind the new foundations in the north-east, when the earldom of Moray was suppressed, and in the south-west on the fringes of rebellious Galloway, where Ayr and Dumfries were founded. Trade, however, was the essential factor without which a burgh would not develop, and as the burghs increased in number in the early medieval period, they came to follow a common commercial code, the Laws of the Four Burghs (Edinburgh, Stirling, Berwick, Roxburgh), whose underlying principles came directly from the laws of Newcastle-upon-Tyne (Mackenzie, 1949). Early trading was largely in the export of agricultural produce from the east coast burghs to the Low Countries and Flanders. Munro (1888) gives the example of the Aberdeen vessel pirated in 1273 of 56½ sacks of wool, 5½ dacres of ox hide (about 60), 150 salmon, 200 boards of oak, and a quantity of deer's hide and lamb's skins.

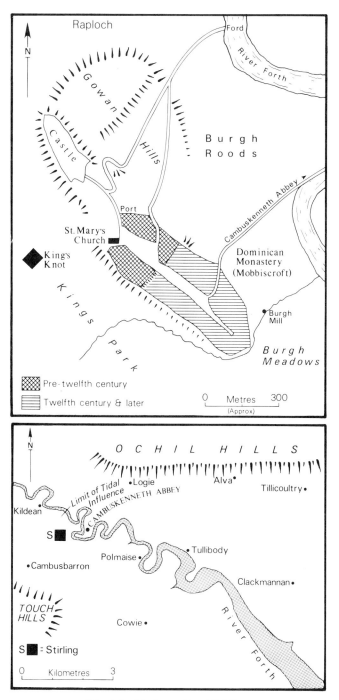

Fig. 4.3 Early medieval Stirling

THE MEDIEVAL PERIOD

After the initial period of burgh foundation, the impetus of establishment slackened. Figure 4.1d shows that fewer burghs were founded in the thirteenth and fourteenth centuries, although the total was 45 royal burghs, 11 ecclesiastical burghs and 14 baronial burghs by 1400. Pryde (1963) comments that the arithmetic of burgh foundation was not simple: there was movement both within and between the groups of burghs. The royal burghs were reduced by ten through alienation to the strongest families of the realm. Thus Renfrew passed to Walter FitzAlan, the earls of Moray and Ross held Elgin, Forres, Nairn, Dingwall and Cromarty, and the Douglases held the burghs of Wigtown and Kirkcudbright in Galloway. To redress the balance, Irvine was promoted to royal status when the Stuarts succeeded to the throne, and Renfrew was reinstated. The crown also lost Berwick and Roxburgh in the south through English action, while Clackmannan and Airth were royal burghs which failed through being economically unsound; the baronial burghs of Urr and Buittle met a similar fate. Too much, however, should not be made of the distinctions between royal and other burghs; the crown measured their success in economic terms and in this period taxed virtually all flourishing burghs accordingly.

Figure 4.1b shows that many of the new burghs were located in the same areas that had been colonized by 1200. The concentration of burghs was therefore higher in the Lothians, Fife, Stirlingshire, Perthshire, Aberdeen and the lands bordering the Moray Firth. Urban settlements were also found across the central lowlands and to the south-west in Galloway.

Scotland's Exchequer Rolls record the economic importance of the burghs in the early fourteenth century. Table 4.1 shows the amounts paid to the crown for the great customs of the ten largest burghs and the yearly rental due under their charters of feu-ferme. The great custom was levied by the king on exports of hides, wool and woollen fleeces and reflects the trading importance of each burgh. The feu-ferme charters allowed each burgh as a community to pay a fixed annual sum to the king for the burgesses' rentals of land, the petty customs levied at the tron and the fines paid to the burgh court.

The pre-eminence of Berwick is immediately apparent; it was followed by a group of east-coast burghs headed by Aberdeen, Edinburgh and Perth. Ayr and Rutherglen were the only western burghs of any significance. Edinburgh's status rose steadily in the fourteenth century to reach first position in the customs record by 1366–1376. Fox (1981) maintains that the feu-ferme data depict an undeveloped urban heirarchy. The triumvirate of Berwick, Aberdeen and Perth give the rank–size distribution a primary pattern; these three were followed by a group of much smaller 'middle-sized' burghs, for example

Table 4.1 Amounts paid to the crown for the great customs of the ten largest burghs and the yearly rental due under their charters of feu-ferme (£ s. d.)

Great Customs 1327				Feu-Ferme 1327			
Berwick	673	0	2½	Berwick	266	13	4
Edinburgh	439	3	9	Aberdeen	213	6	8
Aberdeen	349	10	4	Perth	160	0	0
Dundee	240	4	8½	Inverness	46	0	0
Perth	108	1	9	Stirling	36	0	0
Linlithgow	14	9	1	Edinburgh	34	18	8
Cupar–Fife	13	6	0¾	Ayr	30	0	0
Inverkeithing	8	2	10	Rutherglen	30	0	0
Ayr	3	4	0	Haddington	29	6	8
Stirling	2	11	8	Peebles	23	6	8

Source: Stuart and Burnett (1878)

Stirling, Ayr, Roxburgh and Dundee, and below these was a further tier of minor burghs such as Kirkcudbright and Lanark.

This economic pattern is not reproduced when a measure of political or administrative significance is examined—the place-dates of royal charters. Table 4.2 shows that between 1329 and 1346 the seat of government was to be found in towns across the whole breadth of central Scotland; Berwick, of course, had been eliminated by its passing to England. Between 1357 and 1371, however, the pendulum had swung firmly to the east coast with Edinburgh, Perth/Scone, Aberdeen and Dundee being pre-eminent. These latter place-dates are probably more significant due to the better survival of records; the small number of early charters must cast doubt on any conclusions drawn. Webster (1975) explains that the earlier period was affected by the capture of Edinburgh and Perth by the English, while Dumbarton became the centre of

Table 4.2 Place-dates in Royal Charters

1329–1346		1357–1371	
Dumbarton	13	Edinburgh	266
Scone	10	Perth	98
Edinburgh	9	Scone	40
Aberdeen	9	Aberdeen	27
Dundee	8	Dundee	21
Perth	8	Stirling	17
Ayr	6	Montrose	12
Stirling	5		

Source: Webster (1975)

Scottish resistance. Therefore, by the end of the fourteenth century, government was focusing upon Edinburgh, although sessions of Parliament and the Exchequer were still held at Scone. This century witnessed the complete decline of Berwick and the steady rise of Edinburgh. Throughout the medieval period, the east coast lowland areas dominated.

The Scottish burghs continued to enjoy their trading monopolies in the medieval period, and in this respect practice in Scotland was distinct from the Continent and England. Houston (1954) shows that modifications were forced on the early constraint of restricting trade to the liberty (often a sheriffdom) of the burgh since many new burghs were being founded. A sheriffdom still possessed the royal burgh as the caput of the sheriff, but major portions of the territory within it may have been allocated to subsequent foundations; thus Irvine acquired large tracts of northern Ayrshire. Furthermore, 'rival' royal burghs whose trading limits were uncertain were founded in the same shire. Not surprisingly, medieval burgh records are littered with litigation claiming the right to levy tolls on their neighbouring burgesses. Houston delimits the trading regions in existence by 1400, and perhaps the most salient feature was the smaller size and greater number of the eastern sheriffdoms. Once more the importance of an east-coast location for trade is apparent; the largest market for Scottish trade, which was still principally in wool, lay in the Low Countries.

The two most important innovations in burghal constitutions in the fourteenth and fifteenth centuries were the adoption of feu-ferme tenure and the rise to power of merchant oligarchies on burgh councils. Originally royal officials collected the burgesses' rents, received the fines of the burgh courts, and collected the petty customs and the tolls imposed on the sale of produce in the burgh. Pryde (1937) describes how burghs originally obtained short leases from the crown under which an annual sum (approximating to the burgh's income) was due from the burgh's *prepositi*. This evolved into a system of perpetual feu-ferme tenure in the fourteenth century after Aberdeen instigated the process in 1319. Once the burghs gained this degree of autonomy, they leased out the 'common good', the source of the burgh revenue, to tacksmen who hoped to make a profit above their yearly rent. In this way the burgh's common lands came to be subdivided, and the mills, fishings and customs were fermed (leased) to the prominent burgesses of the town. Munro (1888) gives a good account of Aberdeen's experience and the abuses which this system allowed—it was easy to gain long leases at low rates, thus diminishing the town's revenue.

The earliest burgh officials were the four bailiffs who collected the king's revenue. Before standing councils evolved in the fourteenth century there was an informal body composed of four liners (who established the Town's boundaries) and other semi-official burgesses such as the flesh apprisers and ale tasters. By 1400 the freemen of Aberdeen (Dickinson, 1953) were electing their own aldermen and successive acts of parliament subsequently placed power in the hands of one section of the burgesses, the merchants, whose status was higher than that of the craftsmen. Despite the limited representation of the incorporated crafts (the butchers, blacksmiths, masons, bakers, weavers, etc.) a small group of merchants elected their own friends and families to the highest official positions. As a consequence much of the town's common good became alienated to these families.

In the three centuries following the period of burgh foundation most burghs slowly prospered. As a consequence the burghs inevitably extended their bounds; the initial qualification of the burgess membership was the holding of a burgess plot. Thus new blocks of land were subdivided into plots at the end of the street (or streets) and occupied by burgesses. The size and alignment of St Andrews' medieval burgage plots support this argument (Brooks and Whittington, 1977), and Stirling also follows this pattern.

An accurate impression of the rate of growth of each burgh can be gained from the location of the Dominican convents in the town. Convents were founded from the middle of the thirteenth century onwards (1230 in Ayr and Berwick, 1246 in Glasgow, c. 1270 in St Andrews), and as Cant (1971) suggests, the sites chosen were always just beyond the built-up area of the town because the mendicant orders needed economical (and therefore peripheral) sites which were as near as possible to their congregation. Many of the burghs were therefore bounded at one end by a castle or cathedral and at the other (usually little more than half a mile away) would be a Dominican convent.

The location of substantial properties such as convents can be traced from early royal and ecclesiastical charters. However, the remainder of the burgh's buildings and plots only come to light in the protocol books which survive from the mid-fifteenth century. These books may record property transactions as dispositions and transfers of sasine (for example, Storer Clouston, 1914). They show us that tenements were built on the long, narrow burgage plots that ran back from the market street to the town limits (Figure 4.4). The tenements were set end-on to the market with fore-booths for the selling of goods. Behind the house, linked by a pend, was a courtyard and vegetable garden. The evidence from St Andrews suggests that buildings were of timber, no more than two storeys high, built on a stone foundation. In fourteenth-century Ayr stone houses were unusual enough to be used as prominent points of reference in deeds. Kellet (1969) is further able to use this element of the townscape to differentiate between 'upper' ecclesiastical Glasgow and 'lower' secular Glasgow. By 1440, Glasgow had 32 manses located around the bishop's castle and St Mungo's cathedral. The manses belonged to the canons of Glasgow, and each was a two-storey stone building with towers, balconies and gardens. In contrast, one of the few secular stone buildings was the tolbooth, located at the junction of the four main roads of the lower town, Trongate, Gallowgate,

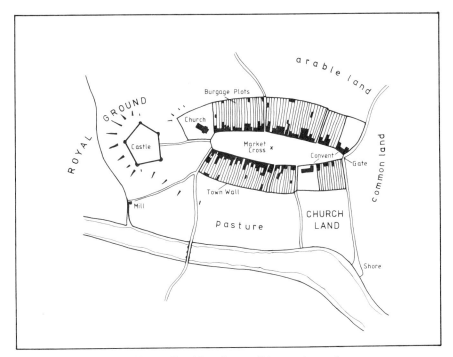

Fig. 4.4   The medieval burgh: possible constituent features

Saltmarket and High Street. The streets were fronted with wooden buildings with thatch and turf roofs and possessing kilns, small barns and malting troughs on the 'tails' of the plots. Other prominent features of the medieval townscape of the secular town were the market cross, the tron or weigh beam, and the ports or gates, which were slowly moved out from the central market place as the burgh extended.

Finally, the small population size of the medieval burghs was one of their most characteristic features. It is difficult to estimate population totals because no systematic surveys have survived, but Dickinson (1957) and Pryde (1949) give us some information and estimates for a few fifteenth century burghs. In 1426, 110 burgages were recorded in Selkirk, in 1429 Ayr had 106 burgesses, and in 1477 Stirling had at least 120 burgesses. These figures suggest a population of around 600 people in medium-sized Scottish burghs. In 1450 Glasgow is estimated to have had 1500 inhabitants, placing the town in the top rank. Aberdeen, the second city of the kingdom, lists 344 burgage holders in 1408, giving a population of around 2000 persons. The leading burgh,

Edinburgh, is estimated to have had 400 houses in the fourteenth century, and these probably sheltered over 2500 inhabitants.

The medieval period is revealed to us through the Royal Charters, the Chartularies of the great religious houses, and the Exchequer Rolls. By the sixteenth century these sources are greatly augmented by burgh records (council minutes, registers of sasine, protocol books), guildry records, proceedings of the trade incorporations, and records of the Convention of Royal Burghs. When these are further supported by the nationwide surveys, such as the Hearth Tax of the 1690s, post-medieval developments appear in greater detail and variety than the features of the earlier periods.

THE PRE-INDUSTRIAL BURGH

The period from 1400 to the Union of the Parliaments in 1707 witnessed many major changes to the type, number and fabric of Scottish burghs. Figure 4.1d shows that the overwhelming majority of new towns founded in this period were burghs of barony or regality. These burghs of barony may be distinguished from the royal and ecclesiastical burghs since their trading was restricted 'in ipso burgo', that is, they had no monopoly over a landward hinterland, or over foreign trade. Also, the founding of the burgh favoured the superior rather than the burgesses; thus the ports and customs of Pittenween and Anstruther Wester did not belong to the townsfolk. These burghs were strictly local centres serving local trading needs and sometimes founded with another function, that of providing way stations on prominent routes, for example Merton on the pilgrims' route to Whithorn. The burgh of Prestwick in 1470 gives us some idea of their size; there were 56 holdings of burgh land supporting a population of 200–300 persons. Pryde (1963) gives us this description 'the average burgh of barony . . . afforded a stable enough social unit, based on small scale agriculture and pastoral farming, with a superstructure, so to speak, of petty trading and the needful crafts, endowed with some sense of community, and reasonably free from oppression or arbitrary misrule'.

Figure 4.1c shows how these baronial burghs spread throughout lowland Scotland and up the major straths into the highlands. Pryde suggests that baronial foundation charters of this period should be treated cautiously, and estimates that as many as 140 of the 350 burghs erected after 1450 may have been 'parchment' burghs. Despite this, we clearly have a lower tier of urban life emerging in pre-industrial Scotland.

The innovation of 'unfree' markets in the seventeenth century introduced a second type of urban centre to this lower tier. Adams (1978) estimates that there were only eleven markets or fairs not held in burghs up to 1661. By 1707 approximately 150 non-burghal market centres had been founded; they had no burghal status, but their market or fair was licensed by Act of Parliament. Their purpose was to serve the agricultural trading needs of areas far from extant burghs, and so complete was their cover that by the Union of the Parliaments few areas of lowland Scotland were more than ten kilometres from a market centre. The final type in the lower tier were the small industrial nuclei that developed between 1650 and 1700. These small settlements were based on the extraction of salt, coal or lead, for example Culross, Alloa, Leadhills, and when these towns were subsequently enlarged they were often afforded burgh status.

Scotland therefore possessed a considerable urban hierarchy by the seventeenth century. In addition to the rapid increase of small urban centres the older-established burghs displayed an approximately log-normal rank–size distribution (Fox, 1981). Three tiers were found on the Extent Roll of 1601 and Taxt Roll of 1670; the leading group of burghs was headed by Edinburgh, followed by Aberdeen, Glasgow, Dundee, Perth and St Andrews; a middle group of under ten burghs included Stirling, Ayr, Dumfries, Haddington and Inverness; finally there was a large number of small burghs such as Crail and Queensferry. One major feature of the seventeenth century was the rise of Glasgow to rival Edinburgh by the turn of the eighteenth century. Up until this time the custumar's accounts show that the medieval dominance of the east coast persisted (Murray, 1975).

The inevitable consequence of the creation of new burghs and market centres was that they encroached upon the rights of the early medieval burghs—particularly the monopolies of domestic and overseas trade. The royal burghs were destined to lose these, by now, anachronistic privileges which were hampering the development of the nation as a whole. Throughout the seventeenth century, however, the Convention of Royal Burghs fought a staunch rearguard action (for details see Pagan, 1926), until a resolution was reached in 1698 whereby 'unfree' burghs were granted the right to overseas commerce if they agreed to pay a proportion of the tax burden (the stent) of the royal burghs.

In the pre-industrial period the Scottish burghs were subject to changes in their town plan and ownership patterns. The legacy of the medieval era was a deterministic framework of streets, burgage plots, and, in one or two places, town walls that overlay an equally influential pattern of land ownership. Expansion could involve either the taking up of undeveloped burgage plots within the urban area or the more intensive use of space within the area already tenanted. The former was common in the vast majority of small baronial and royal burghs, and the latter only applied to the larger, long-established burghs. The intensification of urban development (Conzen, 1960) was usually either in the form of building higher tenements, the infilling of burgage plots behind the street frontage (known as repletion), or the occupancy of the street area itself with the setting up of permanent buildings on the market place (market colonization). These new urban forms are a characteristic of this period.

St Andrews was one of Scotland's leading burghs in the pre-industrial era and John Geddy's 'Birds Eye View' of $c.$ 1580 gives evidence for two of the processes of concentrating building development. There were larger, three-storey tenements (two was the norm), and repletion of burgage plots was taking place in the commercial heart of the town between the tron and the tollbooth. By the mid-seventeenth century two leading burghs had been accurately mapped by James Gordon of Rothiemay—Edinburgh in 1647 and Aberdeen in 1661. Aberdeen exhibited burgage repletion throughout the *terra burgalis* with three-storey tenements and a market colony. Edinburgh had seven-storey tenements, a complete system of wynds (alleys) giving access to the extensively repleted burgage plots and new tenements spreading beyond the town walls. This clearly shows that the medieval system of plots and streets was being stretched to the limit. Historical records from Stirling, principally sasines and council minutes, reinforce the view that in the larger regional centres a certain degree of repletion and market colonization was an established fact by 1600 (Fox, 1978). In the largest cities these processes were intensified.

The Reformation was to provide the most significant development for burghal land ownership, because large quantities of church land were leased in and around the burghs. These lands and properties, usually granted to the burgh with the intention of funding the common good, were in fact frequently alienated, as the common good was leased out to prominent citizens of the town. Where these lands were extensive, as in the case of the ecclesiastical burgh of Glasgow, virtually all seventeenth- and eighteenth-century develop-ment was channelled on to them. Kellett (1969) shows how developments in the burgage area were determined by the size and availability of the arable rigs. In contrast, the distribution of land-ownership outside the town enabled large blocks of land to be released which were suitable for a new type of urban plan—the grid iron.

In addition to the evolution of the new urban forms, the social and economic life of the burghs was slowly changing. The burgh records show that trade became localized in this period. The markets of Edinburgh (March, 1914), Glasgow and Stirling were specialized, each with a specific location and time. There were markets for linen and woollen cloth, meal, flesh (meat), horses, timber, shoes, fruit and vegetables, and fish. All of the larger burghs had a similar system. These markets influenced the pattern of locational preference which burgesses displayed: it is unlikely that the wealthy merchant, bishop or noble would have his house facing the flesh or fish market, and conversely it would be to the advantage of the shoemaker to have his house and fore-booth fronting on to the shoe market. The unsavoury crafts, such as dyeing and tanning, would be relegated to the periphery of the town, where there was space and raw materials for tan pits, and candlemakers, who threatened the town with fire, were ordered to the outskirts by the council.

By 1600 it is possible to reconstruct districts of distinctive social types through the use of sasine registers (Fox, 1978 and in press). In Stirling there was a definite clustering of the elite members of society (noblemen and clergy) and the highest members of the lower class (wealthy merchants and burgh officials) at the head of the ridge on which the burgh developed adjacent to the castle. The best sites were held by the Duke of Argyll and the Earl of Mar. The lesser nobles and highest members of burgh society lived around the commercial centre of the upper market street with its market cross, tron and guild's house. The lower market street and the wynds running down to the Forth had a patchwork of houses, malt barns, kilns, tan pits, etc., and were largely populated by tradesmen. Different social classes, based on political, religious and economic status, were drawn to these separate foci, much as Sjoberg's pre-industrial model predicts (Sjoberg, 1965).

The Hearth Tax records for the 1690s show that strong variations in the building stock, and by inference in the wealth and social class of the burgh's inhabitants, persisted. The burghs were divided into quarters, supervised by a baillie, and this somewhat arbitrary division formed the basis for the returns from the burghs (unfortunately incomplete). Stirling had 2·7, 2·0, 2·3 and 2·5 hearths per tenant in the four quarters respectively; interestingly the first quarter was the pre-industrial social and commercial focus. Those living on the charity of the burgh had 1·1, 1·4, 1·1 and 1·4 hearths per tenant. These figures show us that houses possessing two rooms with hearths were common in the burgh. They also give an idea of the population size. Adamson (1970) estimates that a figure of around 4·5 persons per house is realistic for this period, and this gives estimates of c. 3500 people in Dumfries and c. 4200 in Stirling, these being two of the country's middle-order burghs. Aberdeen's Poll Tax records of the same period (Stuart, 1844) give a combined total for Aberdeen and Old Aberdeen of 1238 households with 3779 persons over the age of sixteen. Using Adamson's calculations and allowing for the under-enumeration of children over 16, this gives a total population of c. 9000. Dundee possessed a similar number of hearths to Aberdeen and so probably had about the same number of inhabitants. Glasgow and Edinburgh were larger, but it is difficult to rely on the records: Wood (1951) only records 1000 households and a population of c. 4500 for Edinburgh's parishes, but Pryde suggests that the total population of Edinburgh was in the order of 30 000 persons.

Poll Tax and Hearth Tax returns not only provide valuable aggregate data about Scottish burghs, they also present important social, functional and locational information about the town's inhabitants. For instance Mary Hardie of Old Kirk Parish, Edinburgh, is found to be the widow of Nicol Hardie, whose profession was that of Writer to the Signet. She had three children, Robert, Janet Anna and John, and two servants, and she possessed six hearths in the fourth and fifth storeys of a tenement in the Cowgate and a further four hearths in her dwelling and brewhouse in the same close. These data can be used to build up a detailed picture of the social and functional character of the town.

CONCLUSION

This chapter has focused upon three aspects of urban development. These themes have been the principal concern of both geographers and historians, and this is partly because Scotland's experience of urban foundation, diffusion and townscape is quite different from England's. Also it is clear that the type of sources available lend themselves to this type of analysis. In conclusion, however, it must be stressed that only the salient features have been introduced above, and as the study of Scotland's urban development is still in its infancy, these will almost certainly be challenged and modified.

REFERENCES

Adams, I. H. (1978). 'The Making of Urban Scotland'. Croom Helm, London.
Adamson, D. (1970). The Hearth Tax. *Transactions, Dumfriesshire and Galloway Natural History and Antiquarian Society* 47, 147–77.
Ballard, A. (1915). The theory of the Scottish burgh. *Scottish History Review* 13, 16–29.
Barrow, G. W. S. (ed.) (1960). 'The Acts of Malcolm IV King of Scots 1153–1165.' Edinburgh University Press, Edinburgh.
Barrow, G. W. S. (ed.) (1971). 'The Acts of William I King of Scots 1165–1214.' Edinburgh University Press, Edinburgh.
Bateson, M. (1900). The laws of Breteuil. *English Historical Review* 15, 73–78, 302–318, 496–523, 754–757.
Bateson, M. (1901). The laws of Breteuil. *English Historical Review* 16, 92–110, 332–345.
Brooks, N. P. (1977). *In* 'European Towns, their Archaeology and Early History.' (M. W. Barley, ed.), pp. 19–33. Academic Press, London and New York.
Brooks, N. P. and Whittington, G. (1977). Planning and growth in the medieval Scottish burgh: the example of St Andrews. *Transactions, Institute of British Geographers New Series* 2.3, 278–295.
Cant, R. G. (1948). 'The Scottish Tradition in Burgh Architecture.' Nelson and Sons, Edinburgh.
Cant, R. G. (1971). The development of the Burgh of St Andrews in the Middle Ages. *Annual Report, St Andrews Preservation Trust for 1970*, 12–16.
Clouston, J. S. (ed.) (1914). 'Records of the Earldom of Orkney 1299–1614.' Edinburgh University Press, Edinburgh.

Conzen, M. R. G. (1960). Alnwick, Northumberland: A study in town-plan analysis. *Transactions, Institute of British Geographers* **27**.

Dawson, A. H. (1975). *In* 'An Historical Atlas of Scotland *c*. 400– *c*. 1600.' (P. McNeill and R. Nicholson, ed.) pp. 1–2. University of St Andrews, St Andrews.

Dickinson, W. C. (1957). 'Early records of the Burgh of Aberdeen, 1317, 1398–1407.' Scottish History Society, Edinburgh.

Dickinson, W. C. (ed.) (1953). 'A Source Book of Scottish History II.' Nelson and Sons, London.

Dodd, W. (1972). 'Ayr: a Study of Urban Growth.' *Ayrshire Archaeological and Natural History Collections, Second Series* **10**, 302–382.

Duncan, A. A. M. (1975). 'Scotland, the Making of a Kingdom.' pp. 467–470. Oliver and Boyd, Edinburgh.

Ellison, M. (1976). *In* 'Archaeology in the North.' (P. A. G. Clark and P. F. Gosling, ed.), pp. 147–164. HMSO, London.

Fox, R. C. (1978). 'The Morphological, Social and Functional Development of the Royal Burgh of Stirling, 1124–1881.' Unpublished Ph.D. thesis, University of Strathclyde.

Fox, R. C. (1981). The burghs of Scotland, 1327, 1601, 1670. *Area* **13**, 2.

Fox, R. C. (in press). *In* 'Scottish Urban History.' (T. R. B. Dicks and G. Gordon, ed.). Aberdeen University Press, Aberdeen.

Houston, J. M. (1954). The Scottish burgh. *Town Planning Review* **25**, 114–127.

Kellett, J. R. (1969). *In* 'Historic Towns.' (I. Lobel, ed.) pp. 1–13. Lovell Johns, London.

Lawrie, A. C. (1905). 'Early Scottish Charters prior to A.D. 1153.' Maclehose and Sons, Glasgow.

March, M. C. (1914). The trade regulations of Edinburgh during the sixteenth and seventeenth centuries. *Scottish Geographical Magazine* **30**, 483–487.

MacKenzie, W. M. (1949). 'The Scottish Burghs.' Oliver and Boyd, Edinburgh.

Millar, A. H. (ed.) (1898). 'The Compt Buik of David Wedderburne, Merchant of Dundee 1587–1630.' Edinburgh University Press, Edinburgh.

Munro, A. M. (1888). 'The Common Good of the City of Aberdeen, 1319–1887.' Wylie and Son, Aberdeen.

Murray, A. (1975). *In* 'An Historical Atlas of Scotland *c*. 400–*c*. 1600.' (P. McNeill and R. Nicholson, ed.) pp. 74–76. University of St Andrews, St Andrews.

Murray, D. (1924). 'Early Burgh Organisation in Scotland I.' Maclehose and Sons, Glasgow.

Neilson, G. (1902). 'On some Scottish burghal origins.' *Juridical Review* **14**, 129–140.

Pagan, T. (1926). 'The Convention of the Royal Burghs of Scotland.' Glasgow University Press, Glasgow.

Pryde, G. S. (ed.) (1937). 'Ayr Burgh Accounts 1534–1624.' Edinburgh University Press, Edinburgh.

Pryde, G. S. (1949). The Scottish burghs. *Scottish Historical Review* **28**, 155–164.

Pryde, G. S. (ed.) (1963). 'The Court Book of the Burgh of Kirkintilloch 1658–1694.' Scottish History Society, Edinburgh.

Pryde, G. S. (1965). 'The Burghs of Scotland: A Critical List.' Oxford University Press, Oxford.

Renwick, R. (ed.) (1887). 'Extracts from the Records of the Royal Burgh of Stirling I, 1519–1666.' Scottish Burgh Record Society, Glasgow.

Ritchie, R. L. G. (1954). 'The Normans in Scotland.' Edinburgh University Press, Edinburgh.

Sjoberg, G. (1965). 'The Pre-Industrial City.' Free Press, Toronto.

Stuart, J. (ed.) (1844). 'List of Pollable Persons within the Shire of Aberdeen, 1696.' Spalding Club, Aberdeen.

Stuart, J. and Burnett, G. (ed.) (1878). 'The Exchequer Rolls of Scotland I, 1264–1359.' Register House, Edinburgh.

Webster, A. B. (1975). *In* 'An Historical Atlas of Scotland *c*. 400–*c*. 1600.' (P. McNeill and R. Nicholson, ed.) p. 62. University of St Andrews, St Andrews.

Whitehand, J. W. R. and Alauddin, K. (1969). The town plans of Scotland. Some preliminary considerations. *Scottish Geographical Magazine* 85, 109–121.

Wood, M. (ed.) (1951). 'Edinburgh Poll Tax Returns for 1696.' Scottish Record Society, Edinburgh.

5

Population Patterns and Processes from c. 1600

H. Jones

Although parochial perspectives have sometimes encouraged an impression of the uniqueness of Scottish demographic evolution, particularly in relation to the socio-economic vicissitudes of the Highlands and Islands, a more tenable view is that Scotland conforms closely to wider European demographic experience and thus to demographic transition theory. Such theory should be regarded as a paradigm which links socio-economic and demographic change through economic and socio-psychological arguments and through the empirical observation of demographic evolution in more developed countries but which is sufficiently open-ended to leave several problems for researchers to resolve in particular spatio-temporal contexts.

The essence of transition theory is that a particular pattern of demographic change accompanies a nation's progression from a largely rural, agrarian and illiterate society to a pre-dominantly urban, industrial and literate one. During the course of this essentially irreversible progression there are major reductions in both fertility and mortality, and in the past two centuries average life expectancy in developed countries has doubled and fertility halved. If fertility and mortality declines had been concurrent, population growth would have been modest, as was uniquely the case in France. But elsewhere in the developed world, mortality decline preceded fertility decline by about a century, leading to the replacement of a demographic steady-state situation by the population explosion of nineteenth-century Europe and North America. Figure 5.1 is a schematic representation of the standard demographic transition. It shows that in pre-industrial societies the birth rate is relatively constant, while the death rate fluctuates from year to year in response to epidemics and variable food supply. After the transition the roles are reversed:

93

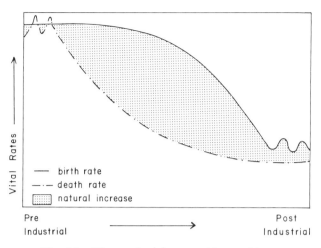

Fig. 5.1   The standard demographic transition

the death rate remains constant, while fertility oscillates in relation to contemporary forces not yet fully understood.

Although Scotland conforms broadly to this model of interlinked socio-economic and demographic transformation, there are spatial leads and lags within the country that are obviously of particular interest to geographers. This is not to say that a spatial perspective in population studies is the unique preserve of geography. In fact, the only full and systematic treatment of Scotland's population evolution—an invaluable recent study by a group of economic historians (Flinn *et al.*, 1977)—consciously adopts and well sustains a regional approach that geographers should find entirely acceptable. Geographers involved in population analysis would be better advised to emphasize more their special skills and technical versatility as practitioners of a spatial science, involving advanced cartography, the assembly and handling of small area data, and multivariate analysis of spatially ordered data sets, with an appreciation of the accompanying problems of scale, spatial auto-correlation and 'the ecological fallacy'.

There has been a growing awareness in human geography that too much attention in teaching and research has been given to the identification of spatial patterns, from which formative processes are inferred, and too little attention to the direct study of the processes themselves. Accordingly, the structure of this chapter has been designed specifically to recognize the prime explanatory importance in contemporary population geography of the dynamic components—fertility, mortality and migration—and the processes that fashion them. It is *their* spatio-temporal interaction which produces the patterns of population distribution, growth and composition that are considered in the final section of the chapter and that embrace the bulk of traditional geographical work on Scotland's population.

MORTALITY

Civil registration of births, deaths and marriages was not instituted in Scotland until 1855, and before this date the only systematic records of vital events are contained in the parish registers kept by clergy from the mid-sixteenth century and now housed in General Register Office, Edinburgh. The extraction, analysis and interpretation of demographic data from such ecclesiastical registers throughout Europe form the core of the interdisciplinary field of historical demography, whose methods (Henry, 1967; Wrigley, 1966a) have been applied to Scottish data by Flinn *et al.* (1977) and Tranter (1978).

Invaluable as the registers are as demographic data banks and ingenious as are the extractive methods often adopted, they are subject nevertheless to major problems of error, bias and uncertainty. There was rarely any check on an individual's diligence in register keeping, the deaths of paupers, plague victims and infants, particularly if dying before baptism, were often unrecorded, and the growth of religious dissent and anti-clericalism from the eighteenth century further promoted under-enumeration, since the events recorded by the established church were essentially religious—baptisms and burials rather than births and deaths. Adjustment of data is difficult because of the temporally and spatially varying nature of these and other deficiencies. In Scotland the survival rate and general standard of upkeep of registers have been poorer than in England and in many parts of Europe, with a particular dearth of extant registers (assuming they were kept at all) for the Highlands and Islands until well into the eighteenth century.

Careful analysis of these registers has, however, illuminated our understanding of mortality patterns in pre-industrial Scotland by locating in time and space the major surges of mortality from the beginning of the seventeenth century. The Edinburgh historians (Flinn *et al.*, 1977) have located just over a hundred, seemingly well-kept registers with burial series extending over periods varying from a few years to two centuries. Obviously they could not use such data to calculate conventional mortality rates because the population 'at risk' in the individual parishes is simply not known before the institution of regular census-taking. Nevertheless, they were able to calculate regional indices of mortality by a method which allows for temporal and spatial gaps in the registers. For a particular region in a particular year, the index is represented by:

$$\frac{\text{the sum of burials in those of the region's parish registers available that year}}{\text{the sum of burial means in the same parishes for all the years for which records exist between 1615 and 1854}} \times 100$$

To be entirely satisfactory, such a method depends on little or no change in population size over time, and although this is a reasonable assumption for most of the period under consideration, there is no doubt that the increased population by the nineteenth century would by itself cause an increase in death numbers and index level at that time, regardless of overall mortality conditions. Nevertheless, the index retains considerable diagnostic value, particularly in the seventeenth and eighteenth centuries, in pinpointing the periods and places of abnormally high mortality, particularly when confirmed by literary evidence from kirk session records, burgh records, estate papers, diaries and the like. Such occurrences, known by historical demographers as demographic crises or catastrophes, have been recognized throughout Europe as the critical repressors of pre-industrial population growth, but whether these crises were of a Malthusian subsistence nature or the result of random attacks from disease, or some combination of both, is more uncertain.

It is likely that such crises affected all parts of Scotland—Lowland and Highland, rural and urban—at one time or another, but Flinn et al. (1977) recognize three crises of exceptional severity and wide spatial impact in seventeenth-century Scotland. That of 1623 was clearly the result of disastrous harvests in 1621 and 1622 induced by poor weather, and its impact is well illustrated in the quarterly totals of burials for Kelso and Dunfermline (Fig. 5.2). Some deaths would have been due to starvation, at a time when the movement of bulk foodstuffs was primitive, particularly in districts remote from ports, but medical historians like McKeown (1976) now place more emphasis on the way in which a malnourished population would have little resistance to infectious diseases like typhus. It has also been argued (Langer, 1974; Sauer, 1978) that at such times the inability of parents to feed their growing families would be reflected in infant neglect—hence the designation of smallpox as 'the poor man's friend'. The 1645–48 crisis was the result of bubonic plague diffusing from a Scottish landfall at the port of Leith. Its impact was clearly most severe in crowded burghs, where the fleas associated with infected rats played a critical role in disease transmission. Flinn et al. (1977) estimate that about a fifth of the Scottish urban population perished of plague at this time. The third great crisis, widely known as 'the seven ill years' or 'the black years of King William', devastated much of Scotland in the latter 1690s, when at least three harvests were seriously deficient and when grain

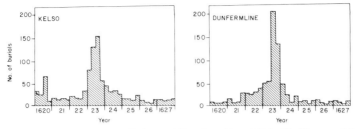

Fig. 5.2   Quarterly burials at Kelso and Dunfermline, 1620–27. (Source: Flinn *et al.* (1977), fig. 3.2.2.)

imports were difficult to secure because of similar, climatically induced harvest failures elsewhere in northern Europe.

The coming of the eighteenth century seems to have heralded demographic transformation in Scotland: the evidence from the mortality index, supported by increasingly useful literary comment, is that there was no major demographic crisis for some 130 years after 'the seven ill years'. The beginnings of mortality reduction throughout northern Europe at this time have been ascribed to three major factors:

Nutritional Improvement

Langer (1975) attributes nutritional improvement to the widespread adoption of the new wonder crop from America, the potato, with its enormous calorific yield and its ability to provide subsistence more reliably than traditional grain crops in agriculturally marginal climates like Norway (Drake, 1969) and much of Scotland. Yet it was not until the end of the eighteenth century that the potato was widely adopted as a commercial field crop in the Scottish Lowlands and as a subsistence crop in the Highlands. Likewise, the agricultural advances, known traditionally, but increasingly controversially, as the Agricultural Revolution, had made little headway outside south-eastern Scotland by the end of the century.

Medical Advances

Despite the founding of infirmaries in the major towns of Scotland during the eighteenth century, it is now widely recognized that medical developments had little or no influence in reducing mortality at that time (McKeown and Brown, 1955), essentially because there was no appreciation until the work of Pasteur and Koch in the 1870s and 1880s of the existence of germs, their manner of reproduction and transmission, and their specificity in causing disease. The treatment of smallpox was an important exception. Controversy surrounds the demographic effect of inoculation—infecting a healthy person with pus from a mild case of the disease in an attempt to confer protection against a serious attack—widely practised in eighteenth-century Scotland, but there is no doubt about the favourable effects of vaccination using the cowpox vaccine developed by Jenner in 1798. Vaccination was not only extolled by the General Assembly of the Church of Scotland but was carried out extensively by its parish ministers from 1803. The effect is shown clearly in the much reduced death toll from smallpox recorded in the bills of mortality issued at that time by several urban parishes (Flinn *et al.*, 1977).

Infrastructural and Institutional Improvements

In Scotland, as throughout northern Europe, the culling of population by regional famine was eased in the eighteenth century by the growing economic integration of national territory promoted by port, road and canal construction. Flinn *et al.* (1977) place more emphasis in Scotland, however, on the emergence of a reasonably efficient system of famine relief, involving Poor Law authorities, landlords and, eventually, central government. Such relief was aided by one entirely fortuitous factor: the virtual absence in the eighteenth century of consecutive harvest failures.

Scotland departs somewhat from the standard demographic transition model (Fig. 5.1) in that progress towards significant mortality decline was interrupted by a last fling of mortality surges in the second quarter of the nineteenth century. The decimation by blight in 1836–37 and 1845–46 of the potato harvests on which the population of the western Highlands and Islands had become dependent was a contributory factor, although in marked contrast to the equivalent, but much larger-scale, Irish situation, major mortality tolls were prevented by extensive famine relief and emigration (Gray, 1955). Demographically more important were the mortality surges in the larger towns where the rapid population growth associated with industrialization outran the ability of civic authorities to provide adequate housing, water and sanitation. Typhus and tuberculosis proliferate in squalid overcrowded conditions, and water-borne intestinal diseases (cholera, dysentery, typhoid) would have responded actively to conditions such as those described for Dundee as late as 1867:

> At this time Dundee was wholly devoid of sanitation. Drainage . . . was barely in evidence and what there was consisted of stone built rubble, allowing the liquid to percolate through and soak into the ground, thus poisoning the soil. A few public sewers were put down but these were confined to the leading thoroughfares. There

was no proper supply of water for domestic, culinary or flushing purposes. All there was was largely obtained from wells. . . . Under such conditions water closets were an impossibility. There were five such places only. . . . The only other conveniences of this nature were wooden or brick privies, with holes sunk in the ground of from four to five feet deep under them as dung pits. . . . The emptying of these pits was attended with the most horrible odours. The scavengers, equipped with sea boots, started about 4 a.m. to empty them and wheeled the contents out to the streets, on which they were deposited prior to being carted away (Kinnear, 1912, 148–9).

From evidence presented in Creighton (1894), Longmate (1966) and Flinn *et al.* (1977), it seems that the four cholera epidemics of 1832, 1848–9, 1853–54 and 1866 followed similar diffusion patterns, which might well merit a spatial diffusion modelling study such as that provided by Kwofie (1976) for West Africa. In each case the Scottish origin of this highly contagious disease seems to have been the Edinburgh area—derived in the first epidemic from the British landfall at Sunderland, and in others through the port of Leith. Subsequently the spread was westwards to Glasgow and northwards to Dundee, Aberdeen and Inverness, although large parts of the countryside escaped, particularly in the Highlands and Islands.

The coming of civil registration in 1855 puts the study of mortality in Scotland on a much firmer statistical footing. The data (Table 5.1) indicate that the resumption of significant mortality reduction was delayed until the 1870s and that there were considerable variations, although diminishing over time, in mortality level by degree of urbanization. Certified cause of death data indicate that the whole of mortality decline between the 1860s and the 1890s, and about 60% of that between the 1890s and 1930s, was attributable to reduction in infectious disease categories, particularly in childhood, a pattern

Table 5.1 Crude death rates by settlement units, 1861–1931 (annual average deaths for three-year period astride census year per 1000 census population)

Year	Rural areas	Towns[a]	Cities	Scotland
1861	17·9	23·4	28·1[b]	21·5
1871	18·4	23·8	28·2	22·3
1881	17·3	20·3	23·3	19·7
1891	18·2	19·5	22·0	19·7
1901	16·6	17·3	20·0	17·9
1911	14·2	15·0	16·6	15·1
1921	13·0	13·6	15·7	14·2
1931	12·8	13·1	14·1	13·4

[a] Towns over 5000 population at each census, except the four cities
[b] Glasgow 29·4, Dundee 29·1, Aberdeen 26·6, Edinburgh 25·5
Source: Flinn *et al.* (1977), tables 5.5.6 and 5.5.7

closely comparable to that in England and Wales (McKeown, 1976). What then were the likely causes?

In the case of one disease, scarlet fever, it has been argued that there was a random biological influence at work, involving a spontaneous or autonomous reduction in the virulence of the infective micro-organism (McKeown, 1976). But for the other infectious diseases, most notably the major killers at the beginning of the period, tuberculosis and typhus, the critical factors appear to be, first, the improved diet and general living conditions associated with continuing economic development, and, second, the major public health improvements, particularly in the cities. The basis of the latter (Chalmers, 1930; Brotherston, 1952) was the provision of abundant pure water (brought, for example, from Loch Katrine to Glasgow in 1859 and from Lintrathen to Dundee in 1875), the construction of water-closets and piped sewer systems, improved facilities and practices in dairies, and the removal of at least some of the most overcrowded and squalid slums. The effect of specific medical therapy was probably slight until the introduction of chemotherapeutic agents in the 1930s (McKeown, 1976), although Razzell (1974) has argued that earlier there had been significant improvements in health education, so that a general awareness had emerged by the beginning of the twentieth century of the need for cleanliness in body, food preparation and domestic waste disposal.

The detailed spatial pattern of Scottish mortality decline from the 1870s has yet to be researched. Flinn et al. (1977) provide a preliminary analysis of county and regional crude death rates, concluding reasonably that differing degrees of urbanization appear to control the patterns. But areal data sets exist—in the Registrar General's breakdown of both deaths and census populations by age and sex—for the calculation, portrayal and analysis of mortality measures fully adjusted for variable age- and sex-structures; an example is the Standardized Mortality Ratio, profitably used in medical geography to elucidate recent spatial mortality experience in Britain (Howe, 1970). Such refined measures can be calculated not only for total deaths but also for particular causes of death, although for lesser causes in smaller populations statistical reliability will be low.

FERTILITY

Before the coming of civil registration, the analysis of fertility within Scotland is hazardous. Parish baptismal registers, where they survive, suffer from the same crippling analytical problems as burial registers; indeed, the underenumeration of baptisms in dissenting areas, because of the sacramental nature of the event, is likely to be even higher than that of burials. In parts of Europe historical demographers have engaged profitably in studies of family reconstitution—an essentially genealogical approach which pieces together life histories from parish registers so that individuals can be traced from baptism, through marriage and the births of their children, to burial. Such studies (e.g. Wrigley, 1966b) have provided invaluable data on age at marriage, birth intervals and family size, but for Scotland, Flinn et al. (1977, xv) 'were unable to find even a single parish with a set of registers for an adequate run of years and of a sufficiently high quality to meet the exacting requirements of reconstitution'. Tranter (1978) has made a brave attempt at reconstitution for the parish of Portpatrick in the nineteenth century, but his study is bedevilled by missing data and the associated problem of possibly biased samples.

The fragments of fertility data and literary comment available before 1855 suggest a pattern which conforms to that elsewhere in pre-industrial northern Europe. During crisis periods of high mortality in Scotland baptisms fall quickly in the affected parishes, doubtless reflecting fetal deaths, deaths of women of reproductive age, an impairment of fecundity (the physiological capability of women to bear children) and the postponement of marriages. However, the effect is often short-lived: marriage inheritance theory (Ohlin, 1961; Berkner and Mendels, 1978) suggests that periods of high mortality provide the land vacancies which promote earlier marriage and consequently higher fertility.

Similar inducements, although based on economic development rather than high mortality, may well have elevated fertility in parts of Scotland towards the end of the eighteenth century. Literary evidence from the *Old Statistical Account* and elsewhere suggests that marriage was made easier, and therefore of younger occurrence, in the western Highlands and Islands by the subdivision of holdings permitted by the spread of the potato and kelping economy in a fashion described for Ireland by Connell (1950). Proto-industrialization may also have had a similar effect, as it certainly did elsewhere in Europe (e.g., Braun, 1978). Scottish evidence is hard to come by, but the Kilmarnock marriage registers do show that the mean age at first marriage for females between the 1730s and 1760s was three years younger in the textile town itself than in its farming hinterland (Flinn et al., 1977).

The temporal and spatial pattern of fertility within Scotland becomes reliably known only after the beginning of civil registration of births in 1855. The Registrar General's county data have been aggregated by Flinn et al. (1977) into six regions (Table 5.2). These data show that the modern period of fertility decline associated with the Demographic Transition commenced in Scotland in the 1880s, as it did in many parts of northen Europe. The common causes, which lie in changing norms and values relating to childbearing and parenthood rather than in advancing contraceptive technology, have been discussed extensively (e.g. Andorka, 1978) and need not be summarized here. More relevantly, throughout the period covered by Table 5.2 there are

Table 5.2 Crude birth rates, 1861–1931 (annual average births for three-year period astride census year per 1000 census population)

	Census Year					
	1861	1871	1881	1891	1901	1931
Far North	27·4	25·9	24·5	22·9	21·7	15·1
Highland Counties	27·0	25·7	26·0	23·2	22·0	14·8
North East	32·7	33·0	32·7	29·5	28·7	19·8
Western Lowlands	39·9	39·8	37·5	34·9	33·3	20·8
Eastern Lowlands	33·9	33·7	32·7	29·5	27·8	17·7
Borders	32·0	31·0	30·3	25·5	22·5	16·6
Scotland	34·8	34·7	33·6	30·8	29·5	19·1

Far North Caithness, Orkney, Shetland. *Highland Counties* Argyll, Bute, Inverness, Ross and Cromarty, Sutherland. *North East* Aberdeen, Banff, Kincardine, Moray, Nairn. *Western Lowlands* Ayr, Dumbarton, Lanark, Renfrew. *Eastern Lowlands* Angus, Clackmannan, East Lothian, Fife, Kinross, Midlothian, Perth, Stirling, West Lothian. *Borders* Berwick, Dumfries, Kirkcudbright, Peebles, Roxburgh, Selkirk, Wigtown. Source: Flinn *et al.* (1977), table 5.3.2

appreciable regional variations in the level of crude birth rate, with the high rates of west-central Scotland (the Western Lowlands of Table 5.2) contrasting in particular with the low rates of the Highlands and Islands (the Far North and the Highland Counties).

Variations in age structure, themselves the result of age-selective migration streams, clearly contribute to this regional pattern. Extensive out-migration of young people from the Highlands and Islands following economic collapse and social disorganization in the first part of the nineteenth century had left the region with an age structure predisposed to high crude death rates and low crude birth rates, while the industrial advance of west-central Scotland had the very opposite effect there.

Another contributory factor is the spatially varying marital pattern within Scotland. Table 5.3 indicates that throughout the 1861–1931 period about 80% of Scotland's women had married by the end of their reproductive period, but the proportion was significantly lower in the Highlands and Islands and significantly higher in west-central Scotland. Data from the 20–24 age group in Table 5.3 also indicate appreciable differences between these same regions in the extent of early marriage. The Highlands and Islands were obviously showing the same response of little and late marriage to the pressure of population on limited resources that Ireland exemplified at the same time. A map by Coale (1969) of female marriage incidence in 700 areas of Europe in 1900 shows clearly that it was lower in the Highlands and Islands than in any other part of Europe outside Ireland. It would be naïve to attribute these marital patterns directly and solely to regional variations in economic opportunities and the material means to sustain marriage and family building; there is

Table 5.3 Percentage of selected female age-groups married, 1861–1931

	Census Year					
	1861	1871	1881	1891	1901	1931
FAR NORTH						
20–24	15·9	14·6	16·5	13·8	15·1	18·7
50–54	74·5	69·7	68·1	69·6	68·8	70·1
HIGHLAND COUNTIES						
20–24	15·2	13·5	14·7	11·3	12·0	14·8
50–54	75·5	73·6	72·5	72·2	71·7	70·3
NORTH EAST						
20–24	22·5	23·5	24·2	19·7	22·0	24·5
50–54	76·6	77·7	76·2	77·7	78·9	78·4
WESTERN LOWLANDS						
20–24	32·3	33·3	32·4	29·3	28·3	24·0
50–54	84·9	85·8	87·2	87·6	87·5	82·2
EASTERN LOWLANDS						
20–24	24·5	24·4	24·5	21·9	21·4	22·2
50–54	78·3	79·3	80·2	80·5	79·6	77·5
BORDERS						
20–24	22·6	20·0	20·4	15·6	13·7	21·4
50–54	77·4	76·4	75·9	75·7	74·7	72·1
SCOTLAND						
20–24	25·9	26·2	26·5	23·6	23·6	22·9
50–54	79·6	80·1	80·7	81·5	81·4	78·9

Source: Flinn *et al.* (1977), table 5.2.6

the additional, or rather intermediate, influence of regional sex ratios to consider (Table 5.4). Imbalances in the ratio, which obviously prejudice marriage prospects, are the result of out-migration which was particularly male-selective until the later decades of the nineteenth century. The best balanced ratio is found in west-central Scotland, and this must have contributed to its pattern of relatively early and extensive marriage.

Thus far we have attempted to explain the regional pattern of crude birth rates in terms of marital and sex composition. To see whether there are any regional variations in fertility independent of structural factors, and dependent perhaps on regional variations in values and attitudes towards family size, we need to adopt refined indices of fertility which fully standardize for structural factors. Such indices have been used by Wilson (1978) to elucidate the contemporary spatial pattern of fertility in Scotland, but the necessary age-specific data are lacking for earlier periods. Before the 1930s it is only in the

Table 5.4 Number of males per 100 females in 15–49 age group, 1861–1931

	Census Year					
	1861	1871	1881	1891	1901	1931
Far North	70·8	72·4	81·2	82·0	89·5	90·0
Highland Counties	83·7	84·7	92·1	91·0	92·9	95·4
North East	83·5	84·3	88·3	87·5	88·6	88·5
Western Lowlands	88·9	95·5	98·2	99·3	101·7	91·8
Eastern Lowlands	81·4	83·0	86·0	87·9	89·1	89·0
Borders	85·3	89·0	84·7	82·4	83·2	86·0
Scotland	84·5	87·5	91·2	92·3	94·4	90·5

Source: Flinn *et al.* (1977), table 5.2.2.

first year of civil registration, 1855, that the mother's age is given at birth registration. Although Flinn *et al.* (1977) have investigated the 1855 data for Ross-shire and Renfrewshire, there is considerable scope for a more comprehensive spatial analysis. Particularly revealing would be a multiple regression analysis, using a standardized fertility index as the dependent variable and selected socio-economic variables from the 1851 or 1861 censuses as the independent or predictor variables. One hypothesis that could be tested in a Scottish context is the view of Friedlander (1973–74) and Haines (1977) that high fertility in the coalmining areas of Britain was due not only to early marriage but also to high marital fertility. They see this as being stimulated by lack of female employment opportunities, particularly after legislation in the 1840s forbidding underground work by women, and by the nature and health risks of mining which curtailed the effective working life of miners, thereby creating a need for unmarried working sons to support the family. The overall regression results could also be compared usefully with those of Jones (1975) and Wilson (1978) for the modern period showing the influence of religion and female activity rate on the contemporary spatial pattern of Scottish fertility.

MIGRATION

Scotland conforms well to Zelinsky's mobility transition model in which 'a transition from a relatively sessile condition of severely limited physical and social mobility toward much higher rates of such movement always occur as a community experiences the process of modernization' (Zelinsky, 1971, 221–2). Until well into the eighteenth century the subsistence nature of the Scottish economy, the strength of local social ties, poorly developed communications, sharply circumscribed awareness-space and minimal disposable incomes all severely restricted territorial mobility. It needed the spur of emerging spatial inequalities through agricultural, industrial and urban transformation to promote significant, and certainly long-distance, movement.

Of the three components of population change, migration is the most difficult to conceptualize and measure. The definition of birth and death, at least for statistical purposes, is clear cut, but migration is 'a physical and social transaction, not just an unequivocal biological event' (Zelinsky, 1971, 223). In particular, there is a vast range of time and space circumstances relating to movement, so that the broad structural division of Scottish migration adopted here should not be regarded as exhaustive or exclusive.

Temporary Migration

The term *circulation* is used extensively to describe migratory movements in the contemporary Third World which are short-term, repetitive, often cyclical and without any intention of permanent change in residence. Such movements, which emerged in eighteenth-century Scotland and probably peaked in the mid nineteenth century, have been shown by historians (Macdonald, 1937; Devine, 1979) to have been far from the haphazard wandering of vagrants that many observers casually noted at the time. A spatial analysis of the movements, comparable to Johnson's (1967) study of nineteenth century Irish harvesters, remains to be provided.

The Highlands and Islands were the major source of temporary migrants as a response to its growing population pressure and the cash needs generated by an emerging money economy. Initially most of the migrants were seasonal harvesters, often women, employed in the grain and turnip fields of the new enclosed farms of the Scottish Lowlands, although some Scottish harvesters also found their way regularly to eastern England (Redford, 1926). Migration for a period of some years was associated with employment in the Highland regiments, the Navy, the Greenland fisheries and the Hudson Bay Company. More seasonal was migration from the islands and west coast to the fishing, gutting and packing industries of the North East as they expanded from the 1820s; the *New Statistical Account* records an annual influx into Fraserburgh of some 1200 people during the herring season. Railway construction was another outlet for temporary migration, and the reports of the Board of Destitution, set up to organize famine relief after the 1847 potato famine, record how the Board actively promoted such migration, even to the extent of arranging employment and paying travel expenses—a forerunner of current government attempts such as the Employment Transfer Scheme to promote and subsidize the movement of unemployed in pursuit of job opportunities. Finally there was the pull of temporary employment in growing urban centres, particularly in the building industry.

There is no doubt that temporary migration retarded the onset of appreciable depopulation in the Highlands and Islands by providing externally derived cash remittances and, in the case of seasonal migration, by the subsistence provided away from home at the critical part of the year when the previous harvest was running out and the new harvest had yet to be gathered. On the other hand, temporary migration brings familiarity with conditions elsewhere, raises material aspirations, and loosens bonds with the home community. Eventually, therefore, it promotes permanent migration, as shown by Lobban's (1969) study of Highland migration to Greenock.

Immigration from Ireland

From the late eighteenth century Irish harvesters began to compete with Highlanders for seasonal work on Scottish lowland farms, their entry being particularly strong after the provision in the 1820s of cheap steamboat services from Belfast and Londonderry to the Clyde. But it was to the labour-hungry industries of the Scottish cities that most Irish immigrants were drawn, particularly after the 1847 famine, and by 1851 7·2% of Scotland's population recorded an Irish birthplace—more than double the equivalent proportion in England and Wales. Distribution maps by county of the Irish-born in Scotland at various censuses (Jackson, 1963) show the dominance of west-central Scotland, but with an important outlier in the jute and linen city of Dundee, where in 1851 the Irish-born proportion of the population (18·8%) was higher than in Glasgow (18·2%). The extent of Irish residential segregation within nineteenth-century Scottish cities is an unresearched field, although the data exist in census enumerators' manuscript returns for detailed spatial analyses, as a preliminary examination of the 1841 Dundee data shows (S. J. Jones, 1975).

The flow of Irish immigrants into Scotland had receded by the late nineteenth century, and the Irish-born proportion of Scotland's population fell to 4·6% in 1901 and a mere 1·7% in 1951; but the residual social impact of Irish immigration is still very real.

Migration within Scotland

The redistribution of population within European countries in the nineteenth century as a result of labour shedding in the countryside and the rapid expansion of manufacturing and service employment in the cities is a familiar theme exemplified by Osborne's (1958) analysis of Scottish census birthplace data. Not until 1961 was a question asked in British censuses about migration, so before 1961 censuses can provide only an indirect assessment of migration through a comparison of place of enumeration and place of birth. Osborne's aggregation of the county data into inter-regional 'lifetime' migration flows (Figs 5.3 and 5.4) clearly reveals a pattern of accelerating net movement in the nineteenth century from northern and southern Scotland into the mining-industrial-urban belt of central Scotland, although by 1951 there had been a subsidence in centripetal flows and, indeed, a beginning of deconcentration from west-central Scotland.

More detailed patterns of net and gross flows on the basis of birthplace data can be provided when individual counties rather than regions are used as units of analysis. For example, Jones (1967) has mapped net migration balances between both Angus and Perthshire and all other Scottish counties on the basis of 1891 census data. The maps clearly reveal the intermediate spatial and

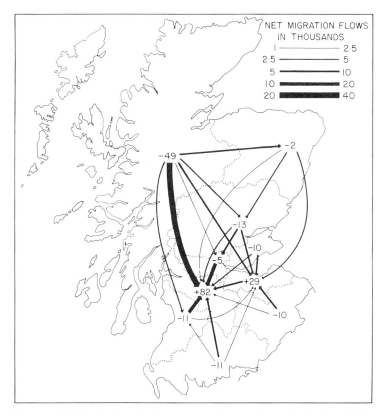

Fig. 5.3 Net 'lifetime' migration between regions on the basis of place of birth and place of enumeration data at the 1851 census. (Source: adapted from Osborne (1958), fig. 4 and table VIII)

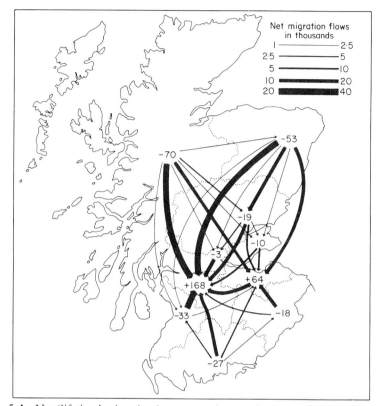

Fig. 5.4 Net 'lifetime' migration between regions on the basis of place of birth and place of enumeration data at the 1901 census. (Source: adapted from Osborne (1958), fig. 5 and table VIII)

economic character of Angus and Perthshire in that both show net gains from counties to the north and net losses to counties to the south. More ambitious, methodologically, has been the attempt of Agnew and Cox (1979) to use birthplace data for Edinburgh and Glasgow at six census years between 1851 and 1951 to evaluate the expansion of metropolitan in-migration fields over time and the erosion of deviations from distance—decay regularity. They adopt a standard social gravity model, put into operation in multiple regression form.

For movements *within* counties, published census data are less revealing, although the power of gravitational forces known to operate on migration generally would almost certainly ensure considerable short-distance migration in nineteenth century Scotland. Apart from literary evidence, sources include: birthplace data from enumerators' books; estate papers, particularly in the case of planned villages (Lockhart, 1980) and the 'clearing' of tenants to coastal sites; and *Reports on the Poor Laws*, which Macdonald (1937) used to demonstrate an important movement of paupers in the first half of the nineteenth century from unassessed, largely country parishes, where little poor relief was available, to assessed, largely urban ones.

Migration to England and Wales

The push factors from the Scottish countryside and the pull factors in urban industrial areas which fashioned much of internal Scottish migration in the nineteenth century also promoted a net movement to destinations south of the border, particularly since the travels of Scottish vagrants, drovers and harvesters in England in the late eighteenth century (Redford, 1926) would have provided some awareness of distant places. Flinn *et al.* (1977) have noted the numbers of Scottish-born enumerated in the rest of the United Kingdom at censuses from 1841, and after making inevitably crude allowances for intercensal mortality, they provide estimates of the movement of Scots to the rest of the United Kingdom for each intercensal period between 1841 and 1931. The intercensal flows are remarkably regular, ranging from 68 000 to 98 000—well below estimated movement overseas. However, reasonably detailed spatial and temporal analyses of Scottish migration to England and Wales have had to await data provided in only recent decades by census migration tables, national insurance cards and the National Health Service Central Register (Jones, 1970; Hollingsworth, 1970; Scottish Economic Planning Board, 1970).

Emigration

The outpouring of Europeans to the temperate latitudes of the Americas, South Africa and Australasia in the nineteenth and early twentieth centuries constitutes the largest migratory movement in human history. It was a response to rural population pressure induced by falling mortality, land consolidation and tenant eviction at a time when New World settlement was being promoted by transport developments on land and sea, by control exerted over indigenous populations, and by spread of information through pamphlets, newspapers and postal services. It is important to view Scottish emigration as essentially representative of this great European exodus, although some distinctiveness accrues from its pioneering origins (Hill, 1972) and its size—vying with Norway for second place to Ireland in overall rate of emigration.

Although the seeds of Scottish emigration lie in the seventeenth century 'plantations' in Ulster and in mercenary service in European armies, migration

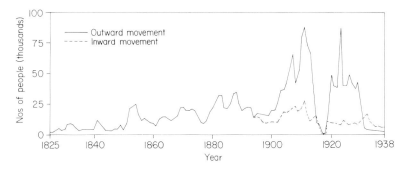

Fig. 5.5 Movement (in thousands) from Scotland to countries outside Europe, 1825–1938, and into Scotland from countries outside Europe, 1895–1938. (Source: data from Carrier and Jeffery (1953), table (1)) Before 1853 the data refer to all departures from Scottish ports, and afterwards to departures from British ports by persons of Scottish origin. Cabin passengers, as opposed to steerage, and emigrants on mail steamers are included only from 1863, but crew–migrants working their passage are never included. From 1912, recorded departures are restricted to those stating an intention to remain abroad for at least a year. In the immigration series, it is likely that the vast bulk of recorded movement is by Scots returning from the New World, although the whole field of return migration, historical and contemporary, is a neglected research area.

to the New World began in earnest in the 1760s. Comprehensive data are lacking, but Adam (1920), Graham (1956), the *Old Statistical Account* and surviving shipping lists (Lancour, 1963) show that most emigrants at this time were Highlanders, often leaving in large parties from particular parishes. An important stimulus was the pool of sponsors created by the disbanding, with land grants, of Highland regiments in parts of Upper Canada, like Glengarry, after the American War of Independence.

It is only from 1825 that a continuous series of Scottish emigration data, assembled from the ship muster rolls required under a series of Passenger Acts, is available. The data, which have been conveniently assembled in a series of tables and commentaries by Carrier and Jeffery (1953), have obvious weaknesses stemming from variable under-recording and from definitional changes, yet they do provide a valuable broad outline of the extent (Fig. 5.5) and selective composition of Scottish emigration to each major destination country. Equivalent, but not always compatible, data at destination may be derived from census birthplace tables and immigrant landing records. Erickson (1972) has used passenger lists of ships arriving in New York to show an appreciable swing from rural to urban origins among Scottish migrants between the mid and late nineteenth century, although it is difficult to distinguish a truly urban origin from an urban staging point. More usefully she demonstrates that the occupational composition, and not merely the absolute number, of Scottish migrants varied appreciably in relation to American labour market fluctuations; in particular, the proportion of unskilled workers rose and fell with the trade-cycle. However, any detailed spatial investigation of Scottish emigration at origin and destination based on a range of literary and statistical sources can be undertaken for only limited areas and periods, as exemplified by Cameron's (1971) study of Scottish emigration to Upper Canada in the early nineteenth century. There is little doubt that such powerful early migration bonds continue to bias the spatial pattern of Scottish emigration (Jones, 1979), reflecting the tendency for international migration streams to be cumulative and self-propagating because of the important role of sponsorship and information feedback in the migration process.

POPULATION DISTRIBUTION AND GROWTH

The hearth and poll taxes imposed in the 1690s to fund the army provide the earliest means of establishing the pattern of population distribution and composition within Scotland on any reasonably wide territorial basis. By and large, hearth taxes were levied on family units and poll taxes on persons over 16, although 'the poor' were exempt from both taxes. It is hazardous to apply multipliers to provide figures of total population, but careful use of the returns can establish relative densities of settlement, although an important qualification is the obvious under-enumeration in those parts of the Highlands where Jacobite support was strong.

Flinn *et al*. (1977) have used county hearth densities (paid hearths per 1000 acres) to outline the broad national pattern of population distribution, and in selected areas they use parish hearth densities to demonstrate the population pre-eminence of those parts, particularly bordering the Forth, which enjoyed a combination of agricultural and sea-trading advantages. It is unfortunate that the territorial coverage of hearth tax returns cannot be matched by that of extant poll tax lists, which are intrinsically more valuable, embracing as they do names, status, place of residence and occupation. Complete poll tax lists are available only for Aberdeenshire, Renfrewshire, West Lothian, Midlothian, and Edinburgh. Walton (1950) plotted the distribution of polled population within Aberdeenshire and provides a model study in perceptive and detailed interpretation of the distribution in relation to the county's physical geography, particularly the depth, drainage and fertility of soils. Such an approach is essential for the pre-improvement era, when soil deficiencies were difficult to remedy. Walton (1961) also used the Aberdeenshire poll tax lists to estimate parish populations as part of a study of population changes in the area between 1696 and 1951, but his conclusions on early population change are invalidated by his appreciable under-estimate of 1696 populations. The error arises, as

Mitchison (1963) has demonstrated, through his excessively conservative addition of one-third to the listed populations to allow for the non-listed (those under 16 and paupers). Poll tax rolls have also been used to determine the 1695 distribution of population and of craftsmen within Renfrewshire (McIntosh, 1956).

At the middle of the eighteenth century two new sources for assessing population numbers and distribution become available: Webster's census and the Roy Map.Alexander Webster was an Edinburgh minister and Moderator of the General Assembly of the Church of Scotland who obtained from parish ministers the number of their parishioners who were old enough (generally 6–10 years of age) to be examined on the Catechism. He converted this figure to one of total population by applying the appropriate ratio calculated from Halley's Breslau life tables. The parish population figures given in his 1755 census (published in Kyd, 1952) are widely regarded as acceptable, although his unexplained age distribution of the total Scottish population is another matter, since it could well be based on returns from a limited number of parishes. The Roy Map, based on a military survey of Scotland between 1747 and 1755, presents a pattern of settlement distribution at a remarkably generous scale (1000 yards to the inch), and although the representation of houses within the characteristic ferm-touns is schematic, it still provides a wealth of information on the settlement pattern just before the redistribution wrought by enclosures, reclamation and planned villages. For example, Coull's examination (1980) of Buchan on the Roy Map confirms the general pattern described by Walton from poll tax returns and in particular indicates the avoidance at a time of low technology of agriculturally marginal interfluves and haughlands.

There are two other significant enumerations of population in the period before the start of government census-taking in 1801, although they cover only small parts of Scotland. Statistics of the Forfeited Estates, collected by factors on government direction in 1755–6, include a breakdown of population by sex and by three age groups (Scottish Record Office, 1973). Then in 1779 the Duke of Argyll conducted a detailed census to assist in planning the redeployment of his estate population at the height of improvement fever. This census, published in Cregeen (1963), has enabled Gailey (1960) to reconstruct the population distribution of southern Kintyre and to interpret it in relation to the physical geography in a manner comparable to Walton's Aberdeenshire study.

The institution of regular government censuses in 1801 places the study of Scottish population distribution and change on a much more secure footing, although the delay in onset of civil registration until 1855 means that the contribution to intercensal population change of natural increase and of net migration, estimated by residual methods, can only be assessed from 1861. The Registrar General for Scotland marked the centenary of civil registration by assembling in the Annual Reports for 1953 and 1954 tables showing total population change, natural increase and estimated net migration for each county in each intercensal period between 1861 and 1951. The tables have been consolidated by Osborne (1956) and Flinn *et al.* (1977) into useful national and regional summaries. They show that although the population of Scotland increased from just over 3 million in 1861 to just over 5 million in 1951, there had been a net loss by migration of some 1·5 million. National migration losses were present in every decade, but were particularly heavy in the 1880s and between 1901 and 1931. Only a few counties at a few intercensal periods show a total population gain exceeding natural increase. They are largely confined to west-central Scotland but are occasionally found elsewhere under particular circumstances of economic growth (e.g. Angus, 1861–71; Fife, Clackmannan and West Lothian, 1891–1900). The county and regional population data also record clearly the internal redistribution of Scotland's population which has been the outcome of the spatially and temporally varying mortality, fertility and migration trends discussed earlier. Thus the Highland Counties, Far North and Borders (as defined in Table 5.2) contained 31·0 of Scotland's population in 1801, but only 10·3% in 1971, at the same time as the share of the Western Lowlands (Table 5.2) expanded from 20·6% to 47·5%. Although nearly all counties in central Scotland recorded their highest populations in 1971, the populations of most Highland counties had peaked just over a century earlier.

   A consideration of population structure and population change at regional or county level masks a good deal of the spatial heterogeneity which shows up on a local authority or parish scale of analysis. Examples of regional studies of census population data adopting these scales are provided by Dewdney (1955) for Fife, Jones (1967) for Tayside, Walton (1961) and Turnock (1968) for the North East, Darling (1955) for the western Highlands, and Soulsby (1972) for the Borders. However, the price to be paid for disaggregation to parish level is the lack of natural increase data.

   Now that the overall pattern of nineteenth- and twentieth-century population change in Scotland is well appreciated, the most rewarding studies of census data will probably be those using the individual family returns from the unpublished enumerators' books available for consultation from 1841, when they were first kept, to 1891, after which confidentiality constraints apply, at New Register House, Edinburgh. Using these returns, it is possible to reconstruct detailed patterns of population and settlement distribution, household structure, and age, sex and occupational composition on any areal basis that researchers prescribe, subject to constraints imposed by the labour-consuming nature of data extraction. Inevitably such reconstructions are confined spatially, but the richness of information provided is demonstrated in studies of Islay (Storrie, 1962, 1967), Ardnamurchan (Gailey, 1962), Great

Cumbrae (Robertson, 1973), Dundee (S. J. Jones, 1975), and Glenlivet (Turnock, 1979). A notable feature of most of these studies is the provision of at least some comparable contemporary data from fieldwork, private census or key contacts.

CONCLUSION

Inevitably, population study is inter-disciplinary, so it is worth while considering where and how the distinctive perspectives and methods of geography can be applied to further our awareness and understanding of Scottish demographic evolution. There are three dimensions of geographical expertise that have much to offer population study. First, there is the traditional ecological approach relating organisms to their habitats, well represented by Walton's detailed Aberdeenshire study. Secondly, there is simulation-oriented work on the spatial diffusion of ideas, behaviour and technology (Hagerstrand, 1967), which arguably has been one of the very few significant strands of theory indigenous to modern human geography. It would be rewarding to consider in a Scottish context the diffusion through space and settlement hierarchies of particular epidemics and also of the overall processes of mortality and fertility reduction. Thirdly, there is the study of spatial assocation, formerly dependent on visual comparison of map distributions but increasingly based on the more rigorous application of correlation and regression methods to geographical data matrices. Many geographical studies of Scotland's population have been restricted in scope—territorially, conceptually and analytically—and a more ambitious consideration of the spatial dimension in Scotland's demographic evolution is now needed.

REFERENCES

Adam, M. I. (1920). The causes of the Highland emigrations of 1783–1803. *Scottish Historical Review* **17**, 73–89.

Agnew, J. A. and Cox, K. R. (1979). Urban in-migration in historical perspective. *Historical Methods* **12**, 145–55.

Andorka, R. (1978). 'Determinants of Fertility in Advanced Societies.' Methuen, London.

Berkner, L. and Mendels, F. (1978). Inheritance systems, family structure and demographic patterns in western Europe 1700–1900.' *In* 'Historical Studies of Changing Fertility' (C. Tilly, ed.) pp. 209–224. Princeton University Press, Princeton.

Braun, R. (1978). Early industrialization and demographic change in the canton of

Zurich. *In* 'Historical Studies of Changing Fertility.' (C. Tilly, ed.) pp. 289–334. Princeton University Press. Princeton.

Brotherston, J. H. (1952). 'Observations on the Early Public Health Movement in Scotland.' H. K. Lewis, London.

Cameron, J. (1972). 'A Study of the Factors that Assisted and Directed Scottish Emigration to Upper Canada, 1815–55.' Unpublished Ph.D. thesis, University of Glasgow.

Carrier, N. H. and Jeffrey, J. R. (1953). 'External Migration: a Study of the Available Statistics, 1815–1950.' HMSO, London.

Chalmers, A. K. (1930). 'The Health of Glasgow 1918–1925.' Corporation of Glasgow, Glasgow.

Coale, A. J. (1969). The decline of fertility in Europe from the French Revolution to World War II. *In* S. Behrman *et al.*, 'Fertility and Family Planning: A World View.' Michigan University Press, Ann Arbor, 3–24.

Connell, K. (1950). 'The Population of Ireland 1750–1845.' Greenwood, Oxford.

Coull, J. R. (1980). The district of Buchan as shown on the Roy Map. *Scottish Geographical Magazine* **96**, 67–73.

Cregeen, E. R. (1963). 'Inhabitants of the Argyll Estate, 1779.' Scottish History Society. Edinburgh.

Creighton, C. (1894). 'A History of Epidemics in Britain.' Cassel, Cambridge.

Darling, F. F. (1955). 'West Highland Survey.' Oxford University Press, Oxford.

Devine, T. M. (1979). Temporary migration and the Scottish Highlands in the nineteenth century. *Economic History Review* **32**, 344–59.

Dewdney, J. C. (1955). Changes in population distribution in the County of Fife, 1755–1951. *Scottish Geographical Magazine*, **71**, 27–42.

Drake, M. (1969). 'Population and Society in Norway 1735–1865.' Cambridge University Press, Cambridge.

Erickson, C. J. (1972). Who were the English and Scots emigrants to the United States in the late nineteenth century? In 'Population and Social Change.' (D. V. Glass and R. Revelle, ed.). Edward Arnold, London.

Flinn, M., Gillespie, J., Hill, N., Maxwell, A., Mitchison, R. and Smout, C. (1977). 'Scottish Population History from the Seventeenth Century to the 1930s.' Cambridge University Press, Cambridge.

Friedlander, D. (1973–74). Demographic patterns and socioeconomic characteristics of the coalmining population in England and Wales in the nineteenth century. *Economic Development and Cultural Change* **22**, 39–51.

Gailey, R. A. (1960). Settlement and population in Kintyre, 1750–1800. *Scottish Geographical Magazine* **76**, 99–107.

Gailey, R. A. (1962). The evolution of highland rural settlement with particular reference to Argyllshire. *Scottish Studies* **6**, 155–77.

Graham, I. C. (1956). 'Colonists from Scotland: Emigration to North America, 1707–1783.' Cornell University Press, Ithaca, N.Y.

Gray, M. (1955). The highland potato famine of the 1840s, *Economic History Review* **7**, 357–68.

Hagerstrand, T. (1967). 'Innovation Diffusion as a Spatial Process.' Chicago University Press, Chicago.

Haines, M. R. (1977). Fertility, nuptiality and occupation: a study of coalmining populations and regions in England and Wales in the mid-nineteenth century. *Journal of Interdisciplinary History* **8**, 245–80.

Henry, L. (1967). 'Manuel de Démographic Historique.' Librarie Proz, Geneva.

Hill, D. (1972). 'Great Emigrations: the Scots to Canada.' Gentry Books, London.

Hollingsworth, T. H. (1970). 'Migration: a Study based on Scottish Experience between 1939 and 1964.' Oliver and Boyd, Edinburgh.

Howe, G. M. (1970). 'National Atlas of Disease Mortality in the United Kingdom.' Nelson, London.

Jackson, J. A. (1963). 'The Irish in Britain.' Routledge and Kegan Paul, London.

Johnson, J. H. (1967). Harvest migration from nineteenth-century Ireland. *Transactions, Institute of British Geographers* **41**, 97–112.

Jones, H. R. (1968). Population, *In* 'Dundee and District.' (S. J. Jones, ed.). British Association. 237–56.

Jones, H. R. (1970). Migration to and from Scotland since 1961. *Transactions, Institute of British Geographers* **49**, 145–59.

Jones, H. R. (1975). A spatial analysis of human fertility in Scotland. *Scottish Geographical Magazine* **91**, 102–13.

Jones H. R. (1979). Modern emigration from Scotland to Canada. *Scottish Geographical Magazine* **95**, 4–12.

Jones, S. J. (1975). 'The 1841 Census of Dundee.' Department of Geography Occasional Paper 3, University of Dundee.

Kinnear, T. (1912). 'Sanitation and pure air in Dundee 50 years ago and now.' *In* 'British Association Handbook and Guide to Dundee and District.' (A. W. Paton and A. H. Millar, ed.). Dundee, 147–53.

Kwofie, K. (1976). A spatio-temporal analysis of cholera diffusion in western Africa. *Economic Geography* **52**, 127–35.

Kyd, J. G. (1952). 'Scottish Population Statistics.' Scottish History Society, Edinburgh.

Lancour, H. (1963). 'A Bibliography of Ship Passenger Lists, 1538–1825.' New York Public Library, New York.

Langer, W. (1974). Infanticide: a historical survey. *History of Childhood Quarterly*, **1**.

Langer, W. (1975). American foods and Europe's population growth 1750–1850. *Journal of Social History* **5**, 51–66.

Lobban, R. D. (1969). The Migration of Highlanders into Lowland Scotland, 1750 –1890. Unpublished Ph.D. thesis, University of Edinburgh.

Lockhart, D. (1980). The planned villages. *In* 'The Making of the Scottish Countryside.' (M. L. Parry and T. R. Slater, ed.). Croom Helm, London, 249–70.

Longmate, N. (1966). 'King Cholera.' Hamish Hamilton. London.

Macdonald, D. F. (1937). 'Scotland's Shifting Population, 1770–1850.' Jackson, Glasgow.

McIntosh, N. A. (1956). Changing population distribution in the Cart Basin in the eighteenth and nineteenth centuries. *Transactions, Institute of British Geographers* **22**, 139–59.

McKeown, T. (1976). 'The Modern Rise of Population.' Arnold, London.

McKeown, T. and Brown, R. G. (1955). Medical evidence related to English population changes in the eighteenth century. *Population Studies* **9**, 119–41.

Mitchison, R. (1963). Dr Walton's population changes in North-East Scotland. *Scottish Studies* **7**, 251–2.

Ohlin, P. (1961). Mortality, marriage and growth in preindustrial populations. *Population Studies* **14**, 190–7.

Osborne, R. H. (1956). Scottish migration statistics: a note. *Scottish Geographical Magazine* **72**, 153–9.

Osborne, R. H. (1958). The movements of people in Scotland, 1851–1951. *Scottish Studies* **2**, 1–46.

Razzell, P. (1974). An interpretation of the modern rise of population in Europe—a critique. *Population Studies*, **28**, 5–17.

Redford, A. (1926). 'Labour Migration in England, 1800–1850.' Manchester University Press, Manchester.

Robertson, I. M. (1973). Population trends of Great Cumbrae island. *Scottish Geographical Magazine* **89**, 53–62.

Sauer, R. (1978). Infanticide and abortion in nineteenth century Britain. *Population Studies* **32**, 81–93.

Scottish Economic Planning Board (1970). 'Migration to and from Scotland.' Scottish Economic Planning Board, Edinburgh.

Scottish Record Office (1973). 'Statistics of the Annexed Estates 1755–1756.' HMSO, Edinburgh.

Soulsby, E. M. (1972). Changing sex ratios in the Scottish border counties. *Scottish Geographical Magazine* **88**, 5–18.

Storrie, M. C. (1962). The census of Scotland as a source in the historical geography of Islay. *Scottish Geographical Magazine* **78**, 152–65.

Storrie, M. C. (1967). Landholdings and population in Arran from the late eighteenth century. *Scottish Studies* **11**, 49–74.

Tranter, N. L. (1978). The demographic impact of economic growth and decline: Portpatrick, 1820–91. *Scottish History Review* **57**, 87–105.

Turnock, D. (1968). Depopulation in North-East Scotland with reference to the countryside. *Scottish Geographical Magazine* **84**, 256–68.

Turnock, D. (1979). Glenlivet: two centuries of rural planning in the Grampian uplands. *Scottish Geographical Magazine* **95**, 165–81.

Walton, K. (1950). The distribution of population in Aberdeenshire, 1696. *Scottish Geographical Magazine* **66**, 17–26.

Walton, K. (1961). Population changes in North-East Scotland 1696–1951. *Scottish Studies* **5**, 149–80.

Wilson, M. G. (1978), A spatial analysis of human fertility in Scotland—reappraisal and extension. *Scottish Geographical Magazine* **94**, 130–43.

Wrigley, E. A. (ed.) (1966a). 'An introduction to English Historical Demography.' Weidenfeld and Nicolson, London.

Wrigley, E. A. (1966b). Family limitation in pre-industrial England. *Economic History Review* **19**, 82–109.

Zelinsky, W. (1971). The hypothesis of the mobility transition. *Geographical Review* **61**, 219–49.

6

Early-Modern Scotland: Continuity and Change

I. D. Whyte

Late sixteenth-century Scotland was a backward and undeveloped country compared with many of her European neighbours. A core area in the Central Lowlands was relatively amenable to control, but it was fringed by a periodically ungovernable periphery (Fig. 6.1a). To visitors Scotland appeared poor and backward, her society dominated by feudal relationships and kinship bonds. Commercial elements in her economy were weakly developed, and capitalist links had scarcely begun to replace the old paternalistic ties between proprietor and tenant, master and man. By the mid-eighteenth century Scotland had made considerable progress towards a more modern society and was poised to undergo the transformations which have been conventionally labelled the Agricultural and Industrial Revolutions. This chapter examines the evolution of Scotland's economic and social geography during this key period of transition between the medieval and modern periods, highlighting changing spatial patterns and the processes that shaped them. After an outline of the frameworks of landownership and rural society in the late sixteenth century, changes in farm, tenurial and rent structures will be examined. Developments in agriculture and their effects on the rural landscape will then be considered. An analysis of continuity and change in Scotland's industrial and urban geography will be followed by an assessment of the strengths and weaknesses of Scotland's economy during the late seventeenth and early eighteenth centuries.

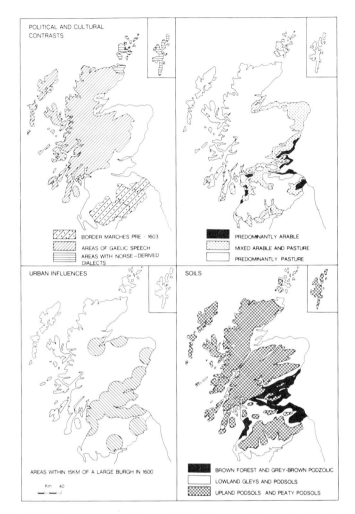

Fig. 6.1   Some core–periphery relationships in early–modern Scotland

THE FEUDAL BACKGROUND

Scotland was dominated politically, socially and economically by the great landowners in the late sixteenth century. The weakness of central authority from the fourteenth century had reinforced their power locally and nationally. They held their lands from the crown by feudal tenures under which military service was often the only burden. In the Lowlands their dominance over tenants and kinsmen allowed them to muster forces to assist the crown or for private warfare. Particularly in the Borders, family loyalties often took precedence over national ones. In the Highlands, the clan system was basically military in character with a feudal landownership structure grafted on to it.

Small landowners did exist. Although rentallers and kindly tenants, the nearest equivalent to English customary tenants, had been virtually eliminated by the early seventeenth century, the newer cash tenure of feu ferme which had spread during the fifteenth and sixteenth centuries had established a class of small proprietors on the land in some districts (Sanderson, 1973). The role of owner occupiers and 'bonnet lairds' in Scottish society at this period awaits detailed examination, but evidence suggests that they were neither numerous nor influential overall. In terms of status and power the gulf between landowner and tenant was wide, theoretically enabling proprietors to effect rapid transformations in rural society and the rural landscape when the time for change was ripe.

In the sixteenth century there was little practical difference between social organization in the Highlands and much of the Lowlands, where kinship played an important role within a feudal landholding system. Social differences between the two regions were of degree rather than kind, and this was reflected in broad similarities in their rural economy and settlement patterns. There were, nevertheless, strong cultural contrasts between the Gaelic-speaking Highlands and the anglicized Lowlands. Mutual distrust and lack of contact had made the Highlands more isolated and less receptive to external influences than the Lowlands, a process which in turn accentuated the differences between the two areas.

In a country that had been imperfectly feudalized in some respects a notable feature was the late survival of feudal rents and duties. Obligations to render military service had vanished over much of the Lowlands by the late sixteenth century (although they survived on the Borders until 1603), but on the edge of the Highlands military service was required for much of the seventeenth century, and tenants along the lower Tay or in the Angus glens had to be prepared to turn out, suitably armed, to repel incursions of Highland raiders. Within the Highlands and even in the north-eastern Lowlands landowners retained the power to call tenantry and followers to arm into the eighteenth century.

Labour services were required on many Lowland estates as late as the mid-eighteenth century. These usually involved providing labour and sometimes draught animals and equipment for cultivating the mains or home farm during the busiest periods of the agricultural year. Carriage services for bringing fuel to the proprietor's house or marketing his grain were general, as was thirlage to the estate's grain mill. Rents in kind were also widespread. In the arable areas of Lowland Scotland rents were paid largely in grain. Over most of the Highlands rents in livestock and their produce were normal. Only in the Southern Uplands and other pastoral areas of Lowland Scotland had cash rents become normal for tenant farmers by the early seventeenth century. The payment of rents in kind isolated tenants from full participation in a market economy, reducing their commercial expertise and incentives to improve their husbandry.

MOVES TOWARDS CAPITALISM

The spread of changes in agriculture and rural society in Scotland during the seventeenth and eighteenth centuries can be viewed in terms of a core/ periphery model in which several related influences are apparent (Fig. 6.1). One of these was the extension of central authority. This brought more peaceful conditions which helped re-orient rural society towards more commercial structures. From the core area of the eastern and central lowlands royal authority, from the late sixteenth century, exerted increasing control over the upland periphery. The Borders were rapidly pacified after the Union of the Crowns in 1603, an international problem being transformed into a purely internal one. The Highlands were more intractable, but here, too, growing control was evident by the end of the seventeenth century. Much of the northern and western Highlands remained beyond effective control until the eighteenth century. The measures taken to remove the Jacobite threat after 1745 hastened the penetration of commercial influences into the more remote parts of the Highlands and precipitated social and economic change.

Another influence on the core/periphery pattern was the larger burghs, particularly those around the Forth and Tay estuaries, but also by the end of the seventeenth century the rapidly growing city of Glasgow (Smout, 1968). The burghs were foci of contact with England and the continent and were centres from which innovations spread. Their demands for food and their role as outlets for exporting the products of agriculture and rural industry encouraged production for the market in their hinterlands. Estates around the largest towns were increasingly being bought by men who had accumulated wealth in trade or the professions and whose attitude to agriculture was often more profit-oriented than those of families which had been entrenched on the land for generations (Smout, 1964).

Core/periphery patterns were, however, modified by influences at various scales. Access to coastal transport was as important as physical resources in determining which areas concentrated on cereal production. By the end of the seventeenth century, closer contact with the English market was bringing innovation to parts of southern Scotland. The development of the cattle trade turned Galloway, formerly a relatively remote and undeveloped area, into a leading producer of store cattle with the advent of selective breeding and large-scale enclosure by proprietors.

Farm structure, and with it rural social structure, also exhibited regional variations. The traditional model of the pre-improvement ferm toun, housing from four to eight joint tenants and a few cottars (Caird, 1964), was far from universal by the late seventeenth century. The poll tax returns of the 1690s show that in the Lothians, Berwickshire and lowland Aberdeenshire, predominantly arable areas, such farms were uncommon. In these regions large farms leased by single tenants, on which most of the work was done by hired servants, were more frequent. Rural society in such areas was polarizing into a small group of wealthier tenants and a rural proletariat which was gradually losing control over the land on which it worked. In the more commercially oriented pastoral areas of southern Scotland, large sheep and cattle farms were also frequently worked by single tenants.

Elsewhere farm structure differed. In Renfrewshire multiple-tenant farms and small family holdings were more frequent. In the interior of Aberdeenshire farms with many small tenants were common. In Orkney townships were sometimes divided between as many as 20 smallholders with few cottars and servants, a pattern which rentals suggest was also common over much of the Highlands.

These regional contrasts were dynamic and not static: a comparison of successive rentals on many estates shows that a gradual reduction in tenant numbers was occurring, particularly in the arable-oriented areas of eastern Scotland. Dodgshon (1972) has shown that in Berwickshire and Roxburghshire this was accompanied by the progressive removal of tenant runrig.

That proprietor/tenant relationships were becoming more commercial is suggested by the spread of written leases (Whyte, 1979b). In the late sixteenth century most cultivators were tenants-at-will, holding their lands by verbal agreements. In practice, paternalistic landlords often allowed continuity of tenure from one generation to another without necessarily selecting tenants for their competence. The granting of written leases for fixed terms spread during the seventeenth century until they had become commonplace on many estates, especially in arable areas where they often specified the use of particular rotations and the application of fertilizers such as lime. There is evidence that by the end of the century some proprietors were selecting tenants for their skill in husbandry and their ability to pay higher rents and were offering long leases as incentives. By the early eighteenth century the first improving leases under which tenants agreed to enclose and improve parts of their holdings with 19 years' security of occupation had begun to appear, and this kind of contract was to be vigorously promoted later in the century by improving landowners.

Another sign of increasing commercial influences was the gradual commutation of rents and services into money payments. As the retinues of Lowland landowners were reduced during the more peaceful conditions of the early seventeenth century the first payments to be commuted were often kain rents, or small payments in poultry, livestock and dairy produce which were no longer required in such large quantities. Conversion of labour services to money may have arisen from baron courts fining tenants who failed to perform their work; by the end of the seventeenth century examples of such commutation occurred throughout Lowland Scotland.

The commutation of principal rents proceeded furthest in the pastoral districts of southern Scotland. Tenants in these areas had probably never been as heavily burdened with classic feudal obligations as their counterparts in arable areas, where estates were often smaller and the proprietor's residence and home farm with its associated labour services were more accessible and more important in the estate's economy. The Borders had inherited a tradition of commercial sheep farming from the medieval monastic houses, and there was a market for livestock across the Border before 1603, as well as a thriving export trade in wool and hides. The ease with which livestock and their products could be transported, compared with a bulky commodity like grain, helped to switch the onus of marketing from proprietor to tenant by converting rents in kind to money payments. By contrast, commutation of grain rents in arable areas made slow progress. Around Edinburgh the first impetus came from mercantile families like the Clerks of Penicuik whose tenants had ready access to the guaranteed market of a large city (Whyte, 1979a). Outside the orbit of the largest burghs, however, commutation of grain rents had made limited progress by the eighteenth century.

RURAL SETTLEMENT PATTERNS

The traditional model of Scottish rural settlement before the changes of the later eighteenth century has been the ferm toun or hamlet cluster spread fairly uniformly over the landscape (Caird, 1964). Although H. L. Gray's assertion (1915) that Scottish settlement units tended to be smaller than those which existed over much of England is essentially true, contemporary sources suggest that the ferm toun model is too simplistic. The character of agricultural units varied temporally or spatially within Scotland, so farms of similar size could have different social structures. In addition, the settlement patterns of some areas contained larger nucleations. In the south east, from Berwickshire to the Forth and possibly beyond, villages existed with origins going back to Anglian times (Barrow, 1973). Such settlements, containing from 40 to 60 households, were minor manufacturing centres with a distributive role which was often confirmed after 1660 by grants of market and fair rights. Other nucleations existed: on some former monastic estates where land had been feued in small units feuar touns had developed. Those in the Regality of Melrose were village-sized with a wider range of functions than the purely agricultural role which has been assigned to the ferm toun (Whyte, 1981). Elsewhere the smaller burghs of barony performed a similar role. Outside the most fertile areas, lower population densities precluded such large settlement units, although the poll tax returns of the 1690s show that within the umbrella term 'ferm toun' considerable variation could exist. A central location around a parish church or adjacent to a landowner's residence could increase the importance and enhance the functions of such a community.

At the other extreme, isolated homesteads existed between the hamlet clusters. The evolution of settlement from medieval times onwards has yet to be studied in detail, but place names suggest that as well as the growth and splitting of larger townships, a process which can often be identified in early charters (Chapter 3), infilling by small-scale intakes from the moorland edge or from more poorly drained land was also occurring, producing a settlement pattern which was complex in detail and whose regional variations are as yet unclear.

THE RURAL ECONOMY

Contrasting settlement patterns should make us wary of expecting too much uniformity in the rural economy. Over the country as a whole the emphasis was on pastoral farming, particularly in the Highlands where environmental constraints, combined with primitive technology, often made arable farming precarious. A pastoral economy also predominated over most of southern Scotland, specialization in cattle-rearing in the moister western dales and lowlands, and sheep-raising in the east having intensified after 1603 with the pacification of the Border. By contrast, the most fertile and best-drained soils from the Berwickshire Merse to the Moray Firth and even Orkney supported an economy which emphasized cereal production to a greater extent and in which, in some areas, livestock rearing had little importance. The limitations of communications meant, however, that most communities grew some grain, although much of the uplands was not self sufficient.

From East Lothian to the Outer Hebrides arable farming was conducted on a system which varied in degree rather than kind. Apart from the experimental enclosures constructed by some landowners on their home farms in the later seventeenth century, infield–outfield farming was virtually universal. Variations in arable farming were largely expressed by the extent of infield in relation to outfield and by the proportion of cultivated land to unimproved pasture. In the most fertile areas, probably influenced by the demands of the larger burghs, more intensive arable systems developed with the use of lime, urban refuse, and seaweed. These raised yields and allowed infields to expand to cover high proportions of the arable area (Whyte, 1979c). In the best-favoured districts around the Forth and Tay estuaries and in a few other parts of the lowlands, farmers grew higher-priced wheat, as well as bere (a hardy four-row variety of barley) and oats, and had integrated nitrogen-fixing legumes into their rotations with occasional fallow courses. Elsewhere infields occupied smaller areas in relation to outfields, and more punishing rotations were used based on continuous crops of bere and oats with animal manure as the principal means of maintaining soil fertility.

The yields provided by infield–outfield farming were relatively low. Even in the best-favoured areas average returns on infields probably did not often exceed six to one; over the rest of Scotland three or four to one was more usual. Arable farming was not, however, completely static during the seventeenth century. The margins of cultivation expanded in some regions, while the intensification of cultivation in certain districts increased the contrast between areas that concentrated on crop production and areas that did not. The adoption of liming early in the century caused dramatic changes in parts of the Central Lowlands (Smout and Fenton, 1965). Where limestone and coal for burning it were available, liming allowed the reclamation of large areas of moorland with acid soils which had previously been permanent pasture. It also raised yields on existing arable land, allowing more frequent cropping of outfields, and encouraged the conversion of outfields to infields further intensifying the cropping system (Whyte, 1979a). Other land was made available for more intensive use by proprietors agreeing to divide their commonties, rough grazings in joint ownership (Adams, 1971), a process encouraged by legislation passed by the Scottish Parliament in 1647 and 1695 (Whyte, 1979a).

Change also occurred in pastoral farming. The pacification of the Borders after 1603 allowed more attention to be paid to livestock rearing rather than raiding, and there is evidence of an expansion of both sheep- and cattle-raising in this area following the Union. In the later seventeenth century, cattle droving to England provided growing profits for many landowners, especially in Galloway. Landowners bought lean cattle from their tenants and improved them by fattening and sometimes cross-breeding with better English and Irish stock. The parks in which these beasts were kept represented the first large-scale enclosure movement in Scotland.

The transformation of the rural landscape proceeded slowly during the seventeenth and early eighteenth centuries. With peace and growing, if modest, prosperity, particularly after the Restoration, many landowners converted and extended their old fortified houses and by the end of the century the first neo-classical country mansions were being built (Slater, 1980). Following English and continental traditions these new houses were surrounded by landscaped parklands or 'policies'. Enclosure around country houses fulfilled an economic as well as an aesthetic role though. On some estates the ornamental planting of trees took on a commercial aspect, encouraged from 1661 by legislation to facilitate afforestation and enclosure (Whyte, 1979a). The enclosure of the home farms which adjoined many country houses led to experiments in crop and animal production. Trials of systems of convertible husbandry, the first real break with infield–outfield farming, led in the early eighteenth century to experiments with root crops and sown grasses. English cattle and sheep were introduced on several home farms to improve the quality of landowners' herds, which were effectively segregated from their tenants' livestock for the first time.

These trends were gradual, spanning the later seventeenth century and first half of the eighteenth. The progress of enclosure beyond the mains and the adoption of new techniques by tenants were slow. Several proprietors blamed this on the conservative outlook of their tenants, but the investment of capital and labour by even the most progressive proprietors was limited. They were only prepared to sink small proportions of their incomes into estate improvements, and much of this went into ornamenting their policies, attention only subsequently being turned to the lands of their tenants. Many proprietors were prevented from incurring long-term debts in the course of estate improvement by strict entail settlements. Equally, they were not encouraged by inelastic levels of demand with sluggish population growth and limited rises in living standards. The Military Survey of 1747–55 demonstrates this visually (O'Dell, 1953). In the Lothians and Fife, where there were many small but prosperous estates, policies and mains frequently gave rise to islands of enclosure accompanied in many instances by enclosed tenant farms. In the western and north-eastern Lowlands, however, and even more in the Highlands, the rural landscape had changed little from that of a century before. Nevertheless, the importance of these slow changes should not be underestimated. In the economic climate of their time they represented a notable break with the past in terms of an increased willingness by proprietors to apply long-term investment, on however small a scale, and long-term planning to the development of their estates. It also showed their desire to experiment with new ideas, which in more favourable conditions later in the eighteenth century were to be disseminated more widely.

INDUSTRY IN THE COUNTRYSIDE

Given the unsophisticated nature of Scotland's economy at this time marked regional specialization in rural industry should not be expected though spatial variations did exist. An important source of information on this topic is the fragmentary poll tax records of the 1690s, but there are difficulties in interpreting the occupational categories which they use. There must have been a gradation between, at one extreme, a cottar who occasionally made a pair of shoes or a garment for someone outside his immediate family and, at the other, a full-time craftsman whose activities were tied to urban markets and who may have worked on the land only at harvest time. The people named as 'tradesmen' in the poll tax records probably lay closer to the second category, but it is impossible to know how many tradesmen evaded registration as such, thereby avoiding an additional payment. As a result, absolute percentages of industrial workers in various areas are probably less significant than relative differences.

Figure 6.2 shows the percentages of recorded industrial workers in Aberdeenshire in 1696. The lower limit of 3–5% of the active male workforce listed as having industrial occupations may represent the basic level of specialist craft production which was required by a dispersed farming community: weavers, tailors, leather workers, smiths, and wrights. Percentages above this threshold may indicate an element of specialization for regional and national rather than local markets.

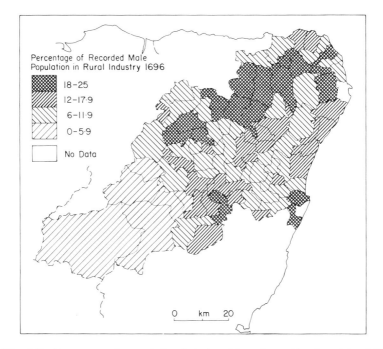

Fig. 6.2 Percentage of recorded male industrial workers, Aberdeenshire, 1696

In Aberdeenshire recorded industrial workers were fewest in the remote upper Dee and Don valleys. Rural industry was concentrated in a belt extending from Buchan, noted for its sheep rearing, through to the pastoral north-eastern interior of the county. Parishes in the predominantly arable Garioch had lower levels of recorded industrial employment. A second concentration occurred around Aberdeen. There were many butchers in the parishes surrounding the burgh, but few elsewhere in the county, and many specialist metal and clothing workers who were not normally found in rural areas. The distribution of textile workers showed a more marked concentration in the pastoral north. In some Buchan parishes one man in five or six was recorded as a weaver.

Elsewhere concentrations of industrial workers existed around large burghs. There were many weavers near the textile centres of Musselburgh and Paisley, and in the Edinburgh region rural industry was located in a zone extending from the capital and Leith eastwards into the Esk basin where coal mining boosted non-agricultural employment and westwards along the coast to Bo'ness and Carriden parishes where salt production and coal mining were prominent.

Little research has been done on the organization of production in Scottish industry at this period, but there does not seem to have been a highly developed putting-out system linking urban capital with rural labour before the later seventeenth century. Rather, merchants travelled from fair to fair in the textile-producing districts, buying cloth on an irregular basis. Glasgow traders frequented the cloth fairs of Galloway and Dundee merchants the fairs of Buchan. This lack of organization and the resulting failure to achieve any uniformity in standards help to explain the poor quality of much Scottish cloth.

A major growth element in the Scottish economy during the seventeenth century was coal mining and salt production. Coal was worked on a small scale in many inland areas but large-scale production for export was tied to coastal locations. In such areas the small coal which was considered unsuitable for sale was used to fire salt pans. The coal and salt industries were concentrated around the Firth of Forth and, to a lesser extent, in North Ayrshire. The eagerness of landowners to develop these industries on their estates led them to establish burghs of barony from which the coal and salt could be exported. A number of new industrial centres with increasingly urban characteristics developed as a result of these industries, including Bo'ness, Irvine and Prestonpans. Nef (1932) has suggested that coal production from the Firth of Forth may have reached 300–400 000 tons per annum by the end of the seventeenth century. Although there may be some over-estimation, this figure indicates the scale of activity, and it is clear that the capital investment involved in sinking some of the deeper mines was on a scale which had not been seen before in Scotland.

THE URBAN HIERARCHY

It is impossible to be certain of the proportion of the Scottish population which lived in towns at this period; a good deal depends on the definition of 'urban', as many burghs were mere villages in size and function. An attempt may be made using Webster's census of 1755 (see Chapter 5). As the urban hierarchy changed little during the first half of the eighteenth century, urban burghs are here defined as those which contributed more than 0·5% of the burghal tax contribution on the eve of the Union of 1707. The parishes containing these burghs, which also included some rural dwellers, held 14·3% of Scotland's population in 1775. This is well below the figure of 20–25% that has been suggested for England (Clark and Slack, 1970). Edinburgh, the capital, contained only 2·5% of Scotland's population in 1755 against London's 11–12% of England's population, suggesting that Edinburgh's role as a market, a centre of innovation, and an 'engine of growth' was less dynamic. Although Edinburgh drew food supplies from as far as Orkney in the late seventeenth century, her demands did not dominate the Scottish rural economy to the extent that London's dominated England. Conversely, the four largest provincial towns, Glasgow, Aberdeen, Dundee and Perth, held between them twice as many inhabitants as Edinburgh, and by the early eighteenth century Glasgow may have been playing a relatively more dynamic role in the Scottish economy than Bristol or Norwich were in England's.

The hierarchy of royal burghs, comprising nearly all the larger towns, changed little during the seventeenth century. A rank correlation of +0·82, significant at the 0·1% level, exists between the tax contributions of the royal burghs in 1612 and 1697. At the upper levels the main change was the rise of Glasgow from fifth to second place. The royal burghs that slipped furthest in rank were all located in Fife: Anstruther Easter, Dysart, Pittenweem and St Andrews, suggesting that Fife's medieval pattern of a dense scatter of small but prosperous trading centres was changing, with more trade gravitating towards the larger burghs.

A few 'unfree' burghs of barony whose economy was linked to new elements in the Scottish economy had also prospered. Thus Bo'ness, Prestonpans and Greenock had developed rapidly, the first two with the expansion of coal mining and salt production, the last with the growth of west-coast trade (Adams, 1978). The economies of these burghs were, however, dependent upon Edinburgh and Glasgow, whose merchants controlled much of their trade and creamed off most of the profits. These towns were only ranked 16th, 18th and 19th respectively in the tax contributions of 1697, and while their assessment may have lagged behind the growth of population and economic activity, the poll tax records for Greenock and Bo'ness suggest that their wealth and occupational diversity were more limited than those of royal burghs of

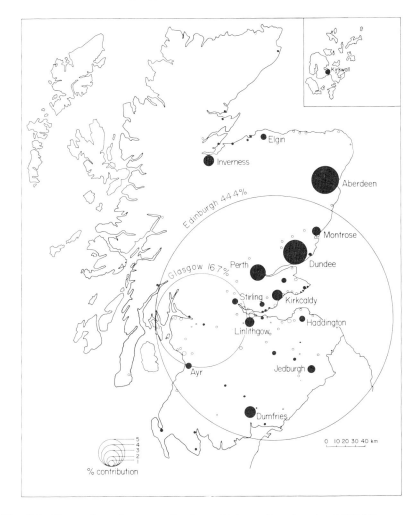

Fig. 6.3 Proportion of tax contribution paid by various burghs, 1697 (● = royal burghs; ○ = burghs of barony and regality)

comparable size. Overall the growth of urban population was modest during much of the seventeenth century, increases in burghs like Glasgow being offset by decline elsewhere.

Figure 6.3 shows the proportion of the total tax contribution paid by royal burghs and burghs of barony in 1697. It is a good indicator first of the distribution of urban wealth and economic activity and secondly, setting aside Edinburgh and Glasgow which were wealthy out of proportion to their populations, of relative sizes. The extent to which the wealth and economic activity of Glasgow and Edinburgh dominated the country is evident; they were respectively only twice and three times the size of Aberdeen or Dundee yet their tax contributions were four and nine times as high.

A second feature is the concentration of urban development. Some 68% of the tax contributions came from towns located in a triangle whose base lay between Stirling and Dunbar with its apex at Montrose. It is not surprising that so much of Scotland's economic development in this period occurred around the Forth and Tay estuaries. The second focus of urban wealth, the Clyde and North Ayrshire, contributed only 21% of the taxes, although this proportion had more than doubled since 1612. Outside these two regions large areas of Scotland, including most of the Highlands, were remote from burghs possessing a full range of urban functions.

URBAN OCCUPATIONS

A study of 40 burghs from the fragmentary poll tax returns of the 1690s suggests that elements of functional specialization existed within the Scottish urban hierarchy. Table 6.1 shows the non-agricultural functions of the 15 largest burghs studied. These are grouped into broad type-of-activity categories, and functional specialization has been measured by values of the standard deviation above the mean of the percentages employed in each category. It may be suggested that towns with one standard deviation or more above the mean in any category showed a degree of specialization. The concentration of professional services in Edinburgh shows how its position as the capital distinguished it from other large towns, while the head burghs of sheriffdoms and regalities, e.g. Aberdeen, Paisley, Perth and St Andrews, were also strong in this function. Trading did not dominate in the larger royal burghs, whose economies were characteristically diversified. Intense specialization in trading marked rapidly growing burghs of barony, such as Bo'ness, Grangepans and Newark. In Greenock the poverty of other service functions suggests that the expansion of trading activity had outstripped growth in other sectors. Concentration on manufacturing was based on textile production in Musselburgh and Paisley and, to a lesser extent, leather-working in Selkirk.

The occupational structures of individual towns cannot be considered in isolation from those of their hinterlands and neighbouring towns. A striking example of this is the way Edinburgh dominated the occupational structures of surrounding burghs. Bo'ness, Dalkeith, Grangepans, Leith and Musselburgh were deficient in professional and mercantile classes, with high proportions of their recorded workforces in manufacturing or low-level services.

In terms of their occupational structures at least 23 out of the 40 burghs

Table 6.1 Percentage of male workforce in type-of-activity groups with standard deviations above the mean

	Manufacturing (% + SD)	Services (% + SD)		
		Trade	Professional	Other
Edinburgh	33·5	11·0	16·4 (2·4)	39·1 (0·8)
Aberdeen	28·0	27·7 (0·3)	10·5 (1·1)	33·8 (0·7)
Musselburgh	55·2 (1·3)	4·7	2·1	38·0 (0·7)
Leith	38·1	16·5	1·8	43·6 (1·2)
Perth	42·4 (0·2)	13·9	8·1 (0·5)	35·6 (0·5)
Bo'ness	29·8	37·9 (1·0)	2·1	30·2
Dalkeith	49·7 (0·8)	7·3	2·9	40·1 (0·9)
Paisley	58·3 (1·7)	12·0	9·2 (0·9)	20·5
Greenock	33·6	52·1 (2·0)	3·1	11·2
Selkirk	48·0 (0·8)	13·7	4·0 (0·1)	34·3 (0·3)
St Andrews	37·8	5·2	11·4 (1·3)	45·6 (1·4)
Grangepans	42·2 (0·2)	26·4 (0·2)	0·6	30·8
Fraserburgh	27·8	48·5 (1·7)	4·1	19·6
Peterhead	58·1 (1·7)	28·0 (0·3)	6·5 (0·2)	7·4
Newark	34·2	37·3 (1·0)	0	28·4

studied could not be considered as truly urban. Small burghs of barony which had a trading function yet which were not true towns must have filled positions in the hierarchy of service centres analogous to nucleated villages in lowland England. There was a distinct break at c. 250–300 pollable persons (corresponding to a population of perhaps 600–700): above this level burghs such as Fraserburgh and Peterhead generally had a full range of professional services and a variety of trades; below it burghs had a more limited range of activities.

THE BURGHS AS TRADING CENTRES

The pattern of urban development in Scotland during the pre-industrial period has been discussed in Chapter 4. All transactions involving middlemen were supposed to take place in an authorized market, so the thin scatter of market centres throughout much of Scotland in the early seventeenth century (Whyte, 1979d) shows the low level of trading activity that existed and emphasizes the importance of regional and local self sufficiency.

As the seventeenth century progressed, the position of the royal burghs was challenged as economic developments placed new demands on the hierarchy of service centres (Whyte, 1979d). This is shown by the foundation of many new burghs of barony between 1600 and 1660 and by the establishment of non-burghal markets and fairs between 1660 and 1707 (Chapter 4). Many of the latter were established in competition with existing centres, but others were located within the Highlands, suggesting that this region was moving towards a more commercialized economy.

It is difficult to determine to what extent the increase in the number of market centres reflected a growth of trading activity or merely a redistribution of existing commodity flows. Many of the new centres did not attain viability. Some were never properly founded; others, established in good faith, failed to prosper. In some cases one suspects that the legislature was giving official sanction to existing illegal customary assemblies. On the other hand some of the new centres thrived and many royal burghs were losing trade to them by the end of the century. It was becoming apparent to the legislature that the monopolistic position of the royal burghs was imposing undesirable constraints on the economy. This was reflected in 1672 by the granting to burghs of barony of the right to engage in foreign trade in most basic commodities at the expense of the royal burghs. The problem of competition for foreign trade between royal and baronial burghs was finally solved in 1698 (Chapter 4).

THE LATER SEVENTEENTH CENTURY:
DEVELOPMENT AND CRISIS

The years from 1660 to the mid 1690s represent the traditional economy of early-modern Scotland at its zenith. It was a period when elements of stability and continuity operated with increased efficiency in an economy freed from war, famine and major epidemics. Yet it was also a period in which incipient changes were apparent. If economic growth was slow, at least low food prices brought better conditions to most of the population. Nevertheless, this well-being was precarious, and there were warnings which emphasized the dangerously narrow confines within which economic development was strait-jacketed.

There were signs of an expansion in agricultural production, especially cereals, but indications are that structural changes and the expansion of the cultivated area were less important in causing this than political stability and a run of favourable seasons. Grain exports grew to such proportions that the Scottish Parliament actually restricted imports, so sure were they that the domestic market could be satisfied internally. There are no indications though that average yields rose significantly: static rents on many estates show that investment in agriculture was still regarded mainly in terms of acquiring more land rather than in raising output per unit area through improvements. With a small home market whose demand for grain was inelastic, abundant harvests with low prices did not necessarily mean great profits for either proprietor or tenant, and the export drive in this sector may have been as much a desperate attempt to dispose of a commodity which could not be sold profitably at home as a sign of positive enterprise.

The growth of the droving trade in livestock, particularly cattle, to England shows an element of dynamism in pastoral farming. By the early eighteenth century Galloway, the Borders and, increasingly, the Highlands were sending 30000 cattle a year to England (Woodward, 1977). As mentioned above, selective breeding and improved feeding in new enclosures were important advances in livestock husbandry. Such improvements were, however, instituted only by landowners. Where the output of pastoral farming increased among the tenantry it was by raising stocking levels or, as in the eastern Highlands, by extending grazings into previously under-utilized deer forest.

The century closed with a run of bad seasons, and the resulting famine, if not as severe as some of those of the late sixteenth or early seventeenth centuries, was more devastating for occurring after more than thirty years of generally favourable conditions (Flinn, 1977). Crop failure and livestock mortality highlighted the bottlenecks in arable and pastoral farming. In upland areas the crisis was more protracted and more serious. In the Borders hard winters, cold springs and wet summers underlined the weaknesses of livestock husbandry— the lack of winter fodder, overstocking, poor grazing management, and the susceptibility of poorly conditioned animals to disease—and, it is from such areas and from the interior of the North East that the grimmest stories of starving tenants and abandoned farms come (Walton, 1952). Tenant farmers in lowland arable areas were not hit so disastrously, but the system of recording arrears in kind after bad years at a money equivalent based on the high market prices then prevailing could leave tenants a burden of debt that could lead to bankruptcy several years afterwards.

Weaknesses in Scotland's trading position were also apparent (Smout, 1963). Her principal exports were unprocessed primary products such as grain, lean cattle, wool, fish, coal and lead ore. Some of the most dynamic growth sectors during the late seventeenth century—the rise of the coal industry and the expansion of lead production from the mines at Leadhills— were still within the realms of primary production.

The only manufactured products which were prominent exports were coarse woollen and linen cloth. Between the Restoration and the Union of 1707 Scotland's unfavourable trading position was worsened by political difficulties. Wars with the Dutch and, after 1688, with France, disrupted trade with two of Scotland's major markets, and she was denied free access to England, the most obvious and immediate market, as well as with England's colonies (Smout, 1963).

After 1660 the Scottish legislature strove to encourage textile production. The development of a fine woollen cloth industry on an English model was seen as a way of improving Scotland's economic position, by adding value to wool, one of her most abundant resources, by saving foreign exchange, and by providing employment for the fluctuating but always disturbingly high proportion of the population which was destitute. Legislation on classic mercantilist lines encouraged the formation of joint stock companies to produce woollens and other commodities (Scott, 1910–11). These companies received various privileges, including the protection of their home market by restricting imports of competing foreign goods. Raw materials were allowed in duty free, and the manufactories were given the sole right to market their products, freeing them from the constraints of the burghal system, while encouragement was given to foreign entrepreneurs to invest in Scottish ventures and to foreign labour to bring in new skills.

Several woollen manufactories were established, and although some, like the New Mills company near Haddington, which was directed with vigour and enterprise, enjoyed a degree of success, they faced difficulties which ultimately caused their failure. Their home market was inadequately protected by inefficient customs administration and by legislation which was disregarded with impunity. The lack of skilled native labour and the high cost of foreign workers were a perennial problem. Additional costs were incurred by the fact that Scottish wool was generally unfit for making fine cloth so production depended on imported English and Spanish wool. The end product was uncompetitive in quality or price with the manufactures of other countries. Fine Scottish woollens even failed to capture a substantial share of the home market, owing to consumer prejudice (probably justified) and the ease with which import restrictions on foreign cloth could be evaded. After the opening years of the eighteenth century the 'high tide of protection' (Gulvin, 1971) ebbed, and exposure to unrestricted competition from the English woollen industry after 1707 caused the rapid demise of many manufactories or their reversion to making coarse cloth. The essence of the economic policy contained in the Articles of Union was that Scotland's economy should be developed to complement that of England. Scottish fine woollens were competitive and could not be supported financially.

THE IMPACT OF THE UNION OF 1707

In the long term the Union marked a social and economic as well as a political watershed, but this was not necessarily apparent at the time. Undoubtedly it was not an immediate panacea for Scotland's economic ills, and there were both gains and losses in the short term. The foundering of the woollen industry, which was in difficulties before 1707, was inevitable in the face of English competition. The Barons of the Exchequer and later the Board of

Trustees for Manufactures who were responsible for allotting funds to assist Scottish industrial development were keener to encourage the linen industry as a complementary sector to English textiles (Durie, 1979). The coarse woollen industry, tied more closely to the home market than fine woollens, continued with belated financial aid from the 1720s. With the demise of fine woollens, linen became Scotland's premier manufacture. England provided a major market with protection from Dutch and German cloth and, from the 1730s, the finance provided by the Board of Manufactures aided rapid growth.

The traditional problems of the Scottish economy remained though. One curb on development was sluggish growth in agriculture. The droving trade expanded after 1707 but not dramatically. Grain exports also increased, but it is uncertain how much of this was due merely to better weather conditions after the disastrous 1690s. Agricultural improvement did take place during the first forty years of the century but very slowly. Such developments as occurred were essentially indigenous and owed little to the Union, being continuations of trends which had existed before 1707 (Campbell, 1977). The Military Survey of 1747–55 shows how little enclosure had been accomplished in most areas by the middle of the century. In progressive districts like East Lothian areas of improvement on the policies and home farms of landowners were frequent and a start had been made on many estates on enclosing the lands of the tenants. Elsewhere improvements were more limited. A good deal of enclosure for cattle rearing had occurred in Galloway, but such land was mostly managed directly by proprietors. In a sense it was still a medieval-style demesne economy touching the rest of the rural population only indirectly.

Some landowners, such as John Cockburn of Ormiston and Archibald Grant of Monymusk, have earned fame as early improvers, promoting the new husbandry of sown grasses and root crops and encouraging enclosure. At Ormiston Cockburn pioneered the planned village, providing a focus for rural industry and forming a nucleus around which the rest of the estate could be reorganized. Unfortunately Cockburn overreached himself, facing opposition from neighbouring landowners and most of his own tenants who were too set in their ways to respond positively to sweeping innovation. Bankrupt, he was forced to sell his estate, although his example had attracted much interest. More representative and, within the scope of their more cautious approach, more successful were contemporaries such as Sir John Clerk of Penicuik and George Dundas of Dundas (Whyte, 1981). They started by ornamenting their policies and planting trees partly for decoration, partly for investment, but by the 1730s and 1740s they had extended their work to the lands of some of their tenants, enclosing, planting and consolidating from runrig.

These improvements were undertaken using limited inputs of capital and labour over extended periods. Strict entail settlements and innate caution militated against investing large sums borrowed on credit, and this slowed the pace of change. Organizational improvements such as removing tenant runrig cost little and may have improved productivity. That output did not rise substantially, however, is suggested by static rents on many estates during the first half of the century. With limited population growth and little improvement in living standards, caution was advisable. The economic climate within which agriculture operated had changed little from before the Union and was not greatly modified until late in the century with sharper increases in population and demand.

CONCLUSION: CONTINUITY AND CHANGE

Between the late sixteenth and mid eighteenth centuries Scotland experienced no revolutionary changes in her economic and social geography or in her cultural landscape. Developments were gradual and occurred against a background of continuity in basic institutions. Where development can be identified, its scale and significance are often difficult to establish and the forces which promoted it are even more obscure. Traditional feudal elements in Scotland's society were not replaced overnight by capitalist ones. The balance between feudalism and capitalism merely altered, and the extent of this alteration is open to debate.

The difficulties of the late seventeenth century demonstrated to contemporaries many of the weaknesses of Scotland's essentially medieval spatial organization and underlined the need for change. For example, the flurry of writing on agricultural improvement in response to the famines of the 1690s indicated both a perception of the need for change and a determination to accomplish it (Whyte, 1979a). We must, however, beware of viewing the Union in purely economic terms as an attempt to reorient Scotland on to a more prosperous course. Ferguson (1977) has demonstrated the importance of the sordid role of political management in bringing about the Union. Even so, the poor state of Scotland's economy was a preoccupation at the time and influenced the Union debate. In the early eighteenth century, Scotland was not yet ready for radical change. However, although she was poor compared with England, the potential for development existed. Defoe, writing in the 1720s, suggested that 'they [the Scots] are where we [the English] were . . . and they may be where we are' (Defoe, 1724–6). To realize this, as he appreciated, determination was not enough; capital, and the time to accumulate it were needed. Understandably it took Scotland's economy a while to adjust to the opportunities presented after 1707, but by the opening of the second quarter of the eighteenth century these adjustments were beginning to bear fruit.

The changes which accelerated during the later eighteenth century were revolutionary in many ways, but the foundations on which they were laid extended further back than has sometimes been appreciated. The importance of continuity and evolution has been neglected in favour of better-documented revolutionary developments. Geographical changes in early-modern Scotland were slower and less spectacular than in later times, but this does not diminish their importance. It is the difficulty of interpreting such shifts of emphasis which makes this period tantalizing yet at the same time fascinating and challenging for the historical geographer.

REFERENCES

Adams, I. H. (1971). 'Directory of Former Scottish Commonties.' Scottish Record Society, Edinburgh.

Adams, I. H. (1978). 'The Making of Urban Scotland.' Croom Helm, London.

Barrow, G. W. S. (1972). 'The Kingdom of the Scots.' Edward Arnold, London.

Caird, J. B. (1964). The making of the Scottish rural landscape. *Scottish Geographical Magazine* **80**, 72–80.

Campbell, R. H. (1977). The Scottish improvers and the course of agrarian change in the eighteenth century. *In* 'Comparative Aspects of Scottish and Irish Economic and Social History, 1600–1900.' (L. M. Cullen and T. C. Smout, ed.), 204–15. John Donald, Edinburgh.

Clark, P. and Slack, P. (1976). 'English Towns in Transition 1500–1700.' Oxford University Press, Oxford.

Defoe, D. (1724–6). 'A Tour Through the Whole Island of Great Britain.' London.

Dodgshon, R. A. (1972). The removal of runrig in Roxburghshire and Berwickshire 1680–1766. *Scottish Studies* **16**, 121–37.

Dodgshon, R. A. (1977). Changes in Scottish township organization during the medieval and early-modern periods. *Geografiska Annaler* **58B**, 51–65.

Durie, A. (1979). 'The Scottish Linen Industry in the Eighteenth Century.' John Donald, Edinburgh.

Ferguson, W. (1977). 'Scotland's Relations with England: a Survey to 1707.' John Donald, Edinburgh.

Flinn, M., Gillespie, J., Hill, N., Maxwell, A., Mitchison, R. and Smout, T. C. (1977). 'Scottish Population History from the Seventeenth Century to the 1930s.' Cambridge University Press, Cambridge.

Gray, H. L. (1915). 'English Field Systems.' Cambridge University Press, Cambridge.

Gulvin, C. (1971). The Union and the Scottish woollen industry 1707–60. *Scottish History Review* **50**, 121–37.

Nef, J. (1932). 'The Rise of the British Coal Industry.' 2 vols. Cassel, London.

O'Dell, A. C. (1953). A view of Scotland in the middle of the eighteenth century. *Scottish Geographical Magazine* **69**, 58–63.

Sanderson, M. H. B. (1973). The feuars of kirklands. *Scottish History Review* **52**, 117–48.

Scott, W. R. (1910–11). 'The Constitution and Finance of English, Scottish and Irish Joint Stock Companies.' 2 vols. Cambridge University Press, Cambridge.

Slater, T. (1980). The mansion and policy. *In* 'The Making of the Scottish Rural Landscape.' (M. L. Parry and T. Slater, ed.), 223–48. Croom Helm, London.

Smout, T. C. (1963). 'Scottish Trade on the Eve of the Union 1660–1707.' Oliver and Boyd, Edinburgh.

Smout, T. C. (1964). Scottish landowners and economic growth 1650–1850. *Scottish Journal of Political Economy* **11**, 218–34.

Smout, T. C. (1968). The Glasgow merchant community in the seventeenth century. *Scottish History Review* **47**, 53–71.

Smout, T. C. and Fenton, A. (1965). Scottish agriculture before the Improvers: an exploration. *Agricultural History Review* **13**, 73–93.

Walton, K. (1952). Climate and famine in north-east Scotland. *Scottish Geographical Magazine* **68**, 13–21.

Whyte, I. D. (1979a). 'Agriculture and Society in Seventeenth-Century Scotland.' John Donald, Edinburgh.

Whyte, I. D. (1979b). Written leases and their impact on Scottish agriculture in the seventeenth century. *Agricultural History Review* **27**, 1–9.

Whyte, I. D. (1979c). Infield–outfield farming on a seventeenth-century Scottish estate. *Journal of Historical Geography* **5**, 391–402.

Whyte, I. D. (1979d). The growth of periodic market centres in Scotland 1600–1707. *Scottish Geographical Magazine* **95**, 13–26.

Whyte, I. D. (1981a). The evolution of rural settlement in Lowland Scotland in medieval and early-modern times: an exploration. *Scottish Geographical Magazine* **97**.

Whyte, I. D. (1981b). George Dundas of Dundas: the context of an early eighteenth-century Scottish improving landowner. *Scottish History Review* **60**, 1–13.

Woodward, D. (1977). A comparative study of the Irish and Scottish livestock trades in the seventeenth century. *In* 'Comparative Aspects of Scottish and Irish Economic and Social History 1600–1900.' (L. M. Cullen and T. C. Smout, ed.), 147–64. John Donald, Edinburgh.

Agriculture and Society
in Lowland Scotland, 1750–1870

G. Whittington

Because of the wealth of data sources for the period 1750–1870, much attention has been focused on it by scholars in many fields. It is a fertile period for examining agricultural change, both as to method and to attitudes, labour relations, the social hierarchy, housing conditions and developments. Unfortunately many of the works published have not been prepared with a critical approach. Stereotyped attitudes have persisted, although several recent works by economic historians (Campbell, 1977; Devine, 1978; Gray, 1973, 1976) have to be exempted from this criticism, and there has been a failing to consider the perceptions of the people involved in the life of rural areas at this time. Moreover the writings from the early part of this period, which have been used extensively by later workers, have not been properly evaluated by considering the actual aims of those publications.

It is possible to think of 1750–1870 as consisting of three time units, each dominated by certain events: the years *c.* 1750–1800 have been regarded by many authors as experiencing an Agricultural Revolution; the years 1800–1836 were a period of adjustment to the earlier events and a grappling with the problems of an extended war and its attendant depression; the years 1836–70 were typified by the development of high farming. However, the identification of such clear-cut time slices is inherently dangerous. Indeed it encompasses degrees of generalization which have led many workers to come to conclusions which careful sifting of the multitude of sources available does not warrant. In the flight from the study of the unique to a concern with the generality of events, there has been a tendency to make unsupportable statements about Scotland as a whole which the varied social and natural environmental conditions within the country render most improbable. Certain writings have seen possibilism run wild (Adams, 1978, 1980) when what is really needed is a realization that environmental determinism still has worth. There has also been a marked failure, especially by historical geographers, to show any concern for the people who were part, and in large measure the fashioners, of the landscape which forms the basis of study. What was the social condition of the rural dweller? Much has been written on the agricultural improvements which are alleged to have amounted to 'the complete subversion of an established system' (Adams, 1980, 155) but little regard has been paid to the people caught up in them. Did their lot improve also? Did it improve in an equitable fashion? What was the contribution to the development of the landscape features by the various strata of society which, if subversion of an existing system occurred, must have been brought into existence? Some fresh air has been introduced into this period of landscape and societal development in recent years (Adams, 1978; Parry, 1976; Whittington, 1975; Whyte, 1978), but the time is now ripe, because the research base is more secure, to review this period and to assess our present understanding and viewpoints.

Topics which need to be considered, but which are not conveniently done so within the constraints of the time slices earlier identified, are many and varied and are of course closely intertwined. The concept of the Agricultural Revolution and the evidence for its existence, mode of occurrence and achievements have to be further examined. In Chapter 6 Whyte has shown that a move from feudalism to capitalism was occurring in Scotland. How did this develop and what effect did it have on the social fabric of the country? This chapter is concerned specifically with events in the Lowlands; this is a term which suggests some homogeneity, but it has already been pointed out in Chapter 6 that farming variation was developing during the late seventeenth and early eighteenth centuries. Its further evolution, which led to considerable spatial variation within the Lowlands, must be considered. An element of the Scottish landscape which has so far received only a limited treatment is that of its housing and farm-steadings (Walker, 1977, 1979); changes in agriculture might be expected to have had repercussions here too. The cumulative effects of agricultural improvement, of changing social attitudes and evolving economics aims also meant that new elements were added to the existing settlement pattern. The rejection of the time-slice approach must indicate that these developments are seen as having had their roots in the period before 1750 and that they continued after 1860.

THE AGRICULTURAL REVOLUTION

Recent writings on the changes experienced in Scottish agriculture during the eighteenth century, which have challenged long-established views, have shown either modifications or hardenings of viewpoints (Adams, 1980; Caird, 1980; Whyte, 1979). The idea of a totally static and unprogressive agriculture seems hard to accept. Farmers, even those working under the undoubted constraints existing in medieval and early-modern Scotland, were still people concerned with the soil and its exploitation. Furthermore they were not entirely insulated from changes both within and outside Scotland; nor indeed were the landowners. Scottish agriculture before the second half of the eighteenth century has been described as backward (Gray, 1973, 107), perhaps an unfortunate term in that it seems to exclude the perceptions and desires of the people involved in it. Nevertheless it did have many features that contrast sharply with the farming practices and aspirations of the nineteenth century. However, the hallmark of a totally static situation is complacency and the lack of a desire for change. Elsewhere (Adams, 1978, 198) the present author has been criticized for making 'a classic mistake' in quoting a seventeenth-century Act of Parliament as evidence against the occurrence of an Agricultural Revolution in Scotland during the eighteenth century. However, the point which needs to be understood from these so-called 'dead letter Acts' is that they show that the state of Scottish agriculture, at the time of their passing, was not acceptable to all. There was a recognition that change could be achieved and, moreover, was desirable. That such change occurred when it did was due to a combination of events of which the least important in many areas were the improving instincts of a narrow group of blood-related landowners. It is perhaps more instructive to regard Scottish agriculture as being in a constant state of flux due to a continually varying set of pressures and aims. Pre-eighteenth century agriculture can only be judged in the context of what went before and what came after; and what came after can only be put into proper perspective after some points about earlier agriculture have been considered.

It has been suggested (Robertson, 1829) that until the middle of the thirteenth century agricultural surpluses had been common over long periods. Arable practices included the growing of wheat, peas and beans, with the latter two crops being not only grown in sufficient quantity to feed the army investing Dirleton (Rothwell, 1957, 324) but also, in this period, mature by late June, a remarkably early date but one which accords with evidence from various *Annals* regarding the hot summer and plentiful harvest of 1289 (Britton, 1937). Throughout the succeeding centuries Acts were passed (Whyte, 1979) to try to restore this state of affairs, and by their very repetition it is clear that the attempts were a failure. Agriculture clearly had deteriorated and it took a long time to recover. Why should this have been? No one cause at any time can be considered to have been exclusively to blame. Certainly internal strife, from inter-family struggle to civil war, must have hampered any change which the Acts of Parliament had indicated were desirable (Alexander, 1877). However, only a scant mention (Adams, 1978, 201), and that wrongly located in time, has been given to the environmental conditions prevailing during the period in which agriculturally oriented Acts were passed. From about 1450, and especially after 1500, climatic conditions were less favourable for many crops (Lamb, 1966). Increased rainfall, lowered temperatures and increasing soil acidity would have forced farmers to reduce peas, beans and wheat in their rotations or even remove them entirely. No matter how many Acts were passed concerning their cultivation, physical conditions were against their implementation.

If such arguments can be put forward to account for agricultural change during the medieval period, it can be legitimately asked how change, let alone revolution, later became possible during the Little Ice Age. As Whyte (1979) has shown, agricultural improvement did occur in the seventeenth century, and it can be contended that split townships, an early phenomenon (Dodgshon, 1977) which continued to proliferate, was a much underrated element of this. Perhaps, however, it is also necessary to challenge the accepted view of the achievements of the Agricultural Revolution. Was it such an all-embracing and synchronous event as has been claimed. (Adams, 1978, 198)? With the identification and consideration of the efficacy of some of its main elements, the reality of the Revolution may be judged.

Of all the events that have been quoted to demonstrate an Agricultural Revolution that of enclosure has been the most frequent because it was seen as a fundamental feature of the agricultural change. Indeed Adams (1980) has used the emergence of the land surveyor, the progenitor of enclosure, as a major plank in his arguments for the Agricultural Revolution. That enclosure was planned and often carried out on a widespeard scale in the eighteenth century is undeniable, but that alone is not evidence for agricultural improvement. What was the motive for enclosure, did the landlords understand why they were undertaking it, how efficient was it, and how much change did it actually produce in the agrarian practices of the time? To answer such questions it is necessary to leave aside the numerous estate plans, which demonstrate the great activity of the land surveyors but not necessarily, their success, and go to those commentators of the time who are demonstrably not evangelists or propagandists.

The view put forward here is that the concentrated burst of enclosure in the late eighteenth century was often a failure, a fashion in a period when being 'progressive' was desirable. Like the early improvements made by Cockburn of Ormiston or the earlier referred to Acts of Parliament, it was a forerunner of better things to come, of a continuing interest in agricultural change. One of the most percipient commentators on the agricultural scene was Alexander Wight (1778), who cast his eye over virtually all of Scotland in the late eighteenth century. A synthesis of his comments on enclosure is very revealing. Far from being a simultaneous event, it was clearly well established in the

Lothians, although even here it often only amounted to a ring fence around a whole farm, and of long standing in Ayrshire and other parts of the West, but in Fife it had hardly started and throughout Central Lowland Scotland, page after page of Wight's commentary notes: 'No enclosure', 'only one tenant has enclosed', 'needs enclosing'. The enclosure that had taken place must also be scrutinized, for there is evidence that the landowners were not practical farmers, but followers of fashion.

> Enclosed with hedges but full of gaps . . . This farm is mostly enclosed with stone dikes but still in infield and outfield . . . inclosing of this estate has been executed at great expense, but without any judgement . . . winter herding has never been in force here, a clear proof that improvements are going on with no spirit; for to allow cattle to go at random, is destruction to new made hedges, to clover, to young grass and to every improvement (Wight, 1778).

As a later writer, having read Wight, put it:

> Many enclosures he saw fenced with dry stones, some new, some decayed, and some tumbling down; but not a gap made up, nor the slightest reparation of any of them. This surprised him. To be at the expense of building fences, and yet never to think of keeping them in repair, appeared unaccountable. But at last he discovered the cause; for, upon looking back he remembered that in every one of these enclosures there was corn as well as grass. In point of fact, 'inclosing', as known to the farmers of the time, was simply a delusion and a snare. It did not partition off the pastures from the cereal and the other crops, and consequently herding was just as much needed as if no enclosures existed (Alexander, 1877, 118).

It is instructive to analyse the rate of enclosing during the eighteenth and nineteenth centuries. The first peak was reached in the 1760s, followed by a distinct decline. The real crescendo was achieved around 1810, after which the rate remained high until the middle of the nineteenth century. Indeed it was the nineteenth century which saw the real advance in agriculture, based upon the new spirit which catalysts had liberated in the late eighteenth century.

This new spirit, it has been maintained, brought about 'an Agricultural Revolution, masterminded by a small, highly motivated group of people with the aim of enjoying the highest standard of living possible' (Adams, 1980, 173). This, however, is too simple a viewpoint, and indeed it might be questioned how effective a group these people were. Again the subject has suffered from over-generalization. There can be no doubt that a landowner like Lord Kames had a great effect on the standard of agriculture on his estates, but it is possible to go to the other extreme and show how variable were the conditions on the estate of the Earl of Findlater, one of the group of blood-related masterminds. The lands around his own house were 'improved': some farms had been developed entirely by tenants at their own expense (Wight, 1778, IV, 60), while on others:

> of good red soil, capable of high improvement . . . the crops were good; but I take the liberty of observing, that more might be done by industry and good management. Here, as in many other parts, crops of oats are taken till the land can produce no more, and then left naked and bare (Wight, 1778, IV, 47).

The importance of the landowners appears to have been overrated in discussions of the agricultural improvements. Many seem to have been involved only nominally, because they owned the land; their own achievements, unless they were actually practising farmers, seem to have been minimal and in some cases even hampering. Throughout the writings of the more objective and less overtly propagandist of late eighteenth and early nineteenth century authors, there are comments on the importance of the tenant rather than the landlord in the upgrading of agriculture. Even one of Ormiston's tenants 'inclosed his whole farm with hedge and ditch, and planted trees, all at his own expense' (Wight, 1778, II, 132). This seemed to be commonplace in south-east Scotland, for George Robertson (1829, 65) commented that:

> Much of the enclosing in Mid-Lothian has been the work of the tenants, without remuneration from the proprietors, even fences of stone and lime walls.

Or again:

> Almost the whole of the improvements specified have arisen from the exertions of the ordinary husbandman; few of them from the proprietors. The views of the latter have been more directed to the introduction of new species of crop, and to enclosing, and to planting of wood (Robertson, 1829, 38).

Indeed the writing into leases of certain rotations, based not on practical farming knowledge but on the theorizing of 'improving writers' was often damaging, and Wight instances a tenant of the Earl of Strathmore, who 'inclosed the land for himself' but who was 'limited by his lease to a certain rotation' (Wight, 1778, 301).

In summing up this important period of Scottish agriculture it seems that a number of events quickened its development. The abortive Acts of Parliament from the period before 1700 could now be acted upon. Change was initiated but it capitalized upon what had gone before. The change was hesitant, piecemeal and frequently inefficient in the short term (Gray, 1973, 112) but it did step up the momentum of agricultural improvement, which was to be capitalized on even further in the nineteenth century once the trauma of the Napoleonic Wars and a series of generally poor harvests between 1793 and 1815 had been overcome. Change which had been initiated early in the Lothians and which led to the high farming, as instanced on the farm of Fentonbarns (Bradley,

1927), had been achieved slowly. Bradley, writing about a time when agricultural improvement was less of a 'fever . . . so common and malignant' (Horn, 1966, 121) which caused emotions to run high, was able, from a more detached point of view, to comment, regarding Fentonbarns:

> that the grandfather of the contemporary farmer working in a comparatively humble way, had begun to bring the land out of the rude and undrained condition common to mid eighteenth century Scotland, and the son and the grandson had perfected it. It is the study in fact, of many Lothian farms the study in cameo of Scottish agriculture generally (Bradley, 1927, 68).

No hint of a revolution here but a continuing improvement with modest beginnings, many of which were achieved by the tenant and not by the landlord; a point made very forcibly by the hero of W. Alexander's novel (1873, 224) *Johnny Gibb of Gushetneuk*. However, the speed, direction and method of improvement were very varied; where the Lothians were early, Kincardineshire and Aberdeenshire were late.

Before closing the main discussion on this period, it should be asked why greater impetus in agricultural improvement did occur in the eighteenth century and why the enabling Acts of Parliament from the previous century in particular were acted upon then. For Adams (1978, 199) the 'push-factor' was the desire for high income and in some instances the furthering of ambition, but this type of argument smacks of rigid cause and effect analysis of a classical physical nature rather than one of the more useful quantum nature. The slow penetration of capitalist aims, the improvement of transport, often predating the turnpike acts, the development of a freer marketing system, consequent upon the decline of Royal Burgh monopoly, and, perhaps above all, greater competition for labour, brought about by the development of the textile industry, all played a part, of varying degree from area to area, in the changing of attitudes. Certainly over much of the eastern Lowlands, north of the Forth:

> when manufactures [especially spinning in the earliest phase] were withdrawn from the hands of the peasantry, landlords had no alternative but to try to cultivate the land in some sound way to make it sustain in comfort its own labourers, from wages wholly derived from the land itself, while it should yield themselves a reasonable return for their outlay in making the new experiment with it (Stuart, 1853, 12).

The replacing of peat as a fuel by coal not only reduced the services to be rendered to the landlords and tenant farmers but also, as a corollary, increased the need for money with which to purchase the new fuel. Furthermore the fact that wages, now in cash rather than in kind, were rising faster than grain prices increased the need for a money income. Noble sentiments about the New Enlightenment affecting the new agriculture are misplaced; self preservation was at the root of the matter with often the only contribution by the landlord being the goad of a raised rent.

THE SOCIAL FABRIC

Controversy occurred during the nineteenth century as to the effect that changes in agriculture were having upon the rural population, not only in terms of its density of distribution but also in relation to the divisions that were developing in society and to the worth and status of labour. Much of the discussion is couched in terms that betray entrenched positions, and indeed the idea that the improvements in agriculture led to a surplus rural labour supply, noted from the nineteenth century, continues to make its appearance in modern writings (Adams, 1978; Lockhart, 1980; Shaw, 1980). In general, recent discussions of these topics has been limited and until the appearance of recent research (Flinn, 1977) could only be conducted at a level which had no firm demographic evidence on which to draw. The majority of Scotland's population was located in the late-eighteenth century in the eastern Lowlands. During this period changes were occurring in the way in which people lived and mixed which were to have profound effects on the social order of later periods. Until the full invasion of capitalist farming, the needs and aims of most active agriculturalists were the same. The landlord–tenant ties were close, because until rent in kind and services were replaced by money rent, the two parts of the community could not live without each other. Once farming for a profit became the normal circumstance, gulfs between the landlord and his tenant and the tenant and his labour began to open, grow wider and consolidate. This was, however, a process which varied both spatially and temporally in the Lowlands and which thus contributed to regional variations within that area.

The changes to the social fabric were not caused by agricultural improvement but were part and parcel of it. As with other parts of this topic, misconceptions have risen over the effects of the improvement on rural population. A common view is that the creation of single tenancies, where formerly ferm touns under multiple tenancy had occurred, was the normal event over Lowland Scotland and that this produced a great uprooting of the rural population which then flooded on to the labour market. This is too gross a generalization. Already multiple tenancy was probably not as common as single tenancy with tributary cot-touns. Furthermore the effect of the new husbandry was to create a multiplicity of new jobs requiring in most instances a steady supply of labour. The introduction of turnips made great demands upon the labour supply. The process of enclosing, continuing throughout the nineteenth century, and its maintenance brought into existence new work in building dykes, planting and cutting hedges, ditching and draining, the removal of setfast boulders, the straightening of ridges, and at first the pulverization of clods on poorly drained soils. During the nineteenth century the introduction of threshing machines removed much labour, but in the earliest period at least the process of land improvement increased employment opportunities. Throughout the early part of the nineteenth century the desire for land brought about the improvement of areas which had only been extensively exploited up to that date. This was achieved by a variety of methods, but such land, at its most extensive in the north-eastern counties (Kincardine to Banff), actually created work. Those moved off the farms, where they had been sub-tenants, were settled on marginal land which they improved as crofters. Whole new settlements were brought into existence in this way and land was made available for engrossment of farms in the mid-nineteenth century. These people were vital to the whole improvement process and were part of it, just as the cottars had been a part of an earlier agricultural system and were not merely living on its margins, except in a physical sense (Adams, 1978, 199).

The growing penetration of Scottish farming by profit-seeking aims however, did, have an increasing effect upon society. The close links between landlord and tenant and tenant and cottar were to be abandoned, and the landlord became more and more distanced from his tenants. This trend, instanced by Bradley (1927), led to the landlord becoming anglicized in speech and orientation, while the tenants, along with the professional classes in the urban urea, retained their Scottish accents until bourgeois aims also overtook them. This distancing, however, meant the development of tensions which built up during the nineteenth century and which were at explosion point during its last decades. The dominant position of the landowning group, aided and abetted by the clergy and the schoolmaster (Sir Simon Frissal of Glensnicker, Reverend Andrew Sleekaboot and Johnathan Tawse in Alexander's *Johnny Gibb of Gushetneuk*), in all walks of life right up to the end of the nineteenth century meant that it was in a position to control through government and the judiciary the groups which rented its land. Certain aspects of life which affected the well-being of the farmer in both his day-to-day farming operations and his way of life became focuses for tension.

There were several causes of friction (M'Culloch, 1879), of which two had their roots in feudalism. Acts of 1621, 1707 and 1772 controlled the right to kill game and vermin. Tenants could kill vermin on their own land and on the proprietor's but had to pay compensation for any damage caused. They could not kill game on their own land, even if it were destroying crops, and the proprietor retained the right to hunt on the tenant's land and even to let out the rights. Farms on the margins of the highland areas suffered badly from the provisions of these Acts. A second source of friction was the Law of Hypothec

whereby a landlord could claim household goods, crops and farming implements as security for rent. This was further exacerbated by one of the very
features which has in the past been held to be an underpinning of the
Agricultural Revolution—the long period lease. This not only contained fixed
and often unsuitable rotations but also was not transferable, so if financial
difficulties or ill-health were encountered, the farmer not only had no claim
upon the proprietor for any improvements he had made but he was charged for
any deterioration on the farm and furthermore could have his goods distrained
under the Law of Hypothec. Those features, added to the competitive bidding
for farms, and in the North-East in particular the effects of disenchantment
with the church (Alexander, 1873), led in the early nineteenth century to a
rupture between proprietor and tenant. The prosperity of farming in the
middle of the century led to a muting of the complaints, but the root problems
remained and when, at the close of the period under review, farming went into
decline, the gulf between proprietor and tenant became even greater, especially in areas where absentee landlordism existed.

While capitalistic development was bringing about a distancing of landlord
and tenant (Saunders, 1950, 28), it was also having a profound effect upon the
group of people now forced to receive cash instead of kind for their labour. The
effect of improvement on the sub-tenant and the cottar was not so much to
remove them from the rural zone but rather to alter their circumstances, both
socially and economically. This did not, however, have the same effect over the
whole of the Lowlands because of the emergence of different farming systems.
Farm labouring systems with different social hierarchies came into existence—
differences which were not only caused by the type of farming pursued but also
by the existence of other employment which could provide extra farm labour
when it was needed.

Perhaps the most distinctive feature of farming in the whole of this period
was its increasing demands upon labour, both in terms of intensity and
specialization. In the eastern Lowlands there was a growing involvement with
cereal cultivation, which meant that the ploughman now became the aristocrat
of the labour force. Because ploughing was no longer confined to one period of
the year and because it now used a more refined and delicate plough and a
higher quality traction, it had to be undertaken by a specialist. In the
South-East this activity, along with other specialist tasks, was undertaken by
the hind, who was resident on the farm in his rented cottage along with his wife
and a bondager, a female helper for the farm in general whom the hind was
responsible for hiring and paying. He had a small-holding (usually about a
sixteenth of an acre) which was exploited variously; often for flax until the
domestic linen industry collapsed and thereafter for potatoes. He also had a
cow, poultry and pigs. Thus he was in a secure position and formed a
conservative and persistent element in the countryside. Outside the South-

East the ploughman was still the most important person on a farm, but instead of living in a cottage he had a place in either the kitchen or bothy system. The bothies were confined mainly to the central and middle eastern counties. In this system the ploughman and the other farmworkers inhabited a zone within the farm buildings and there catered for themselves and dwelt generally under very poor conditions (Cowie *et al.*, 1843; Robb, 1861). In the kitchen system (Robb, 1861) all the labour ate in the farmhouse kitchen where a maid provided the meal. Later in the evening the men all withdrew to the 'chaumer', a sleeping area in the barn or above the stables which again provided them with variable but generally inferior shelter.

The effect of all this was to bring different societal arrangements into being. In the South-East and West married labour was normal; elsewhere in the eastern Lowlands single men and women made up a class of farm servants. Even when they were married, the men would live apart from their wives, who, residing in a village or small town, would be visited on a Sunday. But the general tendency was for the servant of the eastern areas north of the Forth to marry late in life.

The development of the hind system in the South-East and of the kitchen and the bothy elsewhere stemmed largely from the different expectations of the farmer, and particularly of his wife (Alexander, 1873), with the advent of capitalist farming. Material welfare and the desire for 'refinement' led the farmers, especially those with large holdings, to keep workers out of their house, thus giving rise to housing and moral problems which became the concern of many observers of contemporary society (e.g. Robb, 1861; Stuart, 1853).

No review of the social fabric would be complete without a discussion of the position of the labouring class (and it should be pointed out that sharp class divisions did not emerge in Lowland Scotland until the nineteenth century; see Alexander, 1852; Saunders, 1950). Apart from their living conditions, still to be discussed, the labour force did possess one advantage in terms of the method of hiring; this was done at the 'feeing market'. All labour was engaged on a yearly or six-monthly basis. Although this could lead to a certain amount of rootlessness among the rural population, movements at the end of a hiring period tended to be within a severely circumscribed area, for both farm servant and farmer depended greatly upon their known reputations for hiring agreements. If a farmer, or the food provided in his kitchen or bothy, were known to be of low repute, the obtaining of labour at the feeing markets, held at Whitsunday and Martinmas, would be very difficult. Particularly poor housing and food and over-demanding work conditions could be met by the sanction of the 'clean toun'; if the most senior member of the labour force hierarchy, usually the ploughman or the grieve, left at the end of the hiring period then, by an unwritten law, all the other labour left too. Knowledge of such an event would spread rapidly at the feeing market (Alexander, J., 1852; Alexander, W., 1873, 1877).

Working conditions were indeed bad on the farms, especially for the ploughman (Stuart, 1853), due not only to the poor housing and food but also to the very heavy work entailed in ploughing and pulverizing clay soils which until the introduction of tile drains were still liable to be very wet and heavy. The sheer demands on physical strength, the continual dampness of clothing and living quarters and the very long hours worked meant that ploughmen had to give up such employment by the age of fifty. Before long, arthritic conditions meant they were unable to perform any farm work, and this caused the loss of their house and forced them to go to the towns, where they eventually had to rely upon poor relief (Devine, 1978). Such conditions led to some early rural protests, but they were unsuccessful and indeed unionization of farm labour did not take place until the twentieth century (Dunbabbin, 1974).

HOUSING AND FARM BUILDINGS

The continuing reorganization of agriculture during the whole of the period under review brought about changing attitudes to farm accommodation for humans, stock, implements and crops. Thus what was the best form of the farmhouse and its appendages led to much theorizing, the production of many plans and many comments of a social-moralizing nature. The increasingly capitalistic nature of farming demanded that better care be taken of the equipment and produce of the farm. The farmer himself wanted and achieved better living quarters. However, the farm labourer did not share in this general improvement of accommodation; he was trapped in the gulf between landlord and tenant. The dichotomy in housing between that of the farmer, his equipment, stock and crops and that of the farm labour is eloquently summed up in the extremes of Fig. 7.1.

Attempts were made throughout this period to evolve a system of buildings which allowed the most efficient working of the land and the highest possible return for its produce. This meant good accommodation for stock and a location of the various working buildings on the farm which would cut to a minimum the handling of the crops, whether for feeding stock or for storage, and ultimate threshing for sale. The Highland and Agricultural Society gave premiums for good farm layouts and also published plans and descriptions of such buildings (Anon., 1831). However, the process of farmstead reorganization was neither sudden nor achieved in one operation. It was usual for the farmhouse to be rebuilt first, much of this occurring around 1800. The use of lime mortar and slates or tiles and the construction of a second storey became

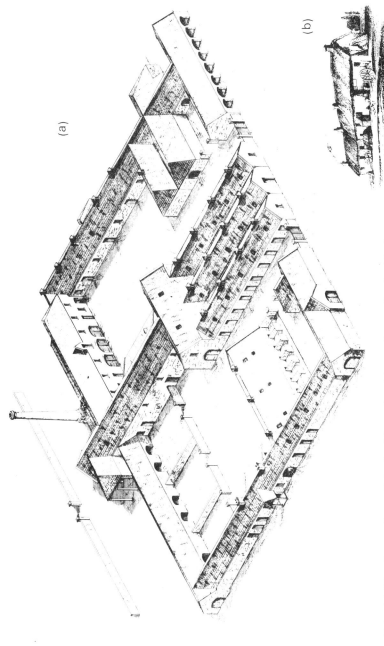

(a)

(b)

Fig. 7.1 (a) The factory farm of the Lothians; the chimney is associated with the steam-driven threshing machinery. The farmhouse is totally detached. (b) Cottages from the North-East in 1850, romantic in appearance but, in hygiene, comfort and construction, rural slums

common. The animal and storage areas, however, although often now detached from the house, were still built of unmasoned stone and continued to
have thatched roofs. The realization that better-housed crops and especially
stock were to the farmer's advantage did not suddenly arise; furthermore, such
improvements had to wait until capital was available. Developments of this
kind were usually the responsibility of the proprietor and with the great
farming prosperity of the mid nineteenth century many farmsteadings and
particularly the non-domestic areas were completely rebuilt in the 1860s
(Morton, 1976).

Continued experiment and change led to a pattern of farmsteadings emerging. Only where crofting retained a hold, especially in the north-eastern
counties, did the elongated farmstead layout continue in any number. Elsewhere the move was to a mixture of scattered, parallel, L-shaped, and
courtyard forms with the extremely complex variations which were feasible
with the last plan (Fig. 7.2). Size and shape depended largely on the type of
farming, the area farmed, and the farm's location. Parts of the Lowlands
showed great homogeneity, but others had considerable variety. Perhaps the
commonest form to emerge was the courtyard with both the open and closed
varieties in existence, the former in the cattle-dominated areas and the latter in
the arable zones. But even by the 1860s a noted authority on farm buildings was
able to pose the question:

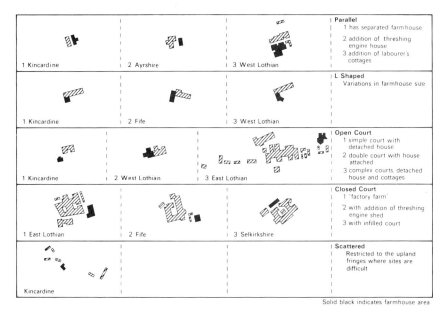

Fig. 7.2 Variations in the layout of farmsteadings

Do existing steadings really possess . . . distinctive characters? We believe they do not. We suspect that very many do not indicate at a glance the purpose for which they were constructed (Stephens and Burn, 1861).

Even at this date of agricultural development steadings were not being constructed to accord with the system of farming they were to serve. Clearly this area of agricultural improvement still had far to go—the Agricultural Revolution was still far from over!

The dwellings of the rurally based population displayed enormous differences. The development of large mansions from the Gothick of the late eighteenth century to the revived Scots Baronial of the mid nineteenth led to new features in the Lowland landscape, especially where it was accompanied by the new passion of the proprietors for tree planting (Slater, 1980). But of greater account was the change in living conditions of the tenant farmer class. Apart from some elaborate buildings, most were plain but substantial stone dwellings of two storeys. Their internal design depended again upon the size of the farm unit and the type of farming; for example, in dairying zones an attic area might well be constructed to accommodate the extra female labour that this activity demanded.

However, neither the proprietor nor the tenant provided the majority of the agriculturally based population. Allusion has already been made to the poor condition of housing for the farm labourer. Indeed the state of housing of this group was a cause which led to passionate outbursts by such men as the Reverend Stuart of Oathlaw in Angus (1853), practical advice from the Highland and Agricultural Society (e.g. Smith, 1835), the setting-up of the Association for Promoting Improvement in the Dwellings and Domestic Condition of Agricultural Labourers in Scotland (1854–61), paternalistic care from certain landowners, and general indifference and handwashing of the whole problem by the majority of proprietors.

It was generally agreed that the lack of cottages throughout the country, and especially outside the Lothians, was one of the main weaknesses in the agricultural system. The continued existence of the kitchen and bothy systems, both capable of providing very bad accommodation but also of a better variety where any care was given to such matters, caused severe social problems which could only produce an inefficient and unsettled labour force. Separation from the family (a teenage child would often leave home for work on a farm and accommodation in a kitchen or bothy), lack of opportunity to marry or even being apart from wife and children, and the high rate of illegitimacy (the cause of which was much debated in the nineteenth century) were conditions closely related to the lack of cottages on farms. Such cottages as did exist were of extremely poor condition. The walls were built of undressed stone and mortared but were scarcely five feet in height, with one doorway and two small windows. The gables were of turf, and the whole structure often had to be supported by buttresses which were little more than piles of stones. The roof was of turves over straw or heather, there was no ceiling and the floor was of earth but at a lower level than the ground outside (Fig. 7.1). The only internal division was by means of box beds, usually the only area free from damp, which produced the two portions of 'but and ben' (Alexander, 1877; Black, 1851; Rob, 1861; Stephens and Burn, 1861).

That this state of affairs could continue late into the nineteenth century, despite the efforts of the Highland and Agricultural Society, the Cottage Association and the Press was due to the poor relations between proprietor and tenant. Tenants either did not have the financial resources to build cottages or they were so constrained by the Law of Hypothec that they would not expend them. Most tenants thought that the provision of dwellings for the farm labourer was the proprietor's responsibilty. The proprietors either ignored the problem, were absentees and so did not know of the situation, for their factors were only concerned with profits and not matters which cost money, or claimed that they did not like to interfere with the tenant's running of his farm (Lindsay, 1854). In some cases, until the Law of Entail (Saunders, 1950; Smout, 1960) was changed, proprietors were in no position financially or legally to invest in their farms. So virtually nothing was done, and even the Cottage Improving Society died from a lack of success in 1861. Thus the bothy and the kitchen were still integral parts of the rural housing system in 1870, and even in 1936 Joe Duncan (Smith, 1973), a campaigner for the rural worker, was able to take a group of visitors to a bothy. Where cottages were built it was to lead to the still persisting rural problem of the tied cottage.

THE SETTLEMENT PATTERN

The view that the rural settlement pattern until the eighteenth century was one of fermtouns occupied by multiple or co-joint tenants has now been dispelled. By the middle of the eighteenth century considerable variation existed in the settlement pattern of Lowland Scotland, even leaving aside the various grades of burghs. The variation also occurred on a regional basis, depending upon the particular specialisms which were being developed in a wider economic sense. The early improvement of agriculture engendered by a favourable climate, good soils, and the availability of the rapidly growing market of Edinburgh had encouraged the engrossment of holdings and the development of village forms throughout the lowlands of the South-East. Fife, Angus and much of the Central Lowlands, due to developments in textile manufacture and mining, had a multitude of hamlets which were not purely coastally located unlike the majority of the burghs. Perhaps the North-East showed the greatest difference in that here the fermtoun was still very important but even the engrossment of holdings did not denude the countryside of dwellings. Here the increased interest in gaining land at the margins, led to the development of small-holdings which were to have a continued existence well into the twentieth century. Some crofting communities even became permanent additions to the settlement pattern, as with Charlestown, south of Aberdeen (Blaikie, 1837; Thomson, 1837). Even where the fermtoun was replaced by the single farmsteading the difference made to the landscape was frequently one of kind and quality rather than in the number of buildings. The rebuilding of the farmsteading and the eventual addition of labourers' cottages created distinct and considerable groups of buildings around many farms. The area occupied by buildings would frequently have been greater on the single-tenant farm than it had been in the fermtoun. This particularly applied in areas dominated by grain cultivation and none more so than in the factory-farm system of the Lowlands.

The greatest change which came to the Lowland landscape, however, was due to the introduction of a regular, ordered form of settlement which had more in common with the street villages of lands colonized during the medieval Germanic expansion than with the village structures of England. The planned village has been scrutinized by Lockhart (1980). It was developed in three distinct phases, the first of which, an extension of existing settlements, had been going on for fifteen years prior to 1750 and was complete by 1769. The second period occurred between 1770 and 1819, but apart from the North-East it was mainly a Highland phenomenon. At this period too there were different types of village being created; in the North-East mostly associated with estate improvement, in the West as a result of expansion in the cotton industry, and in the South-East and Central areas, although few in number, where provision for marketing was needed. The third period 1820–50 saw far fewer planned villages developed. They were smaller and usually associated with new trans-port lines or textile production, the latter especially in Perthshire, Angus and Kincardineshire. The stimulus for the planned village had vanished after 1850 because the advent of the railway and the greatly improved road system encouraged the demise of local markets. Indeed a commentator of the period might well have been viewing the comparable modern effects of supermarket development:

> The facilities of transit which attract the buyer to the cheapest market, thus destroying the business of the small tradesman, who is forced, in self-defence, to remove from country locations,—all lead to a decrease in the rural population (Robb, 1861, v).

What stimulated the planned village or, perhaps more relevant here, what brought about the first two periods of development? Lockhart considered it to be due to several factors but particularly the natural increased in population and a structural change in farming which created a surplus labour supply. This is perhaps an over-simplification. The population trend was not simply one of growth up to 1819: as recent work has shown (Flinn, 1977) mortality rates could fluctuate greatly. Lower mortality rates occurred for several decades after 1750, but at the end of the eighteenth century and at the beginning of the nineteenth Scotland suffered a severe mortality crisis and by 1808 mortality had risen 30% above the levels of the preceding five years. This was not merely an urban phenomenon, whereas the increased fertility, which was leading to population growth, tended to be so. Furthermore the idea of a surplus agricultural labour force cannot any longer be sustained; agricultural improvement was a creator of employment not merely because of specialized labour needs on the land but also because of the greater demand for work from the artisan class by the population at large. Farmhouse building, smithying, textile working, the developing effect of profit-making farming, and the attendant growth of service industry would all have made employment more widely available in the rural zone; at least some of those occupying such jobs would have found dwellings in the planned villages.

The developments in farm building and the erection of the planned villages left enduring features in the landscape. As Lockhart (1980) has shown, very few of the planned villages failed to survive, although many did not fulfil the size or employment structure originally envisaged by their creators; New Leeds in Aberdeenshire is a piquant reminder of this! The rebuilding of farmhouses and their appendages in the 1860s contributed elements to the landscape which in many areas are extensively unchanged even today in both morphology and appearance. Even with technological development, the existing cart shades, threshing sheds and engine houses, barns and stables have often merely been adapted to modern needs.

REGIONAL VARIATION IN AGRICULTURE AND SETTLEMENT

By 1750 agriculture in the Lowlands of Scotland was already showing signs of regional specialization. This trend was to be furthered during the next one hundred and fifty years in recognition of differences in the physical environment, especially that between the drier, more continental east and the wetter, maritime west and also due to differences in market demands. One of the earliest of the distinct regions to emerge was the South-West and West. Several features contributed to this distinctiveness, and perhaps only one or two gave any unity to this area. It was a zone predominantly of cattle keeping, early enclosure and farming based upon the family unit. The aims of the pastoralism were frequently different: in the north the growing urbanization of the Glasgow area provided an increasing market for a fresh milk; the Ayrshire zone became one specializing in cheese and butter making; Wigtown and the Stewartry of Kirkcudbrightshire concentrated on the production of beef. Throughout the area, although farm sizes varied, the medium-sized farm predominated, mainly of the order of up to 100 acres (40 ha). Labour was provided by the farmer's family, supplemented by one or two hired labourers at the most, usually the offspring of farmers who in due course returned to the parental farm, and seasonal labour from the industrial settlements, Ireland and the Highlands. Despite sharing in the general national lack of cottages, farm labour here did not suffer the distancing from the farmer noted elsewhere. The labour fed and lived with the farmer in most instances, a function of the smaller units of farming. This also led to simpler farmsteadings, many being of a linear nature, unless specialized dairying occurred in which case open courtyards were used. Where cottages did exist these usually belonged to crofters who were breaking in the marginal lands and thus creating a myraid of smallholdings.

In stark contrast to all of this were the lands of the south-eastern counties. Here the climate, proximity to Edinburgh as a market and as a source of potential wealthy proprietors, derived from the merchant and professional classes, and the early receipt of new ideas from England, led to an equally early development of the farming so roundly denounced by William Cobbett:

> Almost the whole of the produce of these fine lands goes into the pockets of the lords; the labourers are their slaves and the farmers their slave drivers. The farm yards are, in fact, factories for making corn and wheat, carried on principally by the means of horses and machinery (Cobbett, 1831, 107).

Figure 7.1 shows the type of farm which existed here, although not all were on such a grandiose scale. Apart from the upland areas where linear or open court farmsteadings occurred, the South-East was dominated by large closed courtyard farms, using the hind and the bondager system supplemented by large numbers of hired servants. By 1877 the average land per occupier in the various south-eastern counties was 200 acres (81 ha) for East Lothian, 197 (79 ha) for Berwickshire, 146 (59 ha) for Roxburghshire and 110 acres (44 ha) for West Lothian. One very marked feature of the South-East is inherent in Cobbett's rather extravagant utterance; the chances of anyone rising from farm servant to tenant were utterly remote, a strong contrast with the situation in the South-West, where farms were smaller and available at a lower rent. The power of the landlords, so marked a feature of Scottish history, was virtually undiminished in this area even by the late nineteenth century, as exemplified by the expulsion from his tenancy of one of the most advanced farmers who had the temerity to stand for Parliament as a Liberal (Bradley, 1927, 196).

The Central Lowlands are extremely varied in their physical features and have markedly local climates. They were also open to many different influences. The existence of many small settlements which housed artisans and weavers, the continuation and even the proliferation of the crofting system, encouraged by farmers so as to add the crofter's family to the rural dwellers for use as seasonal labourers, meant that there was little or no need for migrant labour here. The proximity to the Lothians and the difficulty of obtaining farms there also meant that in the area best suited to grain growing there was an influx of Lothian-trained men. All these factors led to the development of a very varied farm structure. An average of about 100–150 acres (40–60 ha) for farm sizes can be calculated, but it is fairly meaningless in an area where farms of over 400 acres (162 ha) occurred in close proximity to small-holdings of 4 to 5 acres (1–2 ha). Thus for Fife in the 1870s a breakdown of farming units in acres gives:

$\leqslant 5$	5–20	20–50	50–100	>100
565	441	201	224	808

Many commentators noted the slow rate of agricultural improvement in Fife as a whole. Wight (1778) gave many examples of greatly changed lands but these were on the large farms. He was also moved to comment on the bad state of many other units, and Thomson, writing in 1800, stated that Fife was still badly in need of enclosure. The slow pace of change may well have been the result of the existence of many small-holdings whose tenants were resistant to change and independently minded enough to support radical political and ecclesiastical movements.

Because of the varied nature of this area the type of farming which developed was also varied. The upland areas remained in grass until well into the twentieth century, with farming predominantly geared to cattle keeping and turnip growing. On the lower altitude lands, mixed farming occurred in which grain growing played a large part, especially so on the raised beach areas where a type of Lothian agriculture flourished. Carse lands such as those in the valley of the Earn, Strathmore and the Carse of Gowrie were mainly arable but difficult areas to farm. The wetness of the soil meant that high crown ridges were retained very late here, and it is interesting to note that it was in the Carse of Gowrie that the first really strong attempt at unionization of labour with a demand for the reduction in the working week's length occurred (Houston, 1958). With so much variation in farming and in the settlement pattern, it is not surprising to find the occurrence here of all styles and types of farm steading and labour housing.

Of the remaining Lowland areas it is tempting to classify them together into a north-eastern region. This would be mistaken: Angus had clear affinities with many parts of the Central Lowlands, while Kincardineshire had many of the attributes of Aberdeenshire and the coastal lowlands of the Moray Firth. Particularly distinctive of the area north of the Mounth was the labour system and its social hierarchy and customs. The work of Carter (1976, 1979) has put this into fine perspective, and Campbell (1977) has shown that in this area the improvement of agriculture was slow and had a distinctive element in its make-up in the very widespread use of crofters for the reclamation of marginal land. This latter feature caused the number of cottages in the landscape to remain high, for although the farm labour was housed in the 'kitchen and chaumer' system, in contradistinction to the bothies further south, the erection of new cottages, albeit of a very low standard, continued on the marginal lands until well into the nineteenth century. Despite the engrossment in many areas, Aberdeenshire and its neighbouring counties remained areas of small farms (preponderantly under 50 acres), some indeed smaller than the crofts of which many continued to be in operation into the twentieth century. Thus the stake in the land remained high in proportion to the total rural population. The crofters were clearly in a stronger economic position than their cottar or sub-tenant forebears had been. They had a land holding and many opportunities for wage earning, either in farming, artisan work or quarrying. However, in terms of acreage farmed the large units were most important and it was on these that the problems of Hypothec, restrictive leases, the distancing of labour by the tenants and the squalor of the chaumers were to be found. Whether it is just that the North-East has been more fully studied or that isolation by the Mounth has made it different, the fact remains that its rural social customs appear to be both distinctive and longer lasting. The actual farming system which came to typify the North-East was based on cattle rearing, with a strong emphasis on sown grass and turnips which gave the region greater stability in times of depression on the grain markets.

CONCLUSION

At the beginning of the period 1750–1870 rural Lowland Scotland was in the process of great agricultural changes engendered by a variety of factors. By 1870 the scene was set for agricultural recession, worst in areas concentrating on the production of cereals, especially wheat, for food imports rose from £77 million in the late 1860s to £140 million by 1877. Thus further change was inevitable, and the succeeding years saw Parliamentary legislation dealing with the problem of unexhausted leases and the game laws, accompanied by an increasing application of improved technology. However, by 1870 Scottish agriculture had evolved to a state which displayed considerable spatial variation, not only in its specialization but also in the varied methods of production.

This was due to a combination of factors which, despite Scotland remaining a land of tenant rather than owner-occupier farmers, had little to do with what Knight (1971) has termed the impress of authority.

REFERENCES

Adams, I. H. (1978). The agricultural revolution in Scotland: contributions to the debate. *Area* **10**, 198–203.

Adams, I. H. (1980). The agents of agricultural change. *In* 'The Making of the Scottish Countryside.' (M. L. Parry and T. R. Slater, ed.), 155–76. Croom Helm, London.

Alexander, J. (1852). 'Prize Essay on the Present Condition of Farm Servants in Scotland.' Aberdeen.

Alexander, W. (1873). 'Johnny Gibb of Gushetneuk, in the Parish of Pyketillin with Glimpses of the Paris Politics about A.D. 1843.' Edmonston and Douglas, Edinburgh.

Alexander, W. (1877). 'Notes and Sketches Illustrative of Northern Rural Life in the Eighteenth Century.' Aberdeen.

Anon. (1831). Designs of farm buildings, drawn up under the direction of a committee of the Highland Society of Scotland. *Prize Essays and Transactions of the Royal Highland and Agricultural Society of Scotland* NS **2**, 365–90.

Black, J. (1851–3). Report on the cottage accommodation in the district of Buchan, Aberdeenshire. *Transactions of the Royal Highland and Agricultural Society of Scotland* N.S. **V**, 92–96.

Blaikie, [?]. (1837). 'Report of the system of improvement followed on the muirs of Drumforskie and Drumquhyle, now called Charlestown', *Prize Essays and Transactions of the Royal Highland and Agricultural Society of Scotland* NS **V**, 97–121.

Bradley, A. G. (1927). 'When Squires and Farmers Thrived.' Methuen, London.

Britton, C. E. (1937). 'A Meteorological Chronology to A.D. 1450.' HMSO, London.

Caird, J. B. (1980). The reshaped agricultural landscape. *In* 'The Making of the Scottish Countryside' (M. L. Parry and T. R. Slater, ed.), 203–22. Croom Helm, London.

Campbell, R. H. (1977). The Scottish improvers and the course of agrarian change in the eighteenth century. *In* 'Comparative Aspects of Scottish and Irish Economic and Social History, 1600–1900.' (L. M. Cullen and T. C. Smout, ed.). 204–15. John Donald, Edinburgh.

Carter, I. R. (1976). Class and culture among farm servants in the North-East, 1840–1914. *In* 'Social Class in Scotland.' (A. A. MacLean, ed.), 105–27. John Donald, Edinburgh.

Carter, I. R. (1979). 'Farm Life in northeast Scotland, 1840–1914.' John Donald, Edinburgh.

Cobbett, W. (1831). 'Tour in Scotland.' London.

Cowie, J., Mitchell, J., Oliphant, L. and Wallace, J. (1843). Digest of essays on the bothy system of maintaining single farm-servants. *Prize Essays and Transactions of the Royal Highland and Agricultural Society of Scotland* **14**, 133–44.

Devine, T. M. (1978). Social stability in the eastern Lowlands of Scotland during the agricultural revolution, 1780–1840. *In* 'Lairds and Improvement in the Scotland of the Enlightenment.' (T. M. Devine, ed.). Glasgow, University of Strathclyde.

Dodgshon, R. A. (1977). Changes in Scottish township organization during the medieval and early modern periods. *Geografiska Annaler* **59**B, 51–67.

Dunbabbin, J. P. D. (1974). 'Rural Discontent in Nineteenth Century Britain.' Faber, London.

Flinn, M. W. (ed.) (1977). 'Scottish Population History.' Cambridge University Press, Cambridge.

Gray, M. (1973). Scottish emigration: the social impact of agrarian change in the rural lowlands, 1775–1875. *Perspectives in American History* **7**, 95–174.

Gray, M. (1976). North-East agriculture and the labour force, 1790–1875.' *In* 'Social Class in Scotland.' (A. A. MacLean, ed.), 86–104. John Donald, Edinburgh.

Horn, B. L. (ed.) (1966). Letters of John Ramsay of Ochtertyre. *Scottish History Society* 4th Series (3), Edinburgh.

Houston, G. (1958). Labour relations in Scottish agriculture before 1870. *Agricultural History Review* **6**, 27–41.

Knight, D. B. (1971). Impress of authority on landscape. *Tijdschrift voor Economische en Sociale Geographie* **62**, 383–7.

Lamb, H. H. (1966). 'The Changing Climate.' Methuen, London.

Lindsay, [?]. (1854). 'Report of the Proceedings of a Meeting held at Edinburgh on 10th January 1854, to form an Association for Promoting Improvement in the Dwellings and Domestic Conditions of Agricultural Labourers in Scotland.'

Lockhart, D. (1980). The planned villages. *In* 'The Making of the Scottish Countryside.' (M. L. Parry and T. R. Slater, ed.), 249–70. Croom Helm, London.

McCulloch, J. (1879). On the history of lands from the earliest times. *Transactions of the Royal Highland and Agricultural Society of Scotland* **11**, 1–23.

Morton, R. S. (1976). 'Traditional Farm Architecture in Scotland.' Ramsay Head, Edinburgh.

Parry, M. L. (1976). A Scottish agricultural revolution? *Area* **8**, 238–9.

Robb, J. (1861). 'The Cottage, the Bothy and the Kitchen; Being an Enquiry into the Condition of Agricultural Labourers in Scotland.' Blackwood, Edinburgh.

Robertson, G. (1829). 'Rural Recollections; or the Progress of Improvement in Agriculture and Rural Affairs.' Irvine.

Rothwell, H. (ed.) (1957). 'The Chronicle of Walter Guisborough.' Camden Society, 3rd Series, lxxxix.

Saunders, L. J. (1950). 'Scottish Democracy.' Oliver and Boyd, Edinburgh.

Shaw, H. (1980). The new rural industries: water power and textiles. *In* 'The Making of the Scottish Countryside.' (M. L. Parry and T. R. Slater, ed.), 291–317. Croom Helm, London.

Slater, T. R. (1980). The mansion and the policy. *In* 'The Making of the Scottish Countryside.' (M. L. Parry and T. R. Slater, ed.), 223–247. Croom Helm, London

Smith, G. (1835). Essay on the construction of cottages, suited for the dwellings of the labouring classes, and adapted to the climate of Scotland. *Prize Essays and Transactions of the Royal Highland and Agricultural Society of Scotland* NS **4**, 205–16.

Smith, J. H. (1973). 'Joe Duncan: The Scottish Farm Servant and British Agriculture.' Scottish Labour History Society, Edinburgh.

Smout, T. C. (1964). Scottish landowners and economic growth, 1650–1850. *Scottish Journal of Political Economy* **11**, 218–34.

Stephens, H. and Burn, R. S. (1861). The Book of Farm Buildings.' Blackwood, Edinburgh.

Stuart, H. (1853). 'Agricultural Labourers, as they were, are, and should be: an Address, Delivered to a General Meeting of the Forfarshire Agricultural Association.'

Thomson, A. (1837). On the settlement of crofters. *Prize Essays and Transactions of the Royal Highland and Agricultural Society of Scotland* NS **V**, 379–83.

Thomson, J. (1800). 'A General View of the Agriculture of Fife.' Edinburgh.

Walker, B. (1977). The influence of fixed farm machinery on building design in Eastern Scotland in the late eighteenth and nineteenth centuries. *Scottish Archaeological Forum* **8**, 52–74.

Walker, B. (1979). The vernacular buildings of north east Scotland: an exploration. *Scottish Geographical Magazine* **95**, (1), 45–60.

Whittington, G. (1975). Was there a Scottish agricultural revolution? *Area* **7**, 204–6.

Whyte, I. D. (1978). The agricultural revolution in Scotland: contributions to the debate. *Area* **10**, 203–5.

Whyte, I. D. (1979). 'Agriculture and Society in Seventeenth Century Scotland.' John Donald, Edinburgh.

Wight, A. (1778). 'Present State of Husbandry in Scotland, Extracts from Reports made to the Commissioners of the Annexed Estates.' 6 vols, Edinburgh.

8

Industrial Development, *c*. 1750–1980

G. Gordon

Between 1750 and 1980 the economic structure of Scotland has transformed from a predominantly rural to an urban-service economy, with an intervening phase when manufacturing was the largest sector of employment. In 1978 only 48 000 worked in farming, forestry and fishing in Scotland, compared to 611 000 in manufacturing industry and 1 191 000 in the service sector.

Formulation of a coherent image of development is hindered by the inadequacies of the statistical base which restrict accurate comparison across the whole industrial spectrum of primary, secondary and tertiary activities for the complete period. The literature has tended to stress the leaders at particular phases, thereby emphasizing innovation and transformation. This treatment is partial in terms of the pattern and the processes of industrial development. The direct contribution of the leaders to the domestic product was often quite small, although indirect employment and production tended to increase in proportion to the scale of the leading industries.

Most major industries associated with industrialization in Britain were present and prominent in Scotland, but there were important differences in the longevity of their success which suggests that industry in Scotland encountered particular problems. Failures were a feature of the initial stage of development in all industrial regions, so the comparatively early decline of leaders in Scotland must relate to such factors as inadequacies of management, high production costs, high transport costs, and a mismatch of product specialization and market demand.

Within Scotland, different regional specializations emerged, such as the making of jute at Dundee or the building of ships on the Clyde. Concentration was the spatial outcome of the progressive definition of the margins of profitability, involving factors such as the source of raw materials, the location of markets, regional variations in the cost and availability of labour, and spatial variations in the application of innovations. Industrial linkage furthered the aggregative process of concentration, notably in cotton textiles and the metal trades.

During the early stages of industrialization in the post-1750 period, the dispersed pattern reflected the importance of water power and the use of agricultural products as industrial raw materials. Gradually the demands of localized urban markets fostered an extensive pattern of small-scale manufacturing involving a wide variety of items united by an ability to operate successfully at that scale of production. Subsequently, the trend towards larger-scale production has eroded the base of the localized industrial sector. Services, including distribution, correlate strongly with urbanization, particularly the size of hinterland of urban centres. Similarly, employment in commercial and public administration is strongly associated with the functional importance of urban centres.

In addition to locational decisions concerning government departments and nationalized industry, the British Government, in the twentieth century, has increasingly been involved in attempts to influence the regional distribution of industries by means of various incentives and initiatives. Previously, government intervention had primarily involved encouraging exports and protecting domestic production.

The potential distribution of mining, quarrying and oil production is dictated by geology, but output depends upon demand, technology and comparative profitability and not merely the presence of the resource.

THE STAGES OF INDUSTRIAL DEVELOPMENT

The process of development was complex, partly aggregative, partly pulsatory, but five chronological stages can be identified to facilitate a detailed examination of trends and spatial patterns. Rostow (1960) proposed a model of the evolution of modern industrial societies which consisted of five stages of economic growth: the traditional society, the pre-conditions for 'take-off', the 'take-off', the drive to maturity, and the age of high mass consumption. According to Rostow 'take-off' involved 'the achievement of rapid growth in a limited group of sectors, where modern industrial techniques are applied'. In Britain, he identified cotton textiles as the leading sector in this stage which occurred during the last two decades of the eighteenth century. Hamilton (1932) propounded a two-phase framework of industrial development in Scotland in which the period from 1780 to 1830 was dominated by the cotton industry whereas from 1830 to 1880 the metal industries became the leading sector. The five stages identified in this chapter are an attempt to reconcile general theses of development with the peculiarities of the Scottish situation.

THE EARLY INDUSTRIAL PHASE, 1750–80

Dating the beginning of modern Scottish industry from 1759 when the Carron Ironworks was established near Falkirk can be justified on the grounds of the application of new techniques and the use of three fundamental mineral ingredients of the Industrial Revolution: coal, limestone and ironstone. None the less, the onset of industrialization was a slow, evolutionary process retaining many links with the pre-industrial era. Coal and ironstone had been worked for centuries, whilst some bloomeries had used indigenous supplies of ore. Traditional agricultural-based industries included brewing, milling and textiles. Finishing trades were represented by the craft guilds. Merchants organized the exchange and distribution of goods. Thus, in the years between 1700 and 1780, there were elements of continuity, albeit with adjustments in relative importance and absolute production, and change.

Wool and Linen

The making of woollen cloth was probably the most important aspect of manufacturing before 1707, although Lythe (1975) suggested that building was the greatest single industrial activity. Despite success as the principal source of Scottish exports, the woollen industry was relatively small-scale and characterized by higher costs than those operating in the major competing regions in England. In the eighteenth century, it was surpassed in importance by the linen industry, but woollen production continued at widely dispersed locations. Regional specialisms emerged, both in type, and quality, of product. Galashiels produced yarns; the centres at Kilmarnock and Stewarton in Ayrshire concentrated upon the making of bonnets and serges.

Campbell (1965) has noted that the linen industry had attained considerable domestic importance by the start of the eighteenth century. It was beset by technical and organizational imperfections: localized markets, inefficient methods of production, and inadequate supplies of raw materials of good quality. Slowly improvements were made, especially after 1727 when the Board of Trustees for Manufactures encouraged the adoption of innovations developed in the leading European centres of linen textiles.

Angus, Fife and Perth became the leading linen-producing counties, benefiting from their strategic location for importing flax from the Baltic countries. Further centres were situated in Ayrshire, Renfrewshire, Glasgow and Edinburgh. Regional specialization resulted in the latter group concentrating upon the making of fine cloth whilst Angus and Fife primarily produced coarse linens. The reasons for the spatial pattern of production were manifold, reflecting traditions and differential responses to newer markets at home and abroad. Turner (1966) suggested that the Glasgow region was more favourably located for trade with the American market and that it had a greater propensity to adopt innovations than the traditional centres around the Tay. Higher value goods could offset above average labour and transport costs, but the exercise would have been pointless unless a buoyant market had existed for finer cloths. This demand was fuelled by the wealthy adopting an elegant lifestyle, typified by the splendid town houses in London, Bath and Edinburgh and by the mansions in the colonies.

Chemicals and Coal

Linen bleaching, a time- and space-consuming process, provided an incentive for development in the chemical industry. Initially sulphuric acid was imported, but in 1749 Roebuck, Garbett and Cadell opened a sulphuric acid works at Prestonpans. The situation maintained traditional localization related to salt-panning, although the choice of site was strongly influenced by the fact that Cadell was a local coalmaster and landowner.

There was also a requirement for mordants and dyes. In 1753 a Liverpool company started the production of copperas at Hurlet, south of Glasgow, using local deposits of aluminous shales. Other ventures included the manufacture of cudbear.

In 1710 John Chamberlayne reported the view that the riches of Scotland lay underground, but the industrial markets for coal developed slowly in the eighteenth century. During the early industrial phase textile mills were water-powered. The market for coal was circumscribed by problems of transport and technical difficulties associated both with the invention of an efficient steam engine and the use of coal as a raw material in iron-making. Domestic consumption probably accounted for more than half of the coal produced from outcrops and vertical shafts which were scattered throughout the Central Lowlands, though rarely located far from water transport.

Iron

Founded by Roebuck, Garbett and Cadell, the Carron Company was the first Scottish concern to use coal in iron smelting. In selecting the site at Carron, Garbett considered it best suited to his locational requirements, with good-quality ironstone and coal available locally, adequate supplies of water, satisfactory communications via the Forth, and the possibility of obtaining supplies of charcoal from forests in the Highlands. Additionally, the purchase of a slit mill at Cramond provided a market for bar iron which was converted into strips and supplied to nailmakers. Within a decade concern about supplies led the company to negotiate access to haematite reserves in Cumberland and timber at Glenmoriston.

Ordnance became a specialism at Carron, aided by the introduction of skilled borers from Sussex. Problems relating to quality control and precision of manufacturing led to a temporary loss of government contracts in 1773, but the successful development of the carronade generated a period of renewed growth.

Natural access to the Forth offered a potential cost advantage in east-coast markets, but Scottish trade was also forging strong links with the Americas through the operation of Glasgow merchants. This trade imposed the costs of expensive overland transport to Glasgow, and the Carron Company was an enthusiastic supporter of proposals for a canal between the Forth and the Clyde. Started in 1769, by 1775 the canal had reached the outskirts of Glasgow. Improved communications facilitated the other specialism of the Carron works, the production of castings such as iron pots, stoves and fireplaces which were destined for the domestic and foreign market.

The difficulties encountered by the Carron Company in the first three decades of operation and the problems of transporting bulky raw materials and heavy finished goods may explain the slow diffusion of modern iron-making in Scotland. Two decades passed before a second works opened, at Wilsontown on the Lanarkshire moors, although a further eight plants were established between 1786 and 1801 at locations ranging from Muirkirk in Ayrshire to Balgonie in Fife.

Trade, Commerce and Banking

The Clyde tobacco trade was a major component of foreign commerce in the eighteenth century. Stevenson (1973) noted that the crossing to Glasgow from the American South on average took a fortnight less than the voyage to Bristol, the other leading British tobacco port. Much of the Clyde-imported tobacco was re-exported to other parts of Europe, although Glasgow still retains manufacturing ties with the tobacco industry.

The Atlantic trade furnished a ready market for Scottish goods such as linen cloth and iron pots and stoves. It also stimulated improvements in the infrastructure of communications, including the engineering works designed to open the Clyde to ocean-going shipping.

Landowners were influential promoters of the linen and woollen industries, coal-mining and mineral-working, transport developments, and the formation of financial agencies. Butt (1975) noted the frequency with which the nobility appeared as directors of the Bank of Scotland (1695), the Royal Bank (1727), and the British Linen Company (1746). The emergence of a national capital market was an important precondition for industrialization, although the degree of capital investment required was largely a function of the scale of operation, extent of mechanization and of land and building costs.

Construction

The building of planned villages, the New Town of Edinburgh, the western extension in Glasgow, industrial premises, and improvements in transport such as the Forth and Clyde Canal collectively provided a major stimulus to the building trades and allied industries. Demand for stone, slates, wood, lime and a variety of internal and external fittings encouraged increased production in a chain of associated activities ranging from quarrying to iron castings. Bulky materials were mostly carried by water, but there was invariably some carting involved. Indeed, increased activity and production in every sector of economic life in eighteenth-century Scotland must have involved the movement at a variety of spatial scales of substantial volumes of materials and manufactured goods.

The small scale of operation of the building trade was a characteristic feature of most sections of industry. In aggregate, however, the numerous individual ventures combined to form dynamic and important areas of industrial growth in the phase which established the pre-conditions for 'take-off'.

THE AGE OF COTTON, 1780–1830

Textiles

In dating the 'take-off' phase in Britain as 1783–1802 Rostow cited as empirical evidence the rapid increase in the imports of raw cotton. A similar situation occurred in Scotland, where cotton imports increased by approximately 700% between 1778–88 and by 500% between 1788–1801. The 'take-off' stage also involved the adoption of factory-based production, increased levels of capital investment in industry, the introduction of new techniques, and the spatial concentration of labour and production. Progressively the development of the cotton industry in Scotland satisfied all of these requirements, although the rate of attainment of the various criteria differed. The average rate of founding of new cotton mills provides further support for the thesis of 'take-off' in the last two decades of the eighteenth century. Between 1787 and 1795, 72 cotton mills were established, at an average of nine per year. Although the total number of mills continued to increase, reaching 192 by 1839, the average rate fell to less than three per year.

Around 1778 the production of raw cotton began to exceed demand, leading to a fall in price at a time when flax prices were increasing. Recognition of the opportunity was probably aided by the existence of strong links between Glasgow merchants and the plantation owners in America. Equally, the rapid adoption of cotton manufacturing was facilitated by the skills developed in the linen industry. West Scotland may have gained an advantage from previous experience in the making of fine linen, but the natural benefits arising from proximity to the points of importation should not be neglected.

At first, the primary locational factor was the need for adequate supplies of water, both for power and for the manufacturing process, which partly explained the scattering of mills between Spinningdale in Sutherland and Newton Stewart in Galloway. The speculative attractions of the industry provided further encouragement for landowners to seek partners in the establishment of a small mill. Despite these divergent tendencies, a pattern of regional concentration soon emerged, notably within a thirty kilometre radius of Glasgow. At the sub-regional level localization was evident with clusters of mills beside particular rivers such as the Levern Water, Gryfe and Cart in Renfrewshire. A group of mills in Perthshire, including the substantial Deanston and Stanley mills, illustrated the attraction of a location in a region reputed for textiles. However, the Glasgow district progressively acquired overwhelming dominance, and by 1839 91% of all the cotton mills in Scotland were located in Glasgow, Renfrewshire and Lanarkshire. The Glasgow mills were strategically located, in relation to supplies of coal which were brought by canal from Monklands, when steam-driven machinery was introduced in the first three decades of the nineteenth century. The adoption of technical innovations was a spasmodic process which reached fruition in the 1820s with the introduction of power-looms. Within a few decades Glasgow became the centre of this activity, replacing a more dispersed pattern of domestic hand-loom-weaving.

A number of large mills, such as New Lanark, Blantyre and Catrine, established in the initial formative surge, increasingly became acentric as the Johnstone–Glasgow district assumed locational supremacy.

An ebbing of the tide of buoyant growth may date from the first decade of the century, when Scottish cotton textiles first experienced stiff competition in foreign markets. However, the graph of employment and production continued to rise, even if the heady conditions of the formative flush had passed.

Cotton was a spectacular leader, but growth occurred in other sections of the textile industry. Between 1780–1830 ten woollen spinning mills were opened at Galashiels, and further mills at Hawick, Innerleithen, Earlston, Walker-burn and Peebles made the Border valleys the principal centre of growth in the Scottish woollen industry.

Although overshadowed by the growth of the cotton industry, the making of linen remained important, especially in the eastern counties, which had acquired prominence in this activity in the eighteenth century. The propensity towards innovation was inevitably slower in an established industry, but gradually new techniques were adopted, mirroring developments in the manufacture of cotton textiles.

Deane and Cole (1967) estimated that cotton contributed about 5% of the British national income at the start of the nineteenth century. Chapman (1972) has questioned the accuracy of their estimates, but at this period cotton was undeniably a minor direct contributor to national income. However, the indirect impact was substantial and cumulative, affecting chemical manufacturing, coal-mining, engineering, construction, transport, distribution, banking, finance, and commerce, in addition to the catalytic impact upon the basis of organization, spatial and structural, of society.

Allied Industries

Many subsidiary industries benefited from the growth in textiles. Finishing trades such as bleaching, printing, tambouring and the weaving of specialized goods were notable examples. In 1798 Charles Tennant started to produce chloride of lime, a bleaching agent, at St Rollox. His plant was situated near the Glasgow terminus of the Forth–Clyde and Monklands Canals, offering advantages in the distribution of manufactured goods and the acquisition of supplies of coal.

Generally, there was a strong spatial association between centres of cotton and linen production and the location of works specializing in bleaching, dyeing and printing, an early example of industrial linkage. Bleachfields and dyeworks also had similar locational requirements to those of the early cotton mills, notably the availability of adequate supplies of clean water.

Construction

In addition to the stimulus of industrial and urban growth, the construction industry benefited from engineering projects associated with the canal era. Although modest, when compared to the mileage constructed in England, several major canals were built in Scotland in this period: the Forth–Clyde, Monkland, Crinan, Aberdeenshire, Glasgow–Johnstone, Union, and Caledonian canals. The projects introduced the phenomenon of camps of navvies which, along with the building work, necessitated the provision of an array of supplies ranging from lime and stone to grain and beer. At the peak of construction, 3000 men were engaged in building the Caledonian Canal.

Paper and Brewing

Cotton manufacturing was unquestionably important in the process of industrialization in Scotland between 1780 and 1830, but the rate of growth and innovative contribution of one industry provide an inadequate statement of the varied pattern of that phase. Industrialization and urbanization created a consumer market which sustained and propagated numerous economic activities.

The importance of raw materials stimulated a variety of port industries, including soap-making and sugar-refining, with Greenock as the centre of the latter activity. Equally, publishing was an early example of a market-oriented industry. Paper-making and brewing serve as two examples of traditional industries which experienced both an increased in demand and an alteration to their geographical patterns of production.

Thomson (1974) stressed five locational factors which influenced the distribution of paper mills: 'The main requirements were a plentiful supply of fresh running water, a good market for the paper and a ready supply of raw material.' He listed the availability of suitable labour and of good transport as lesser factors. At the end of the eighteenth century the principal foci of paper-making were sited beside the Esk and Water of Leith in Midlothian, although important lesser clusters occurred at Aberdeen, Glasgow and the Carron valley. Proximity to major urban centres offered the twofold advantage of a ready supply of rags (the essential raw material of the industry) and a market for the finished product. None the less, the geographical distribution at this period clearly illustrated the prime importance of an adequate supply of water.

In the case of brewing, it might be expected that the importance of barley as the primary raw material would be reflected in the pattern of geographical distribution. Donnachie (1979) noted opposing locational attractions when he observed that 'despite the dominance of the brewing industry in the eastern counties, there was hardly a market town of any consequence in the Lowlands not possessed of at least one brewery'. Edinburgh was the major brewing centre, but the increase in the number of breweries in Glasgow 1800–1825 reflected the growth in demand in that area. Even in barley-growing districts, most breweries were situated in towns, indicating the importance of a market location in this classic example of an industry characterized by gains in weight and bulk during manufacturing.

Technically, paper-making and brewing retained the mantle of traditional industries. Thomson (1974) has recounted the halting introduction of machinery into paper-making with the main phase of transformation commencing in the 1820s. Similar approximately contemporaneous mechanization occurred in many industries, suggesting that a major shift in productive method and skills occurred towards the end of this period and some time after Rostow's 'take-off' stage.

THE AGE OF IRON, 1830–70

Iron

The age of iron correlated broadly with the drive to maturity of Rostow's model of economic development. Increased production occurred in a wide array of industries, partly consequent upon technical improvements but primarily ensuing from the expansion of demand in domestic and foreign markets. Iron-making, and a web of associated activities such as mining and engineering, supplanted cotton textiles as the leading sector in manufacturing. A second transformation of scale marked the transition from 'take-off' to the subsequent stage in industrial development. The leading sector was more extensively based in terms of spatial and organizational linkages. It accounted for a larger share of the total labour force and involved greater volumes of raw materials, fuel and finished goods compared with the period of 'take-off'.

After 1830 the juxtaposition of coal and blackband iron-stone in Monklands parish in North Lanarkshire stimulated a major phase of blast-furnace construction. The commercial application of the Neilson hot blast process of iron smelting transformed the profitability of the Scottish iron industry. Previously the industry had faced recurrent trading and investment problems, in addition to difficulties at certain locations in obtaining raw materials of a sufficiently high quality. The hot-blast process meant considerable savings in fuel costs, variously estimated at between 22/- (£1.10) and 32/- (£1.60) a ton, thereby improving the competitiveness of the Scottish industry. Development also occurred in Ayrshire after the discovery of reserves of blackband ironstone, but by 1848 Lanarkshire remained dominant, producing 426 000 tons of pig-iron compared to an output of 60 000 tons from Ayrshire furnaces. The Monklands (Coatbridge) district became one of the leading British iron-producing regions.

The growth in production is summarized in Table 8.1.

Between 50% and 70% of the pig-iron was either exported or sold in England, and as a result Scottish industry failed to experience the full generative growth which could have occurred if a greater proportion of pig-iron production had been finished and used in Scottish forges and engineering workshops. Few major blast-furnace companies owned works producing malleable iron. Admittedly, the process required special skills and some early ventures failed dismally. Collectively these factors may have persuaded the monopolistic ironmasters that re-investment in additional or

Table 8.1 Growth of Scottish pig-iron production

Year	Number of furnaces	Percentage change	Production (tons)	Percentage change
1796	21		16 000	
1830	27	+29	40 000	+150
1840	70	+159	241 000	+503
1850	143	+104	630 000	+161
1860	171	+20	1 000 000	+59
1870	156	−9	1 206 000	+21

Source: Data for furnaces and production extracted from tables in Lythe and Butt (1975) pp. 192–3

enlarged furnaces was prudent capitalism. None the less, forges were developed, notably at Monklands and in various districts of Glasgow. Iron was brought from other regions and mixed with Scottish pig-iron, which was unsuited to forging. After 1850, rising demand from railways and shipbuilding sponsored the erection of several new ironworks in the vicinity of Coatbridge. Contemporaneously, production costs of Cleveland pig-iron became lower than those in Scotland. The consequent increased use of Cleveland pig-iron favoured forges and ironworks located beside the Forth and Clyde Canal.

Foundries were widely distributed, with spatial concentrations related to urban and industrial development. Localized demand for agricultural or mining equipment, railway goods, and a wide range of machinery encouraged a dispersed pattern of production, but some locations progressively acquired a reputation for particular products or benefited from proximity to major centres of engineering. Thus the Springburn district of Glasgow won fame as the leading Scottish centre of railway locomotive construction.

Coal

Improvements in fuel efficiency between 1830 and 1870 were more than matched by increases in the total demand for coal. The apparently insatiable demands of the iron industry in the growth period after 1830 precipitated the opening of numerous new pits in Ayrshire, Lanarkshire, Stirlingshire and Fife. Butt (1975) recorded that 'In 1854, 368 colleries, employing 32 971 miners, produced 7 500 000 tons of coal'. At that time about one-third of the coal produced was consumed by the iron industry, but although coal output doubled between 1854–73, the amount destined for the iron industry only increased by about 200 000 tons. In the period 1830–70 many ironmasters entered the field of ownership of collieries and ironstone mines in order to

secure essential supplies of raw materials, and these policies enabled ironmasters to effect a considerable measure of integrated production.

It is tempting to deduce that the dictates of ironmasters shaped the character
and locational pattern of the coal mining industry. Fear of insufficient supplies
was certainly a powerful incentive for intervention into this related economic
activity. Yet the colliery giants, like William Baird & Company, could only
operate profitably by seeking appropriate markets for the various grades of coal
produced at their mines. Moreover, there was a growing demand for house coal
and for grades suited to use in steam boilers in factories, railway locomotives,
and steamships.

Textiles

One major exception to the general pattern of aggregative, sustained growth
was the cotton industry. Leading cotton manufacturers, in their evidence to
the Select Committee on Manufactures, Commerce and Shipping in 1833,
noted stiffer competition in foreign markets and speculated that the Manchester district may have assumed supremacy in sections of the British industry. If
the initiative had passed to Manchester, the Scottish industry still remained an
important employer throughout this period. Indeed, the numbers of spindles,
power-looms and employees continued to increase. A decline in the number of
mills after 1838 indicated a phase of consolidation and concentration. Between
1830–60 the cotton industry was overshadowed by the rapid growth of
iron-making. The reversal of growth after the middle of the nineteenth century
has consequently been interpreted as the collapse of the industry. Relative
decline compared to the new industrial leaders was massive, if inevitable, since
the leaders were experiencing the accelerative phase of the growth curve.
Absolute decline was less marked. For example, the net loss of employment
between 1861 and 1890 amounted to some 6000 jobs. Over a period of three
decades the competitiveness of the Scottish cotton industry had been gradually
eroded, and after 1857 there was a phase of redirection and contraction, with
significant structural and spatial dimensions. The making of cotton thread at
Paisley emerged as an important area of growth, but production of other lines
ceased and, notably in Glasgow, mills closed.

In the woollen industry, which in 1838 employed 5076 people, one-seventh
of the number engaged in cotton mills, the most spectacular development of
the period was the growth of tweed manufacturing at Galashiels. Other
specialisms included hosiery, notably at Hawick, and carpet-making at
Kilmarnock and Glasgow.

Aberdeen and Dundee experienced opposing trends in textile production
during the first half of the nineteenth century. The more northerly location of

Aberdeen ultimately operated to the disadvantage of local cotton, linen and woollen manufacturers because of the comparative isolation from the main markets and the high costs incurred in transporting coal from the Central Lowlands. Contemporaneously, the jute industry blossomed at Dundee. In explaining this development, Turner (1966) noted that Dundee was an established producer of coarse and heavy linens. Experimentation in the making of bagging paved the way for the introduction of jute in 1823. The growth of manufacturing created a massive demand for cheap, strong bagging which Dundee mills made from flax-tow and jute. The subsequent boom in jute production meant that by the 1860s employment in jute- and linen-making in Dundee almost equalled that for the Scottish cotton industry.

Transport and Tertiary Activities

In a study of the nineteenth-century Scottish carrier trade, Morris (1980) concluded that by 1861 rail links were dominant in the movement of goods between major urban centres while carters serviced more local connections. The first railways were built to provide access from coalfields to the major centres of consumption and distribution. Thus the Monklands–Kirkintilloch railway (1826) provided a connection with the Forth and Clyde Canal at Kirkintilloch, and thence, with markets in Glasgow and east Scotland. The elaboration of the rail network involved a major phase of construction between 1835 and 1860 which included the building of the major trunk routes and of specialized, often short, connections related to the movement of minerals. Railways also provided a substantial measure of direct employment and created a range of demands for manufactured goods and raw materials.

Economic and urban growth stimulated the development of tertiary activities. In the second half of the nineteenth century there was a marked increase in the number of clerical, sales and supervisory positions, reflecting the enlarged importance of public and professional services and retailing. Equally, the dimensions of society were transformed, with a sharper structural and spatial definition of socio-economic class.

THE LATE INDUSTRIAL PHASE, 1870–1914

Shipbuilding, steelmaking and marine engineering displayed the phenomenon of accelerative growth that had characterized the development in preceding periods of cotton textiles and ironmaking. By contrast, some industries, particularly textiles, iron and coal, were either in decline or experiencing severely reduced rates of growth. The difficulties primarily resulted from increasing competition in foreign markets as industrialization entered the post 'take-off' stage in the United States and Germany.

In general, Scotland failed to achieve even a proportionate share of the growth in consumer industries. The assets of raw materials and industrial skills were insufficient to compensate for the peripheral position in relation to the core of the British markets and for technical inadequacies and a record of declining profitability in several leading industries. The period 1870–1914 was a pivotal one for industrial locational decision-making in Britain, and Scotland only scored a limited measure of success during this phase.

Within Scotland substantial areal variations occurred in the relative import-ance of the major sectors of employment. Farming remained dominant in many parts of the Highlands and Southern Uplands, although manufacturing and service activities were gaining in importance as these areas became urbanized. Within the Lowlands there was also considerable spatial variation. Carstairs (1968) noted that in 1881 manufacturing provided the main source of employment in Dundee and Glasgow (66% and 49% respectively) whereas service activities were dominant in Edinburgh (64%) and Aberdeen (50%). The cities had above average rates of female employment, but the nature of the employment varied: in 1881 in Edinburgh 44% of women and girls were engaged in domestic service, whereas in Dundee over 80% worked in manufacturing.

Iron and Steel

Adams (1978) wrote that 'After 1871 the ironmasters invested heavily in open-hearth steelworks, especially for ship plate, and by the late 1880s Scotland was the leading open-hearth steel district in Britain'.

The first steelworks (Hallside), sited near Cambuslang, was not promoted by an ironmaster. Warren (1965) noted that sites at Coatbridge and on the Ayrshire coast were considered and rejected. The selection of Hallside may have incorporated location prejudices inherited from the age of iron, but it could be justified in terms of local coal and ore supplies and good access by means of the Caledonian Railway. With the exception of the plant at Glengar-nock in Ayrshire, the Scottish steel industry followed the locational lead set by Hallside, and a distinct concentration emerged in a south-easterly corridor beside the Clyde stretching from Blochairn in Glasgow to Wishaw in Lanark-shire.

The pioneers in the Scottish steel industry faced daunting technical prob-lems because the high phosphoric Scottish ores were unsuitable for use in the Bessemer process. This explained the prominence of the open-hearth method in Scotland and it also encouraged the substitution of imported haematite for

Scottish ores. The steel industry specialized in ship plate and was therefore dependent upon the economic health of shipbuilding. Fortunately, the client was enjoying good health, and by 1913 the Scottish production of 1 431 000 tons of steel ingots and castings exceeded by 62 000 tons the output of pig-iron.

Between 1870 and 1914 the iron industry was faced with the need to adapt if it was to succeed in a more competitive international economy. The industry was wasteful of natural resources and technically laggard. Yet the start of the period witnessed a phase of building with 11 new ironworks opening in the Falkirk district. Major reconstruction occurred at Carron, where a new line of blast furnaces, two foundries and a brick-works were built in an attempt to improve the competitiveness of the company. None the less, Campbell (1961) recorded that the Carron works continued to be surpassed by German, American and some English competitors in terms of blast-furnace performance and efficiency of the layout of the plant. Other Scottish producers also struggled to keep pace with the new leaders in terms of costs and profitability.

There was a considerable, if fluctuating, demand for light castings, particularly for the building industry. This offered some encouragement to the iron industry but simultaneously posed serious problems. The crux of the dilemma was created by the scale of the Scottish iron industry. Total output was considerably in excess of the figure which might be expected on the basis of Scotland's share of the population of Britain, so if Scottish production was to be maintained, iron goods had to continue to be sold in English or foreign markets. The problems of the iron industry had repercussions for ironstone- and coal-mining. By 1913 Scottish iron ore production amounted to 600 000 tons, a mere 20% of the volume of output in the 1870s. The impact upon the coal industry was more subtle, involving a weakening of the major causative relationship which had fostered the rapid growth of coal-mining in the nineteenth century. By 1913 coal output reached 41 000 000 tons, and exports had become an important outlet for excess production, particularly from the Ayrshire and Fife coalfields.

Shipbuilding

In 1913 the 39 Clydeside shipyards launched a record 756 976 tons of shipping. Between 1870 and 1914 Scotland was responsible for approximately one-third of the total production from British shipyards and, in the peak year of 1913, it made nearly one-fifth of the world tonnage. Not surprisingly Campbell (1964) commented that 'From the 1870s until the First World War, shipbuilding was the chief growth point of the Scottish economy'. It provided a ready market for iron, and later steel, and stimulated the manufacturing of a wide range of marine engineering. Equally, it was marine engineering that initiated the

major phase of development of shipbuilding on the Clyde through experimental work on steam engines and boilers. Shipbuilding in the nineteenth
century was one industry in which Scotland was uniquely successful in
establishing and maintaining a reputation for invention and the application of
scientific and technological research to commercial production.

By 1850 the Clydeside yards were beginning to specialize in iron ships,
although wooden clippers remained in demand and were built at various
Scottish yards ranging from Dumbarton to Aberdeen. Between 1880 and
1890 steel ships became dominant. Scottish steel-makers negotiated specially
reduced prices with the shipyards in order to compete with imports of
cheaper steelplate.

Engineering

Between 1870 and 1914 the heavy industries (coal, iron and steel, shipbuilding
and engineering) assumed overwhelming dominance of the industrial economy, industrial employment and capital investment of Scotland. A crude
measure of success is provided by the fact that in 1913–14 Scotland had the
lowest unemployment rate of any British industrial region.

To the late Victorian Scottish industrialist the future seemed bright for
heavy engineering. There was a world demand for ships, locomotives, boilers,
bridges and heavy plant, and Scotland offered the prospect of the marriage of
local resources in raw materials and industrial skills. The natural focus for the
industry lay in West Scotland, especially along the corridor which reached
from Clydebank to Motherwell.

Some investors were attracted to light and electrical engineering, but on a
modest scale compared to heavy engineering. It is tempting to infer that the
outsider viewed the prospects for light engineering with greater enthusiasm,
but the only major investment, the Singer sewing machine factory at
Clydebank, was probably primarily attracted by three factors: the manufacture of cotton thread at Paisley, regional skills in engineering and textiles, and
the availability of a surplus of female labour at Clydebank.

Several attempts were made to produce motor-cars in Scotland, but only the
Albion Company in Glasgow, which from 1913 specialized in commercial
vehicles, had lasting success. Various explanations can be proffered for failure,
but none of the ventures succeeded in creating a marriage of technical and
commercial acumen. Most enterprises were located in and around Glasgow,
although in 1914 the Arrol-Johnston car was being made at Dumfries.

Other trends

In textiles the processes of areal and product specialization continued against a general background of declining employment and production in most sectors of the industry. Modest increases in employment and substantial growth in production occurred in brewing. The difficulty of balanced and comparative assessment of industrial importance was highlighted by the fact that while some 48000 people were employed in the textile industries of Dundee in 1911, just over 2400 were engaged in brewing in Scotland. Whisky distilling, another traditional industry, faced severe over-production at the start of the twentieth century. The basic ingredient of blended whisky, grain spirit, was produced from Lowland distilleries whereas malt whisky was centred upon Speyside and Argyll.

Distillation of oil from shale deposits in West Lothian furnished a further example of a resource-based industry. Peak production was reached in 1913 when 3280000 tons of shale were worked.

In several industries the final decades of the period saw distinct trends towards rationalization of production with amalgamations and the establishment of formal connections between associated activities. None the less, the phase was typified by the formation of a multiplicity of new enterprises, both large and small as the Scottish economy reached the zenith of industrialization.

RECESSION AND REDIRECTION, 1914–80

An attempt is made in Table 8.2 to construct comparable statistical employment categories for 1907 and 1976 in order to gain an insight into the changes in the structure of industrial employment. There was a marked decline in the mining and textile categories which contrasted with substantial growth in construction and in chemicals and allied industries. Some categories, such as paper and printing, displayed a pronounced degree of stability in terms of total employment.

The process of structural concentration affected most sectors, producing a small number of giants who exercised control in activities as divergent as shipbuilding, banking and brewing. There was further refinement of geographical patterns involving both regional concentration of particular activities and, especially after 1945, a trend towards decentralization of industrial location with the construction of industrial estates on the outskirts of major cities and at the New Towns.

From 1920 onwards the export-oriented basic industries, with the solitary exception of whisky distilling, faced decline as worldwide industrialization eroded the markets for Scottish goods. Technological change associated with

Table 8.2 Employment by major manufacturing categories in 1907 and 1976 (in rank order)

	1907		1976
Iron and steel, engineering and shipbuilding	230 691	Metal manufacture, engineering, vehicles and shipbuilding	270 000
Textiles, clothing, leather and canvas	223 291	Construction, bricks, pottery, glass and cement	188 000
Mining and quarrying	130 557	Food, drink and tobacco	91 000
Building, clay and stone	80 557		
Food and drink	70 968	Textiles, clothing, leather and footwear	90 000
Paper and printing	44 440	Paper, printing and publishing	44 000
Timber	34 480		
Public utilities	29 395	Mining and quarrying	35 000
Chemicals	9 274	Chemicals and allied industries and petroleum	32 000
Other metal trades	5 555		
		Public utilities	29 000
		Other metal trades	27 000
		Timber and Furniture	20 000

Sources: Lythe and Butt (1975) Table 33; based on Final Report Census of Production 1907, 19
Scottish Abstract of Statistics 1980, 44

new sources of energy and the general development of a wide array of substitutes for traditional materials furthered the cumulative trend towards decline in most major sectors of manufacturing and extractive employment.

Heavy Industry

The nexus which had emerged by 1914 left the heavy industries vulnerable to any recession in trade or demand for capital goods. The worldwide economic recession in the early 1930s produced that situation.

In shipbuilding the nadir was reached in 1933 when production on the Clyde dwindled to 7% of the peak 1913 tonnage. Unemployment soared as work ceased on projects such as the building of the passenger liner the *Queen Mary* at Clydebank. Periodic and seasonal fluctuations in output and demand for materials were normal, but the scale of amplitude of fluctuation was exceptional. Government intervened and attempted to stimulate demand for ships.

Paradoxically, the Scottish share of British output increased in the inter-war period, probably because Clydeside specialized in passenger liners.

Structural re-organization between 1918 and 1939 led to larger groupings of Clydeside yards through horizontal integration and the acquisition of controlling interests in steel firms. Both measures indicated growing concern about the competitiveness of Scottish shipbuilding.

The steel industry was also beset with problems resulting from inefficient plant and high costs of production. Modernization proceeded with the extension of the Dalzell steelworks, the making of steel billets at Glengarnock, and the reconstruction of two works at Clydebridge to produce an integrated plant. Output of steel increased between the wars, but by 1939 the production of pig-iron amounted to less than one-quarter of the 1912 tonnage. Scottish steelmakers had increasingly turned to foreign pig-iron and imported and local scrap iron.

In the decade after 1945 demand exceeded supply, rekindling interests in new projects. Although support was voiced for new locations at Rosyth and Inchinnan, the major new development was sited in the heart of the existing steelmaking region at Ravenscraig. Colvilles estimated that in doing so they saved 45% compared to the costs of a new greenfield location.

Government also decided to favour a strip mill being built at Ravenscraig. Changes in the markets for steel had left the Scottish mills at a disadvantage because of their inability to produce the correct form of finished steel. Government hoped to solve that deficiency and simultaneously to remove a major obstacle standing in the way of relocating part of the dynamic car industry in Central Scotland. With the opening in the early 1960s of the Rootes factory at Linwood and the British Motor Corporation tractor plant at Bathgate it finally appeared that a new growth leader had been found. In fact both plants faced considerable teething troubles, exacerbated at Linwood by various changes in ownership and management policy.

As recently as 1967, when the steel industry was nationalized, forecasts suggested an expansion in the demand for steel and a substantial, if reshaped, output in Scotland. In fact, the projections were over-optimistic, and the industry has been pruned to a cluster of plants in the Ravenscraig–Gartcosh axis and a solitary outlier at Glengarnock. A final flirtation with the notion of a coastal location resulted in the development of a deepwater ore terminal at Hunterston, linked by rail with Ravenscraig.

From the mid 1950s there has been a pronounced downward trend in the tonnage of shipping launched from Scottish yards. In the mid 1960s the industry was in a state of crisis as yards faced mounting losses and lacked the ability to re-organize production, to adopt new techniques and meet new market demands. Massive re-organization led to the creation of two regional groups based upon the Lower and Upper Clyde. Further moments of crisis occurred, and doubts still remain about the viability of particular yards and the future size of the industry.

Success occurred in particular sectors, notably at the yards of Scott Lithgow and Yarrow. Yarrow had specialized in the production of sophisticated naval vessels, thereby gaining a degree of independence from the vicissitudes of the commercial market.

Between 1913 and 78 coal production in Scotland declined from a peak of over 41 000 000 tonnes to a mere 11 400 000 tonnes. The 1978 figure was produced by 17 collieries whereas, in 1930, some 400 collieries were in production. By 1978 almost a quarter of coal production came from open-cast workings using large-scale modern excavation techniques. The decline in output reflected the changes in the markets for coal and the sources of energy (Fig. 8.1). Although the electricity industry is now the major market, the use of coal is spatially concentrated into the South of Scotland Electricity Board (SSEB) area. Within that region 56% of electricity is produced by coal-fired plants, and so the fate of the coal industry is inexorably linked to decisions relating to future demand and the satisfaction of that demand in the SSEB area. Much depends upon the comparative costs of various competing methods of electricity generation.

Light Industry

From the 1930s a succession of legislation has been enacted with the aim of encouraging diversification and reviving declining industrial regions in Britain. Gradually the spatial extent and financial ramifications increased, until by 1979 (Fig. 8.2) all of Scotland qualified for some measure of financial assistance towards industrial development. These measures have resulted in the creation of a considerable number of jobs which might not otherwise have been attracted to Scotland. By 1979 foreign-owned companies were responsible for about 100 000 jobs, one-sixth of the total in Scottish manufacturing. Their share of the expansion in the light industry sector was appreciable, notably in instrument engineering, electrical engineering and mechanical engineering, in which foreign-owned companies, in 1975, accounted respectively for 61%, 41% and 38% of Scottish employment.

Recent plant closures and consequent redundancies have fuelled fears that Scottish light industry would suffer severely as foreign-owned companies rationalized their European operations. A recent study (Hood and Young, 1979) concluded that this process was occurring and new growth would be required to maintain current levels of employment.

The development of light industry has been accompanied by a considerable measure of success at a variety of locations throughout Central Scotland,

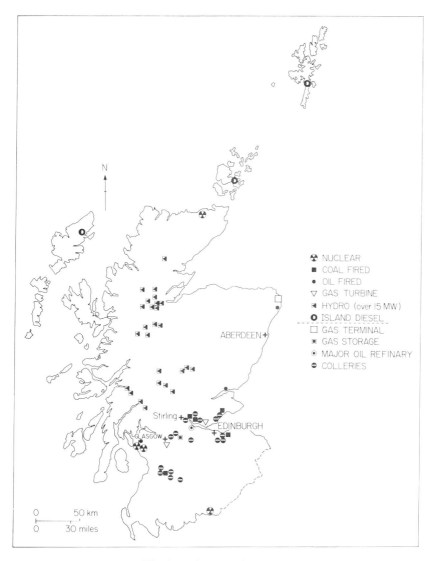

Fig. 8.1   Sources of energy, 1980

especially in the New Towns. In particular sectors spatial localization has emerged such as the making of cash registers at Dundee and electronics at Glenrothes, Greenock, Cumbernauld, Newhouse and Edinburgh.

Industries associated with the production of food and drink have experienced modest growth in employment and substantial increases in volume and

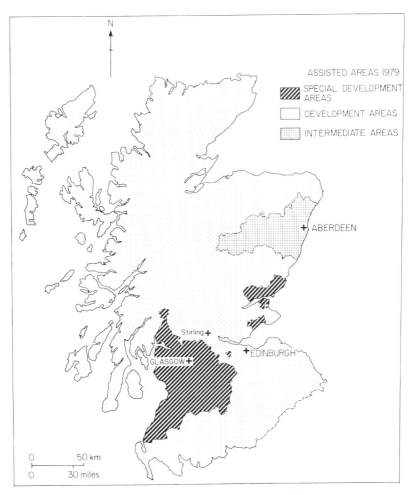

Fig. 8.2   Assisted Areas, 1979. (Source: DOE)

value of their products. Scotland's leading export industry, whisky production, involves a comparatively small labour force, most of which is employed at
the Lowland grain distilleries and bottling plants. In the late 1950s a phase of
amalgamations quickly reduced the number of brewery companies to a
handful of giants. Modernization also favoured the closure of many breweries
with production concentrated into a small number of large plants in Edinburgh, Glasgow and Alloa.

Jute, woollen and cotton textiles continue to be important specializations at
Dundee, the Border towns, and Paisley respectively. In every case employ-

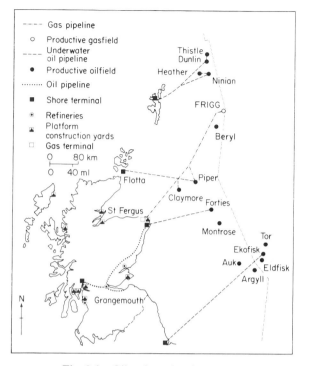

Fig. 8.3   Oil and gas developments

ment has declined, and market problems continue to affect these industries. Glasgow has retained a significant centrally located cluster of clothing trades.

The discovery of North Sea oil and gas resources in the 1960s initiated a flood of speculative writing about the possible effects on the Scottish economy. By the 1980s views have moderated. Although the production of oil has increased rapidly and a considerable number of jobs have been created, particularly in construction and the servicing of offshore production platforms, many platforms yards (Fig. 8.3) have failed to attract orders. In addition, several protracted planning battles may have generated an apparent climate of opposition to the building of refineries and related projects at new locations.

Between 1946 and 1978 the volume of crude oil handled at Grangemouth increased from 460 000 to 8 600 000 tonnes. It was identified as a growth centre in the economic plans of the early 1960s, but the anticipated accelerative growth has not ensued. In part, this was due to a misunderstanding of the nature of the industry and also to over-optimism about cumulative growth.

Conclusion

With the emergence of the tertiary sector in the twentieth century there appeared the prospect of stability in employment because the tertiary sector is primarily related to the size and economic health of the domestic market. Recently, technological and demographic changes have called this assumption into question.

The new industrial developments associated with North Sea oil maintain the established locational attractions of natural resources and strategic situations. On various occasions it has been argued that Scotland offered an industrial bridgehead position between America and Europe. Indeed American investment can be viewed in these terms. Can natural resources or situational advantages attract a new major industrial leader or will decline become the leading sector?

REFERENCES

Adams, I. H. (1978). 'The Making of Urban Scotland.' Croom Helm, London.
Butt, J. (1967). 'The Industrial Archaeology of Scotland.' David and Charles, Newton Abbot.
Butt, J. (1971). 'Robert Owen, Prince of Cotton Spinners: A Symposium.' David and Charles, Newton Abbot.
Campbell, R. H. (1961). 'Carron Company.' Oliver and Boyd, Edinburgh.
Campbell, R. H. (1964). Scottish shipbuilding: its rise and progress. Scottish Geographical Magazine 80, 107–113.
Campbell, R. H. (1965). 'Scotland since 1707.' Oxford University Press, Oxford.
Campbell, R. H. and Dow, J. B. A. (1968). 'Source Book of Scottish Economic and Social History.' Oxford University Press, Oxford. 83–6.
Carstairs, A.M. (1968). In 'Dundee and District.' (S.J. Jones, ed.). British Association, Dundee. 320–1.
Chapman, K. (1974). The structure and development of the oil-based industrial complex at Grangemouth. Scottish Geographical Magazine 90, 106–7.
Chapman, S. D. (1972). 'The Cotton Industry in the Industrial Revolution.' Macmillan, London. 63–8.
Cmnd. 2188 (1963). 'Central Scotland: A Programme for Development and Growth.' HMSO, London.
Coull, J. R. (1963). The historical geography of Aberdeen. Scottish Geographical Magazine 79, 89–90.
Deane, P. and Cole, W. A. (1967). 'British Economic Growth 1688–1959.' Cambridge University Press, Cambridge. 185–8.
Donnachie, I. (1979). 'A History of the Brewing Industry of Scotland.' John Donald, Edinburgh.

Gordon, G. (1977). *In* 'A Geography of Scotland.' (K. J. Lea, ed.). David and Charles, Newton Abbot. 207–10.

Habakkuk, H. J. and Deane, P. (1965). *In* 'The Economics of Take-off into Sustained Growth.' (W. W. Rostow, ed.). Macmillan, London. 71.

Hamilton, H. (1932). 'The Industrial Revolution in Scotland.' Oxford University Press, Oxford. 1.

Hood, N. (1973). A geography of competition: The Scottish woollen textile industry. *Scottish Geographical Magazine* **89**, 74–80.

Hood, N. and Young, S. (1979). 'European Development Strategies of US-owned Manufacturing Companies located in Scotland.' HMSO, London.

Houston, J. M. (1948). Village planning in Scotland 1745–1845. *Advancement of Science* **5**, 129–32.

Lythe, S. G. E. and Butt, J. (1975). 'An Economic History of Scotland 1100–1939.' Blackie, Glasgow.

Macpherson, A. (1964). Scotch Whisky. *Scottish Geographical Magazine* **80**, 99–106.

Miller, R. and Tivy, J. (ed.) (1958). 'The Glasgow Region.' British Association, Glasgow.

Miller, T. R. (1958). 'The Monkland Tradition.' Nelson, Edinburgh.

Morris, A. S. (1980). The Nineteenth Century Scottish Carrier Trade: Patterns of Decline. *Scottish Geographical Magazine* **96**, 74–82.

Murray, G. T. (1973). 'Scotland: The New Future.' Blackie, Glasgow. 85–106.

Robertson, C. J. (1964). New Industries and New Towns in Scotland's Industrial Growth. *Scottish Geographical Magazine* **80**, 114–23.

Robertson, C. J. (1979). *In* 'Looking at Lothian.' (J. B. Barclay, ed.). Royal Scottish Geographical Society, Edinburgh. 9–10.

Rostow, W. W. (1970). 'The Stages of Economic Growth.' Cambridge University Press, Cambridge.

Salmon, R. B. (1979). *In* 'Looking at Lothian.' (J. B. Barclay, ed.). Royal Scottish Geographical Society, Edinburgh. 14–17.

Scottish Economical Bulletin (1980). Overseas investment in Scottish manufacturing industry. **20**, 11.

Slaven, A. (1975). 'The Development of the West of Scotland 1750–1960.' Routledge and Kegan Paul, London.

Smout, T. C. (1969). 'A history of the Scottish people 1560–1830.' Collins, London.

Stevenson, W. I. (1973). Some aspects of the geography of the Clyde tobacco trade in the eighteenth century. *Scottish Geographical Magazine* **89**, 19–35.

Thomson, A. G. (1974). 'The Paper Industry in Scotland 1590–1801.' Scottish Academic Press, Edinburgh.

Turner, W. H. K. (1964). Wool Textile Manufacture in Scotland. *Scottish Geographical Magazine* **80**, 81–9.

Turner, W. H. K. (1966). The concentration of the jute and heavy linen manufacturing industry in east central Scotland. *Scottish Geographical Magazine* **82**, 29–45.

Warren, K. (1965). Locational problems of the Scottish iron and steel industry since 1760, Part I. *Scottish Geographical Magazine* **81**, 18–36.

Warren, K. (1965). Locational problems of the Scottish iron and steel industry since 1760, Part II. *Scottish Geographical Magazine* **81**, 87–103.

Welch, R. V. (1974). Manufacturing change on Greater Clydeside in the 1950s and 1960s. *Scottish Geographical Magazine* **90**, 168–78.

West of Scotland Plan (1975). 'Strathclyde: the Economic Impact of Offshore Oil.' Glasgow.

Wilson, G. (1980). 'Industrial coal markets in Fife 1760–1860. *Scottish Geographical Magazine* **96**, 83–90.

Youngson, A. J. (1966). 'The Making of Classical Edinburgh.' Edinburgh University Press, Edinburgh.

9

The Highlands: Changing Approaches to Regional Development

D. Turnock

Today the Highlands constitute a part of rural Scotland which has experienced a sharp decline in population during the present century (Osborne, 1958). The 'Outer Regions'* in general have failed to match the resources of the Central Belt, where urban-industrial development has been concentrated, and have evolved complementary economies with an emphasis on the primary sector. At a time of falling employment in agriculture and fishing, some expansion of industry in suitable 'growth centres' is being stimulated, and interesting experiments have been carried out to further this process (Ashton and Long, 1972). Undoubtedly the most impressive efforts have been made in the Highlands by the *Highlands and Islands Development Board* (abbreviated HIDB) on whose area of responsibility this essay concentrates. (Adjacent areas to the east and south-east are also involved in some of the discussion covering the earlier periods.) In view of the great extent of Scotland's rural periphery it is necessary to explain why the Highland area should be supported by the elaborate machinery of a development board and why this one region should merit special attention in a volume of essays pursuing a thematic approach to the historical geography of Scotland. It is possible to present statistical tables to demonstrate the particular gravity of depopulation in the Highlands, yet in shifts of relative demographic strength the region is different only in degree from other Outer Regions (Table 9.1). It is also true that unlike the Grampian and Tayside regions the Highlands focus on a relatively small regional capital.

* Such an area was first mentioned by Scottish Office (1966) (*The Scottish economy 1965–1970: a plan for expansion* Edinburgh: HMSO Cmnd. 2864). The Outer Regions covered 83.5% of the area of Scotland but only 26.5% of the population and 19.0% of employment in manufacturing. Table 9.1 includes the equivalent area expressed in terms of the new administrative regions.

191

Table 9.1 Population trends of Scottish regions

Region	Census Year										
	1801		1921			1961			1971		
	A	B	A	B	C1	A	B	C2	A	B	C3
Highlands & Islands[a]	325·4	20·2	371·4	7·6	14·1	304·2	5·9	−18·1	307·5	5·9	1·1
Grampian	211·9	13·2	438·6	9·0	107·0	440·4	8·5	0·4	438·6	8·4	−0·4
Tayside	214·7	13·3	388·4	7·9	80·9	397·8	7·7	2·4	397·6	7·6	0·0
Borders	79·9	5·0	112·9	2·3	41·3	102·2	2·0	−9·5	98·5	1·9	−3·6
Dumfries & Galloway	106·7	6·6	143·3	2·9	34·3	146·5	2·8	2·2	143·2	2·7	−2·2
Outer Regions	938·6	58·4	1454·6	29·8	55·0	1391·1	26·9	−4·4	1385·4	26·5	−0·4
East Central[b]	335·3	20·8	1163·2	23·8	246·9	1275·5	24·6	9·6	1335·8	25·6	4·7
West Central[c]	334·5	20·8	2264·7	46·4	557·0	2512·7	48·5	10·9	2506·5	47·9	−0·3
Central Belt	669·8	41·6	3427·9	70·2	411·8	3788·2	73·1	10·5	3842·3	73·5	1·4
SCOTLAND	1608·4		4882·5		203·3	5179·3		6·1	5227·7		0·9

Column A Total regional population in thousands
Column B Percentage share of total Scottish population
Column C1 Percentage change in regional population 1801–1921
Column C2 Percentage change in regional population 1921–1961
Column C3 Percentage change in regional population 1661–1971

[a] HIDB area
[b] Central Fife and Lothian Regions
[c] Strathclyde Region less Argyll & Bute districts and islands of Arran and Cumbrae
Source: Census of Scotland

Yet Inverness with 34.4 thousand people in somewhat larger than Dumfries (29.4) and Hawick (16.7), the largest towns in Dumfries & Galloway and Borders respectively. The aim of this essay is to consider, broadly, in what ways the region has been regarded as a problem area (Fig. 9.1). It appears that government has shown concern ever since Scotland was first established as a state in medieval times, but the nature of the problem to be solved and the strategies to be contemplated show distinct variations.

THE MEDIEVAL PERIOD: RESISTANCE TO FEUDALISM

The medieval Scottish kingdom successfully extended its authority over virtually the whole country with the exception of the Highlands. In the north-west this anomaly is understandable in view of the extremely tenuous communication links and the lack of any significant economic potential to

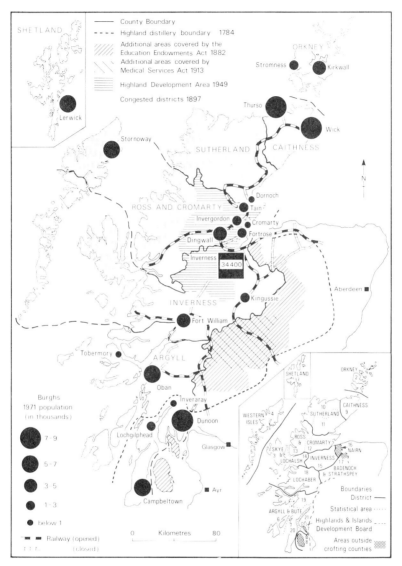

Fig. 9.1   Problem regions in the Highlands

justify completing the system of royal burghs. Hence the inevitability of very large sheriffdoms which would make it virtually impossible for the king's representatives to enforce law and order efficiently. It is remarkable how closely the modern Highland region corresponds with the sheriffdom of

Inverness erected in 1136 (Muir, 1975). But the historical geography does not spring directly from the logistical problems inhibiting effective administration, serious though these were in the far north and west where the periphery disperses into island chains which account for a third of the region's population today. Remoteness, accentuated by rugged terrain and insularity, was merely a precondition for *de facto* autonomous regimes inspired fundamentally through cultural values which assumed a powerful political force. The process of unification in Scotland involved the emergence of a 'core area' largely external to the kingdom of Alba, the state created by the union of Pictland and Scotland in the ninth century in the face of Viking pressure (Small, 1968). Not only did these provinces find themselves remote from decision-making processes but the imposition of a feudal system on the English model and the adoption of the English language created resentment which inevitably found political expression (Crawford, 1971). The cores of Dalriada and Pictland (especially North Pictland), Argyll and the inner Moray Firth respectively, thus remained politically active and thereby posed a serious threat to the survival of Scotland as a nation state (Henderson, 1975). Although Scotland's independence continued to be upheld by a population of distinct racial origin (Donaldson, 1974), it was almost inevitable that the clearing of the 'Celtic ways' from the Lowlands would assure their persistence in the Highlands (Kermack, 1972). Equally it was predictable that 'feudalism', a system of measures to provide an efficient chain of command from the sovereign to each individual, with reciprocal rights and obligations, would assume connotations of tyranny and exploitation (Barrow, 1956; Ritchie, 1954).

Moray provides an example of a 'debatable land' that was taken successfully under control through a military campaign and an effective settlement afterwards. The challenge was sharpened by Macbeth's claim to the Scottish throne, and although he was killed in 1057 his descendants were able to sustain a century-long rearguard action against the attempts of Malcolm III and his sons to impose the authority of the central monarchy on this recalcitrant province. An effective settlement was reached in 1163, leading to the founding of royal burghs and the introduction of a new aristocracy: the celtic *mormaer* gave way to feudal agents like the Lord of Duffus, based at the motte and bailey castle built on the edge of the Loch of Spynie (Barrow, 1975). However, in the remoter Highlands centralizing impulses faltered, and William the Lion's forts along the Great Glen were not complemented by any significant urban or monastic communities. In 1293 King John planned new sheriffdoms in Kintyre, Lorn and Skye, but momentum was lost in the Wars of Independence. It was at this time that John of Islay was able to accumulate territories granted by Scottish kings in return for military service and extend them by marriage to cover a vast sea empire controlling the Minch crossings and the Great Glen approaches (Kermack, 1957). This power was only repulsed in

1493, and the last Lord of the Isles died ten years later as a king's pensioner (Munro and Munro, 1975).

The vacuum, however, could only be filled by granting commissions to reliable nobles: Argyll and Huntly, leaders of the Campbell and Gordon clans respectively. These two agents appear to have exercised their authority within close range of their own estates, but they seem to have been powerless to prevent the deepening of local feuds in the islands. The settlement of lowland colonists (Fife Adventurers) in Lewis at the turn of the sixteenth century was a conspicuous failure, but a strategy of civilizing the Highlands through the local chiefs, who were required to accept the Statutes of Iona in 1609, did offer a real prospect of drawing the Highlands slowly into the mainstream of Scottish life. Military bases constituted an important element in a Highland policy, and a start was made in Lochaber during the enlightened occupation at the time of the Commonwealth. Unfortunately prospects of peace were gravely compromised by religious and successional issues which spawned a Jacobite movement (Mitchison, 1970). Although in the ensuing conflict the outcome could hardly be doubted, given the resources of what was now a united Britain, it is also clear that a simple military engagement was endowed with a crusading spirit which overcame Highland resistance with a force which has troubled the Lowland mind ever since. Reaction to the excesses of Glencoe and Culloden, stimulated in part by a sustained migration of Highlanders into the Lowlands, contributed to a willingness to grapple with regional problems and thereby to accept a political importance for the region going far beyond its present demographic strength (Lobban, 1969). The reappraisal of Highland scenery, first evident at the turn of the eighteenth century as part of a romantic movement to which Sir Walter Scott made a powerful contribution, stimulated travel and enabled the Highlands to be viewed constructively as an essential element in Scotland's history and culture.

EIGHTEENTH CENTURY: VISIONS OF IMPROVEMENT

By stressing the events of 1745–6 as a turning point in the economic fortunes of the Highlands there is a tendency to suppose that the defeat of the Jacobites was somehow a precondition for effective modernization (Youngson, 1973). However, changes were occurring before 1745, and it could be argued that heavy-handed military methods of suppression, together with subsequent sanctions against Highland culture, increased hostility to the alien forces of capitalism. The Disarming Act of 1745 was followed by efforts to 'civilize' the Highlanders (Withrington, 1962). Most prominent was an experiment in regional development through conversion of a number of estates (forfeited by owners involved in the Jacobite Rebellion) into a permanent crown holding that would stand as a model for rural development (Smith, 1974, 1975). Some thirteen estates were affected by the Annexing Act (implemented in 1755) and were distributed loosely over an extensive area stretching from Kippen near Stirling in the south to Loch Broom in the north. New villages were seen as an essential component of any agricultural plan. Earlier schemes to develop the Highlands had rested on the creation of new burghs and sheriffdoms, and the commissioners were well aware of contemporary developments at Fort William and Fort Augustus. However, it was evident that success would depend on a substantial economic potential and a tractable disposition on the part of the native population. There is no evidence that many viable industries were started, and attempts to settle former soldiers at various places, including Inverie and Ullapool, were not generally successful. Even the planned settlements established on the eastern coast, most notably at Beauly, made a slow start. Certainly the Commission's objectives were too grandiose and their capital resources were inadequate. When they concluded their activities in 1784 (the estates being restored to the families which had previously owned them) the land was not in a significantly better condition than on other properties. Yet development could not reasonably go beyond the real potential and this may well have been over-estimated.

There was considerable encouragement of the linen industry after Culloden. Many parts of the Highlands were physically ill-suited to flax production (Turner, 1972), and so there was some determination by the Board of Trustees for Manufactures (a semi-public body set up in 1727) to develop the industry on the basis of imported raw materials: manufacturers organized the distribution of raw materials through their intakers based at strategic points (Cowper, 1969). At a time before major road improvements had made any impact, it was difficult to maintain an efficient network, and instruction of the necessary skills through a chain of spinning schools was also problematical in outlying places like Lochbroom and Lochcarron. Even further east in Badenoch, effort could not be sustained because of the high cost of the finished yarn. Although for a time the heavy yarn demands by Tayside weavers led to the search for many spinners further north, recruitment was largely confined to the Grampian region, where there was some invasion of the area previously geared to the knitting of woollen stockings (Durie, 1974). The fisheries were also seen as an excellent prospect, but despite efforts by the British Fisheries Society it was not possible to establish a satisfactory infrastructure for the Minches; only on the east coast, notably at Wick, was a successful large-scale fishery maintained (Dunlop, 1952). Much of the effort in the west was made by stranger-boats based on the Clyde estuary, yet it should not be overlooked that there was a significant small-scale activity by predominantly agrarian communities producing dried fish for local consumption and for export. The industry was particularly well-organized in Shetland, where the landlords controlled the *far haaf*, a very successful fishery in the late eighteenth and early nineteenth centuries (Goodlad, 1971; Smith, 1977). The lairds made some innovations through the use of trading sloops to act as mother ships to the sixerns (open rowing boats with a six-man crew), thereby cutting out much arduous rowing to and from the coastal stations. Their greatest success, however, was in the improvement of fish drying and curing techniques.

There were only modest industrial prospects to justify a programme of planned villages to extend the market network into the Highland margins. Geddes has contrasted the medieval plantations of the Moray coast with the eighteenth-century small towns in the hills, highlighting the complementary environments of laich and brae, with the laich displaying a more compelling potential and attracting attention earlier (Geddes, 1945a; 1945b; Woolmer, 1970). New planned settlements were also built on the Argyll and Sutherland estates, where vigorous programmes of land reorganization and industrial growth were implemented for a time (Lindsay and Cosh, 1973; Richards, 1973a). Although criteria for recognition are not always explicit, recent research demonstrates clearly that a considerable number of villages were built in the Highlands (Lockhart, 1974; Smout, 1970). But the most interesting aspect of the planned village era was the uneven distribution within the region between east and west. D. G. Lockhart's map (1980) shows at least 244 planned villages in Scotland, 51 of which were in the Highlands. The region therefore covered 20·9% of the villages, a share almost identical to the share of the 1851 population (with the principal burghs—over 5000 population—discounted) of 21·5%. But 29 of the Highland planned villages were situated in a belt from Caithness to south-east Sutherland, East Ross, Inverness, Nairn and Badenoch: one village to 4·4 thousand people. This relates favourably to comparable figures for Scotland (7·3 thousand) and the Outer Regions (5·7). But in the rest of the Highlands the ratio was one village to 11·6 thousand people. Yet considerable optimism prevailed, and emigration was generally deplored both by landowners and politicians. There were visions of great changes with reorganization of transport and settlement patterns underpinning more intensive activity in the countryside (Anderson, 1785).

In much of the Highland region, especially the western districts, there was an equivalent to the planned villages in crofting townships with permanently lotted arable strips which induced a linear settlement pattern in contrast to the nucleated form of the old clachan. There was a strong economic motive for this type of development in Shetland, where the prime importance of fishing made it appropriate to resist the option of land reorganization for commercial farms in favour of a smallholding system that would support the fishermen. Elsewhere, however, the profitability of fishing was not normally sufficient for landowners to forego the profits that could be made through a system of commercial sheep farming. It has to be noted that in the late eighteenth century a new generation of Highland chieftains accepted a novel role as landowners on the southern model and set out to develop their estates in a way that would best ensure for them a substantial material prosperity. A rapidly increasing peasant population created awesome problems which the conventional improvement strategy was quite incapable of solving. Yet a smallholding system combined with land reclamation could provide some possibility for subsistence while freeing land for sheep farming. It is evident that many estates applied a spirit of compromise which may well have been first introduced by the Annexed Estates Commissioners. On the forfeited Lochiel estate small tenants were removed from Glen Dessary and the shores of Loch Arkaig, a policy which may have been partly aimed at the flushing out of cattle reivers and army deserters from remote parts of the property: resettlement took place on crofts lotted out on the shores of Loch Linnhe at Banavie and Corpach. In the south-west, where Cregeen considered that the House of Argyll saw its historical function as the modernization of the Highlands, there was great disappointment as industries failed and agrarian reorganization was undermined by a deep mistrust of the Campbells, especially on the northern outposts of their estates (Cregeen, 1964). Changes were made, and on Tiree the Duke of Argyll reversed a doctrinaire plan to create large farms and resettle surplus tenants in fishing villages in favour of a crofting pattern which meant consolidated holdings but with a small average size.

There was still a substantial forest cover, and the rational exploitation of woodland might be seen as an attractive strategy for timber-using industries (Lindsay, 1975a). This is illustrated by the eighteenth-century iron furnaces: the most successful were Goatfield Furnace on Loch Fyne, which closed in 1813 (though a gunpowder factory used the site until 1884), and Taynuilt Furnace on Loch Etive, which survived until 1866 as a going concern and remains to this day as a monument of industrial archaeology. Both works were situated on the coast and could easily import their ore by sea. Timber (for charcoal) was drawn from surrounding estates for up to fifty miles: long-term contracts were negotiated, and although there were some difficulties in getting a steady supply, conservation measures were implemented and in the case of the Taynuilt furnace the woodland area available to the company in 1866 was no smaller than it had been in 1750 (Lindsay, 1975b, 1976). This conclusion is part of a long-overdue assessment of the significance of woodlands in the Highland economy. The negative tone of some early research has been too readily accepted. There were substantial areas of woodland revealed in pre-1914 agricultural returns, and the undeniable case for state intervention should not imply that private enterprise was totally ineffective. However, until the strategic argument became persuasive, the competition from imported timber tended to depress economic interest in Highland woodlands. Certainly there were times of great activity: the range of commercial working was extended during the Napoleonic Wars and the timber of Rothiemurchus was marketed by rafting down the Spey (O'Sullivan, 1973), a procedure dating back at least to the seventeenth century. There was floating also on Loch Ness and on the Beauly–Cannich–Glass system. But as the nineteenth century wore on forestry was weakened by a breakdown of coppice management and increased grazing pressure.

NINETEENTH CENTURY:
FROM *LAISSEZ FAIRE* TO PROTECTION

The compromise remained satisfactory during the Napoleonic Wars with high commodity prices which enabled the smallholders to survive through their sales of cattle and kelp (Gray, 1957). The end of the war brought a reduction in prices which threatened the Highland economy with collapse as a large population was thrown back on limited land resources. The increasing use of steam power in manufacturing and the rise of a new class of industrialists with no commitment to rural employment accelerated the transfer of industry to the towns (Shaw, 1980). The end of war removed any stigma that might previously have made emigration appear unpatriotic: indeed resettlement overseas now appeared inevitable, and those who had advocated controls on Atlantic passenger ships (to discourage emigration through the higher prices that better accommodation would necessitate) pleaded successfully for their removal in 1827. Voluntary migration followed but the process was accelerated by eviction policies which provided a 'final solution': creating more opportunity for sheep farming while reducing the scale of poor law commitments towards the peasantry.

The clearances introduced a clear revolutionary element into a fundamentally evolutionary process of agricultural change (Storrie, 1965). They have been widely discussed, and it is well established that cumulatively they had the effect of demoralizing the Highland peasantry. Yet it is also clear that conditions varied considerably between estates, and historical narratives that follow the nineteenth-century crises can easily mislead with a picture of unremitting gloom (Hunter, 1976). The extent of voluntary emigration was important here (also the migration associated with the departure of many tacksmen in the late eighteenth century), but the physical possibilities for resettlement as perceived by landowners and their agents was apparently crucial (Turnock, 1977a). There is also scope for investigation of the psychological aspects of the clearances. Evictions of subsistence farmers were not unique to the Highlands yet nowhere else are they so deeply resented. A strong attachment to the land is undeniable but it would appear that landlord and peasant were frequently poles apart over the fundamental desirability of modernization, and this mutual incomprehension, deepened by inability (through language difficulty) to communicate directly, reduced the level of landlord 'sympathy' toward tenants and of tenant disposition to cooperate in any programme of estate development. E. Richards (1970) has shown that in Sutherland the relationship between the planners and the people became permanently soured, through a clash between an innovating Lowland society and a fundamentally conserving society in the Highlands (Adam, 1922).

The nineteenth century witnessed a general reluctance by government to sponsor schemes of industrial development in the Highlands. However, this does not necessarily indicate a lack of sensitivity, for appreciation of the special problems of small distilleries in the north of Scotland led to a regime of moderate excise impositions in 1823. It then became clear that when the Highlands produced goods of particular distinction, industries could survive and develop. Demand for high-quality malt whisky in the south encouraged widespread illicit distillation in the late eighteenth century, and after 1823 a growing number of licensed distilleries were able to serve this market. The growth culminated in the late nineteenth century blending boom in which Highland malt whiskies played a decisive role. The unique qualities of the malt whisky of each distillery (somewhat mysteriously induced by the utensils involved and the secondary constituents of the water supply) make imitation impossible. But it has emerged that the generally medium malts of Speyside and the heavy malts of Islay are essential ingredients of acceptable blended whiskies. Hence a remarkable concentration has arisen, with the great major-ity of distilleries in Islay (along with Jura and Kintyre) and round the inner Moray Firth, representing an extension of the Speyside concentration which lies predominently in the Grampian region (Storrie, 1961).

Communications continued to be an important preoccupation. The military road system was extended considerably during the eighteenth century and then gave way to a programme inspired by economic requirements (Mathieson, 1924; Richmond, 1974; Salmond, 1934). Commissioners were appointed in 1804 to administer the Road and Bridge Act and they took over the military roads in 1814, although only the roads of economic significance were kept in repair (Haldane, 1962; Stephen 1936).

Government was also concerned over moral and spiritual matters. In 1823 funds were made available for building additional churches, and between 1824 and 1840 some thirty churches and forty manses were completed. Thomas Telford carried out this work, which formed part of a powerful effort by the established Church of Scotland to improve its organization (Dodd, 1971). The more extensive civil parishes were divided for ecclesiastical purposes, and eventually schools as well as churches were provided in these *quoad sacra* parishes.

The famine of 1846 brought a government response through a Central Board of Management which gave out meal in return for labour on public works such as the 'famine' roads (Gray, 1954–5). For the first time there was an attempt to bring together a related complex of programmes covering not just infrastructure (roads and piers) but also industrial development, related especially to fishing and hosiery manufacture. Unfortunately there was no progress over the important issue of landholdings because the estate owners were anxious to maintain a profitable farming system. Indeed the withdrawal of the Board in 1850, coupled with a statement in favour of emigration by the Board of Supervision (responsible for the poor) put landowners in a mood for further clearance.

However, change was on the way. The crofters hung on grimly to what they had, and some clearance plans were abandoned when it became clear that violence would arise (Richards 1975b, 1974). A new crofter leadership, bred in the harsh climate of the mid nineteenth century, gained the ear of government so effectively that the crofting system became accepted as a pillar of regional development policy for the Highlands. After a Royal Commission (1884), privileges of security of tenure, fair rents and compensation for improvements were achieved in 1886. Shortly after, the most overpopulated districts were given relief through the provision of new holdings and the enlargement of some existing ones and common grazings (MacCuish, 1976–8). In some areas, such as the Western Isles, smallholders have been restored to virtually all the lands from which they had previously been evicted. This success may be related to action taken by the crofters themselves, and Hunter (1974) shows how the Free Church helped to weld the crofters into a community with a distinct outlook and a capacity for collective action. Hanham (1969) provides a complementary perspective through Scotland's readiness for a period of political and social reform. The case for regional protection reflected a consensus in British politics at the time, so that despite frequent changes of government there was a continuity of effort through to the First World War. Support for crofting was fundamentally a political gesture, but it was economically rational in recognizing that employment off the land was too spasmodic and unstable to justify the same clear separation of agricultural and non-agricultural occupations that was feasible in other parts of the country. There was abundant evidence to support this view at the time through the decline in local fishing, brought about by rapid technical change in the industry which left Hebridean crofter-fishermen unable to compete by virtue of capital shortage (Gray, 1973). Unfortunately the crofting legislation shows a preoccupation with agricultural matters, and this had tended to beguile planners into regarding agricultural development as a worthy objective in itself, overlooking the fact that agricultural efficiency cannot be reconciled with the maintenance of the crofting population (Caird and Moisley, 1964). Regional development on the basis of the crofting system is required.

It is not without significance, however, that the support for crofting came at a time when sheep farming was becoming less profitable and landowners were beginning to capitalize on their deer forests (Hunter, 1973; Mather, 1978a). The high moorlands formed traditional hunting grounds, but sheep ranged over them during the summer when the grazings were reasonably attractive (Mather, 1972). In the late nineteenth century when the Highlands were first opened up by the railways the interest in deer stalking by affluent southerners was sufficient to justify the exclusion of sheep from extensive areas of mountainous country. In many cases new mansions and houses were built as shooting lodges, to be occupied by successions of fashionable parties during the autumn season. They were important centres of local employment, requiring numerous domestic servants not to mention additional staff to look after the kennels, stables and access routes (Duff, 1929). Many of these menial positions were occupied by crofters who would migrate considerable distances to take advantage of the seasonal opportunities for work. The smallholders gained considerable benefit from the sporting boom, and reports of clearance to make way for deer forests are exaggerated. Certainly some crofts situated close to the deer forests might have been damaged by marauding animals, but generally the eclipse of sheep farming and the fall in the value of farm land contributed to an expansion of croft land, continuing after the First World War as part of a nationwide land settlement policy (Mather, 1978b). Government was alarmed at the spread of deer forests and appointed a Royal Commission to see how far land taken for sport could be restored to smallholders previously displaced to make way for commercial farming (Royal Commission, 1895).

The reforms of the late nineteenth century indicated government acceptance of the right of people to stay in their home areas. For about half a century out-migration had been seen as a solution to overpopulation, but now it was clear that other ameliorative measures would have to be taken. The Napier Commission of 1884 had emphasized the poverty of many families living on tiny holdings and saw little future for them. If the security of tenure granted by the 1886 act was to have any real meaning, there would have to be some enlargement of holdings and ancillary employment as well. In the most overcrowded areas action was taken by the Congested Districts Board set up in 1897. It was not sufficiently well financed to make a major impact but did enlarge the land available to crofters, improve local communications and encourage ancillary industries like fishing and tweed manufacture (Moisley, 1961). Furthermore, steps were taken to improve the lines of communication into the Central Belt. Steamer services were developing (Donaldson, 1966; O'Dell, 1939), but the progress of railway construction in the Highlands was hampered by construction costs and limited traffic. The Irish precedent for government support of railways was not followed up immediately in peripheral regions of Britain, no doubt because of a reluctance to discourage private enterprise, such as the initiative of the Duke of Sutherland who built the Golspie–Helmsdale section of the Highland Railway at his own expense. Also the growth of interest in recreation in the Highlands was potent enough to intensify competition between the Highland and Great North of Scotland companies and oblige the former to build a direct line between Aviemore and Inverness (opened in 1898) to forestall a rival project (Vamplew, 1970). However, the Light Railways Act of 1896 made rural branch lines cheaper to build while, specifically for the Highlands, financial concessions allowed the extension of the Inverness–Strome Ferry line to Kyle of Lochalsh and completion of the West Highland Railway from Fort William to Mallaig. Altogether therefore the measures applied at the turn of the nineteenth century were considerable. Although resources were limited, the intervention by the state 'whetted the appetite of enthusiasts for land settlement for more' (Jones, 1926). So important did the task of economic development become that gradually depopulation came to be regarded as the key problem of the Highlands. In a century the wheel had turned full circle, and the out-migration so bitterly resented by the landowners in the late eighteenth century was now seen as an indictment of government policy.

At this point it is worth considering the change in the broad distribution of population that had taken place during the upheavals of the nineteenth century. The Highland share of Scotland's population fell from 20·2% in 1801 to 7·6% in 1921, a far greater loss of relative demographic strength than the erosion encountered in the other Outer Regions (see Table 9.1). However, there was a rapid absolute increase in Scotland during this perimd (1·6 million to 4·9) and even a significant growth of the Highland population, by 14·1% from 324·3 thousand to 371·4 thousand. Yet trends varied considerably between the various districts. The statistical areas adopted by the Highlands and Islands Development Board provide a useful framework for analysis (Table 9.2). There was certainly growth in the core of the region (Inverness, Nairn, and Badenoch & Strathspey areas) from 45·1 thousand in 1801 to 57·9 thousand in 1921. The same situation arose in the most peripheral areas: Caithness, Orkney and Shetland together showed an increase from 69·4 thousand to 77·9 thousand, but the most remarkable growth occurred in the Outer Hebrides, where population more than doubled from 21·6 thousand to 44·2 thousand and in Arran, Bute and Dunoon with a threefold increase from 18·3 thousand to 58·0 thousand. Apart from the Oban area, which showed a significant increase, all other statistical areas showed decreases. These were heaviest in the mainland/Inner Hebridean belt (north-west Sutherland, West Ross and Lochalsh, Skye, Bute, Argyll & Bute, and Argyll Islands): from 90·3 thousand to 62·2 thousand. This is the area where the clearances had their greatest demographic impact, although allowance must be made for a substantial element of voluntary migration. Even so, in view of the low level of urban

Table 9.2 Population Analysis of the Highlands and Islands[a]

	Census Year							Percentage share of Highland population		
	1921			1971						
Area[b]	A	B	C1	A	B	C2	C3	1801	1921	1971
Islands	151·5	35·3	24·6	93·7	24·2	−38·2	−6·2	37·5	40·7	30·4
Shetland	25·5	4·8	14·0	17·6	6·2	−31·2	−1·4	6·9	6·9	5·7
Orkney	24·1	5·4	−1·4	17·3	6·3	−28·4	−8·0	7·5	6·5	5·6
Skye	11·6	—	−32·5	7·5	—	−35·5	−3·7	5·3	3·1	2·4
Lewis & Harris	33·7	4·1	176·7	23·7	5·3	−29·6	−6·0	3·7	9·1	7·7
Uist & Barra	10·5	—	10·4	6·8	—	−35·7	−8·4	2·9	2·8	2·2
Argyll Islands	12·4	—	−48·7	7·5	—	−39·5	−3·8	7·4	3·3	2·4
Bute	19·5	15·2	218·8	8·4	6·4	−56·7	−14·0	1·9	5·2	2·7
Arran & Cumbraes	14·2	5·8	150·6	4·9	—	−65·7	−8·8	1·7	3·8	1·6
Mainland	219·9	71·8	8·5	213·8	98·1	−2·8	−4·7	62·5	59·3	69·6
Caithness	28·3	11·1	25·1	27·9	16·7	−1·3	2·0	7·0	7·6	9·1
N.W. Sutherland	7·0	—	26·2	3·8	—	−46·0	−4·5	2·9	1·9	1·2
S.E. Sutherland	11·9	—	−23·5	10·1	—	−14·8	0·0	4·8	2·6	2·2
E. Ross	31·8	3·9	−6·2	30·5	10·9	−4·0	8·1	10·4	8·6	9·9
W. Ross & Lochalsh	9·6	—	−15·5	6·8	—	−29·3	0·0	3·5	2·6	2·2
Inverness	38·2	20·9	37·2	49·5	34·4	29·5	8·0	8·6	10·3	16·1
Nairn	8·8	4·5	5·5	8·3	5·4	−5·5	−1·4	2·6	2·4	2·7
Badenoch & Strathspey	10·9	1·6	22·7	9·1	1·5	−16·9	0·0	2·7	2·9	3·0
Lochaber	11·4	1·9	−41·3	17·6	8·0	54·0	23·6	6·0	3·1	5·7
Oban & Lorn	16·0	6·3	25·4	15·1	6·4	−5·9	−0·6	3·9	4·3	4·9
Mid Argyll & Kintyre	21·6	6·8	−20·1	18·6	6·0	−14·2	−0·8	8·3	5·8	6·0
Dunoon & Cowal	24·4	14·7	272·8	16·8	8·9	−31·1	3·2	2·0	6·6	5·5

Column A Total population in thousands
Column B Urban (> 1500) population
Column C1 Percentage change in total population 1801–1921
Column C2 Percentage change in total population 1921–1971
Column C3 Percentage change in total population 1961–1971

[a] Figures based on parish statistics with estimates where parishes are divided between statistical areas
[b] HIDB Statistical Areas
Sources: HIDB *Report for 1979* and Census of Scotland

development in this area it was still possible to regard several parishes as 'congested' because the Congested Districts Board balanced population against rateable value (discounting deer forests and shootings) in deciding which parishes should benefit from their assistance. But it can be appreciated that the Outer Hebrides and Shetland would most readily qualify with only a small urban population. By contrast the growth areas round Inverness and in Argyll & Bute experienced a very substantial urban development. Indeed Inverness, Dunoon, Bute and Arran with 25·9% of the total Highland population accounted for 52·9% of urban population (reckoning towns of over 1500 population) and included the three largest towns in the Highlands in 1921: Inverness (20·9 thousand), Rothesay (15·2 thousand) and Dunoon (14·7 thousand).

TWENTIETH CENTURY: REGIONAL DEVELOPMENT

Turning to the period since 1921 it is evident that the overall loss of population has more than wiped out the increase noted above. A decline of 17·2% in fifty years contrasts with a gain of 14·5% over the previous 120 years. Only Inverness and Lochaber have increased their population, although Caithness, Dunoon and East Ross have recovered between 1961 and 1971. It is remarkable that this heavy loss of population which reduced the Highlands' share of the Scottish population from 7·6% to only 5·9% has generated far less public disquiet than the upheavals of the nineteenth century, (although there was then an element of coercion present). Between 1921 and 1961, when the losses in the Highlands occurred (for there was a growth of 1·1% between 1961 and 1971), only one other region, Borders, showed an absolute decline. The basic statistics for the last half century also show only a very modest increase in the urban population, an indication of the failure to expand industry. Clearly the trend has been upward, and a more impressive performance would probably be registered if smaller settlements (500–1500 population) could be examined. Nevertheless, the stagnation in many areas and, especially, the sharp fall in population in the Clyde estuary towns of Campbeltown, Dunoon, Millport and Rothesay from 42·5 thousand to only 22·5 thousand, is a phenomenon that merits greater attention.

Although comprehensive regional policy could not be formulated during the inter-war period, the economic and social importance of land was recognized and the provision of new smallholdings continued. Basic services were being provided by county councils, and special assistance was only necessary in particular cases, as with medical services in 1913 (Day, 1918). The growing nationwide preoccupation with physical planning and the important initiatives taken after the First World War with regard to forestry both had positive implications for the Highlands without the need for a specific Highland policy. The work of the Forestry Commission, established in 1919, had particular significance for the Highlands for it quickly became apparent that the Great Glen (Inverness and Lochaber), along with adjacent areas in East Ross and Argyll & Bute, contained a great deal of suitable land. Many new jobs were provided, and the smallholding movement was extended by the provision of forest workers' holdings (Mather, 1971). In recent years mechanization of forest work has reduced the scale of employment, but planting (both private and public) continues, especially in the more favoured areas just mentioned (Mather, 1979).

Industrial development remained very limited, but without a solution to the problem of power supplies there was little scope for a growth of manufacturing at this time. Distilling remained important in some areas (although prohibition in America forced a temporary recession), while textile industries had provided some compensation for depression in fishing in the Western Isles (particularly Lewis and Harris) and Shetland. Electro-metallurgical industries had made a strong start at Foyers and Kinlochleven, but the much larger size of hydro-electricity schemes in Canada and Scandinavia suggested that the growth of world demand for aluminium would mean a steady decline in Scotland's share of production (Chilton, 1950).

The idea of a special development commission can be traced back to the suggestion of the Liberal Party in 1928 that there should be some organization to coordinate the effort's of various public bodies and implement a development plan. In the 1930s the Scottish Economic Committee (SEC), the forerunner of the present semi-official body known as the Scottish Council (Development and Industry) set up a committee to examine the problems of the Highlands and Islands. Particular stress was placed on the need for better transport facilities (SEC, 1938) and the scope of manufacturing based on hydro-electric power, but the difficulty of interposing a regional authority between the county councils and the Scottish Office limited the institutional reform proposals to the appointment of a Development Commissioner. The Secretary of State eventually appointed an Advisory Panel (1946) to assist over government policy for the Highlands (Thompson, 1979). By this time, however, a special organization had been created to exploit the hydro-electric potential of the Highlands: the North of Scotland Hydro-Electric Board was set up in 1943, and as the number of generating stations increased (supplementing the legacy of inter-war private enterprise) it became clear that a wider spread of light industry was now feasible (Lea, 1961). Probably the potential was exaggerated by an assumption that the wartime disperal of industry would continue, but the potential of the inner Moray Firth area, around Inverness, was clear enough. The designation of a Highland Development Area in 1949 around Inverness represented the first application of development area incentives (designed to help urban regions with high unemployment) to a rural district (Scottish Home Department, 1950).

There is no doubt that the material condition of the Highland population continued to improve rapidly during the early post-war period. The Advisory Panel repeatedly stressed the need to improve communications, and additional resources were made available for various projects, including some new roads and the introduction of car ferry services to the islands (Turnock, 1965). Crofters were encouraged by the reconstitution of the Crofters Commission after a further Royal Commission (1954), while government stimulated the Forestry Commission to evolve a social policy of planting in the remoter parts of the Highlands. The electrification programme proceeded rapidly, not only through hydro-electric schemes but also by experiments with nuclear energy at Dounreay (Caithness) and thermal power derived from peat at Altnabraec (Sutherland): the Dounreay programme was subsequently extended by construction of a fast breeder reactor for grid supply, but the $2 \cdot 0$ MW gas turbine installed at Altnabraec in 1958 was not a viable proposition and an extensive land reclamation programme on skinned land had to be abandoned. The plans for a missile range in the Uists went ahead on a limited basis, but nevertheless created a stimulus for construction of the North Uist–Benbecula causeway (opened in 1960), complementing the Benbecula–South Uist road link previously opened in connection with Balivanich air base. But the staple industries could not provide sufficient employment and depopulation continued; despite government support for hill farming, amalgamation of holdings and a reduction of farm labour took place. The strategic importance of the islands, though considerable in wartime (Fereday, 1971; Ruge, 1973), brought only a modest increment of population under peacetime conditions (Nimlin and Barry, 1979). Moreover, as services improved, accessibility to them became more important and a redistribution of population within the region placed more emphasis on the small towns and key villages, leading to the desertion of some remote glens and small islands (Moisley, 1966).

Interest in a special development authority was maintained, with particular dedication by the Scottish Trades Union Congress, and the idea was included in the Labour Party manifesto of 1965. It is fairly clear that much left-wing support for a development authority arose out of a desire to reduce if not eliminate the influence of private landowners and to introduce a new landholding system to eliminate the unsatisfactory use of land previously noted by the Advisory Panel (1965). Fears of a radical approach ensured that the government's Highlands and Islands Development (Scotland) Bill of 1965 would stimulate heated debate. However, the modest funds made available to it, plus the cumbersome nature of compulsory purchase procedures, effectively ruled out any major innovations on the land. Although the Board has been obliged to co-exist with the established local authorities and other bodies with responsibilities in certain economic sectors, it is able to operate a unique grant and loan scheme and assist enterprises considered worthy of support. Any appraisal of the Board's work must take into account these basic considerations (Marshall, 1975; Williams, 1973). It was inevitable that much time would be spent looking at miscellaneous proposals for the development of light industry and tourist facilities (Spaven, 1979) and finding solutions to difficult tasks of liaison and coordination, for relations with other authorities in the Highlands have not always been harmonious.*

Under the circumstances it is a considerable triumph for the Board merely to have survived and won the confidence of all major political parties in spite of the need to make substantial revisions in strategy (in the range of responsibilities and territorial organization) to accommodate the changes in local government in 1975. But clearly observers with a Marxist approach who expected a greater commitment to socialism (with priority for social as distinct from economic development) have been disappointed (Carter, 1974; 1975; McEwen, n.d.), although it is not clear how far the desired radical approach could have been adopted, given the Board's remit and its status as an agent of central government. Some other reviews tended to envisage a wide range of policy options with choices dictated in large measure by the dispositions of successive chairman (MacGregor, 1978). This is a speculative line of approach which must also take note of the need to adjust policies on the basis of objective assessments of national trends. The attention given to manufacturing, tourism and fishing could hardly have been denied, given the slender, yet significant precedents (Blake, 1964). Equally the opportunities to develop the Moray Firth area, given the recent growth in aluminium and oil-related industry, could not seriously have been resisted (Turnock, 1973, Watts, 1970). With considerable flair and expertise the impact of prevailing national trends has been maximized in the interests of employment.

Much of the controversy over HIDB policy probably relates to regional problems within the Highlands. Caird (1972) has shown the contrasting population trends very clearly. The 'inner' mainland zone lost population marginally between 1951 and 1961 (0·4%), but the 'outer' island zone declined much more sharply by 11·5%. During the following decade 1961–1971 the disparity persisted, with growth on the mainland (6·1%) and decline in the islands by almost the same margin (6·8%). Table 9.2 is laid out in such a way as to elaborate on these points, although minor discrepancies arise over the areal delimitations. Now, although the Congested Districts Board had responsibility for a small overpopulated area covering the majority of the islands, along with the north-west mainland, most government policies for the Highlands have affected a much larger region. The Disarming Act of 1746 applied to the whole area north of the Tay and Vale of Leven, while to varying degrees the upland districts of the present Grampian and Tayside regions were included in *ad hoc* programmes, along with the belt of Highland counties extending from Argyll to Shetland (Campbell, 1920).

It is, however, the latter area alone which has been most favoured in recent

---

* The Scottish Tourist Board leaves the HIDB to operate a chain of tourist offices and does not seek to duplicate the promotional work done in the Highlands. Also the Scottish Development Agency leaves the provision of advance factories in the Highlands to the Board.

times as a suitable Highland region for policies of protection and development. The 'Crofting Counties' were recognized in 1886 as the area within which the economic and social problems of smallholders was most severe (Moisley 1962). It was with some difficulty that the claims of other counties with a significant smallholding population were resisted (Carter, 1979). This same area, somewhat arbitrarily delimited, has now been made the responsibility of the HIDB, apart from small additions made in 1975 to accommodate changes in local government areas. The act allows for the Secretary of State to designate other areas from time to time where this is indicated by their 'character and proximity' in relation to the Highland core, but there is no reason to suppose that the HIDB has ever advocated this and there are good reasons for not doing so (Turnock, 1969). The problem arising from this situation is that an area of relatively high economic potential on the east mainland, Lochaber and Argyll & Bute is complemented by the remoter island zone where a numerous crofting population continues to seek ancillary employment. The existence of a strong sense of community in these remoter areas may appear anomalous, yet there is no doubt that the instinctive response to adversity has been the development of a social system, with its strong independent culture and its distinctive landholding pattern, which acts as a filter through which innovations must pass prior to adoption. Innovations then perceived as inappropriate are rejected like the Leverhulme proposals for industrialization in the 1920s (Nicholson, 1960) and the HIDB proposals for reorganization of the Harris Tweed industry in the 1970s. Others are modified in their impact to minimize disruption, like the oil-related developments in Shetland (Nicholson, 1975).

The problem for the Board is that it has to deal with strongly contrasting situations. Its responsibility to the whole region compels exploitation of potential wherever it exists, yet relatively rapid growth in selected areas on the mainland cannot benefit the islands where *local* wellbeing is the only relevant measure of the Board's effectiveness. To work in mainland factories it is necessary to migrate, and it is of relatively little consequence on which side of the boundary of the HIDB area they happen to lie. The Board has accepted the reality of the 'two worlds' phenomenon, and apart from a short period when there was an enthusiastic recommendation for a policy of mainland growth areas (Carter, 1973) (in sympathy with prevailing concepts of regional development worldwide in the 1960s) a sensitive balance has been sought (Hutchinson, 1969; Macdermott, 1976). The Board now claims to have a 'broadly based balanced approach to regional development' (HIDB, 1978) and accepts that its policies must be designed to achieve 'a significant impact in the more difficult areas' (HIDB, 1977). Nevertheless, economically attractive schemes which are socially acceptable are difficult to find. Conservatively minded communities often react unfavourably to external development proposals, while lacking the leadership to inspire their own initiatives (Caird and Moisley, 1961). In tuning policies to the needs and possibilities it appears that a major determinant is 'the availability of people in each area willing to initiate and operate appropriate developments effectively' (HIDB, 1980). Lack of cooperation from land-owners has frustrated the progressive ideas of the Board for local land-use planning, as proposed for Kildonan and the Isle of Mull (HIDB, 1973). However, there are some promising signs, and the plea made by Geddes (1955) for social surveys to discover the links between environment and society as a base for constructive planning has been heeded to the extent of encouraging island cooperatives in a number of crofting districts. Some form of compulsion to ensure adoption of land-use policies that will maximize employment is now being contemplated (Brydon and Houston, 1976). However, it has been made clear that 'the Board has no aspiration to become a substantial landowner' (HIDB, 1978).

CONCLUSION

Throughout the history of Scotland, considered both as an independent state and as a constituent region of the United Kingdom, the Highlands have been regarded as a problem. The nature of the problem has varied, although economic development to improve material conditions and increase employ-ment has always been a prominent concern. Armed rebellion is no longer a possible consequence of disaffection, but perception of regional inequality by a mature democracy does have a significant political implication, especially in view of the values currently placed on the Highlands as the cradle of the nation: few would deny that the weight of history, although difficult to quantify, has strengthened the case for special measures of regional development. It has inspired some visionaries to advocate support for a new society in which appropriate (though undefined) social policies would underpin the crofting system and extend its hold over the region at the expense of the private estates. Unfortunately, since the Highlands is not the only peripheral region to make demands on government departments, a range of special measures can never provide full compensation for remoteness. Hence income tax concessions could not be contemplated, while even major innovations like relatively cheap electricity for the inner Moray Firth (possibly from a nuclear reactor) or 'road equivalent tariff' for island ferry services have so far failed to win government approval. There is unlikely ever to be complete satisfaction over the amount of assistance and still less over the way in which resources are allocated.

This is not to say that recent policies towards the Highlands have been ineffective. If it is accepted that the prevailing national ideology must be respected, it is evident that at different times in history Highland development agencies have pragmatically sought to exploit as fully as possible the opportunities for growth. Unfortunately efforts to increase exposure to market forces tend to exaggerate the impact of the 'boom and bust' cycles (Prattis, 1977) which are seen as characteristics of the colonial exploitation of peripheral regions (Hechter, 1975). Yet ideal societies cannot survive in an economic vacuum, and the only realistic course is to combine acceptance of the prevailing potential with local initiative and expertise wherever this is available. There can be no once and for all solution to the challenge of development, for the task of accelerating the spread of modernizing innovations across a region, against the tremendous 'friction' encountered in the Highlands and Islands, is a continuing preoccupation. Inevitably the work of any development authority will appear especially inadequate when scrutinized retrospectively, and it is too easily overlooked that the predecessors of the HIDB were reasonably successful given their specific responsibilities and the prevailing possibilities. The fluctuating façade of administrative expedients, arising from the political difficulties of allowing exceptions on a permanent basis, may weaken the validity of the continuity argument put forward, but a pragmatic approach is not without merit given the conditions of rapid economic and social change experienced in the last two centuries.

REFERENCES

Adam, M. I. (1922). Eighteenth century Highland landlords and the poverty problem. *Scottish Historical Review* **19**, 161–79.

Advisory Panel on the Highlands and Islands (1964). 'Report on land use.' HMSO, Edinburgh.

Anderson, J. (1785). 'An account of the present state of the Hebrides and western coasts of Scotland.' n.p., Edinburgh.

Ashton, J. and Long, W. H. (ed.) (1972). 'The Remoter Rural Areas of Britain.' Oliver and Boyd, Edinburgh.

Barrow, G. W. S. (1956). The beginnings of feudalism in Scotland. *Bulletin Institute of Historical Research* **29**, 1–31.

Barrow, G. W. S. (1975). Macbeth and other mormaers in Moray. *In* 'The hub of the Highlands: the book of Inverness and district.' (L. Maclean of Dochgarroch, ed.), 109–23. Inverness Field Club, Inverness.

Blake, J. L. (1964). The Outer Hebrides fisheries training scheme, *Scottish Studies* **8**, 113–31.

Bryden, J. and Houston, G. (1976). 'Agrarian Research in the Scottish Highlands.' Martin Robertson, London.

Caird, J. B. and Moisley, H. A. (1961). Leadership and innovation in the crofting communities of the Outer Hebrides, *Sociology Review* **9**, 85–102.

Caird, J. B. and Moisley, M. A. (1964). The Outer Hebrides. *In* 'Field studies in the British Isles.' (J. A. Steers, ed.), 374–90 Nelson, London.

Caird, J. B. (1972). Changes in the Highlands and Islands of Scotland 1851–1971. *Geoforum* **3**, 5–36.

Campbell, H. F. (1920). 'Highland reconstruction.' Alex. MacLaren, Glasgow.

Carter, I. R. (1973). An evaluative study of the HIDB. *Aberd. Univ. Rev.* **45**, 56–78.

Carter, I. R. (1974). The Highlands of Scotland as an undeveloped region. *In* 'Sociology and development.' (E. de Kadt and G. Williams, ed.), 279–311. Tavistock Publications, London.

Carter, I. R. (1975). A socialist strategy for the Highlands. *In* 'Red paper on Scotland.' (G. Brown, ed.), 247–53. Edinburgh University Student Publications Board, Edinburgh.

Carter, I. R. (1979). 'Farm Life in North East Scotland 1840–1914: a Poor Man's Country.' John Donald, Edinburgh.

Cowper, A. S. (1969). 'Linen in the Highlands 1753–1762.' Edinburgh College of Commerce, Edinburgh.

Crawford, B. E. (1971). 'The earls of Orkney and Caithness and their relations with Norway and Scotland 1158–1470.' Unpublished Ph.D. thesis, University of St Andrews.

Cregeen, E. R. (1964). 'Argyll estate instructions 1771–1805: Mull Morvern and Tiree.' Constable, Edinburgh.

Cregeen, E. R. (1970). The changing role of the House of Argyll. *In* 'Scotland in the age of improvement.' (N. T. Philippson and N. Mitchison eds.), 5–23. Edinburgh University Press, Edinburgh.

Day, J. P. (1918). 'Public administration in the Highlands and Islands.' University of London Press, London.

Dodd, W. E. (1971). Telford's churches. *Scots Magazine* **95**, 113–9.

Donaldson, G. (1966). 'Northwards by sea.' Privately published, Edinburgh.

Donaldson, G. (1974). 'Scotland: the Shaping of a Nation.' David and Charles, Newton Abbot.

Duff, I. D. (1929). The human geography of south-west Ross-shire 1800–1920. *Scottish Geographical Magazine* **45**, 277–95.

Dunlop, J. (1952). 'The British Fisheries Society 1786–1893.' Unpublished Ph.D. thesis, University of Edinburgh.

Durie, A. J. (1974). Linen spinning in the north of Scotland 1746–1773. *Northern Scotland* **2**, 13–36.

Fereday, R. P. (1971). 'The Longhope battery and towers,' Stromness, Rendall.

Geddes, A. (1945a). The foundation of Grantown on Spey. *Scottish Geographical Magazine* **61**, 19–22.

Geddes, A. (1945b). Burghs of laich and brae. *Scottish Geographical Magazine* **61**, 38–45.

Geddes, A. (1955). 'The Isle of Lewis and Harris.' Edinburgh University Press, Edinburgh.

Goodlad, C. A. (1971). 'Shetland fishing saga.' Shetland Times, Lerwick.

Gray, M. (1954–5). The Highland potato famine of the 1840s, *Economic History Review* **7**, 357–68.

Gray, M. (1957). 'The Highland Economy 1750–1850.' Oliver and Boyd, Edinburgh.

Gray, M. (1973). Crofting and fishing in the north-west Highlands. *Northern Scotland* **1**, 89–114.

Haldane, A. R. B. (1962). 'New ways through the glens.' Nelson, London.

Hanham, H. J. (1969). The problem of Highland discontent 1880–1885. *Transactions Royal History Society* **19**, 21–65.

Hechter, M. (1975). 'Internal Colonialism: the Celtic Fringe in British National Development 1536–1966.' Routledge and Kegan Paul, London.

Henderson, I. (1975). Inverness: a Pictish capital. *In* 'The hub of the Highlands: the book of Inverness and district.' (L. Maclean of Dochgarroch ed.), 91–108. Inverness Field Club, Inverness.

Highlands and Islands Development Board (1973). 'Island of Mull: survey and proposals for development.' HIDB, Inverness.

Highlands and Islands Development Board (1977). 'Eleventh Report for 1976.' HIDB, Inverness.

Highlands and Islands Development Board (1978). 'Twelfth Report for 1977.' HIDB, Inverness.

Highlands and Islands Development Board (1980). 'Fourteenth Report for 1979.' HIDB, Inverness.

Hunter, J. (1973). Sheep and deer: Highland sheep farming 1850–1900. *Northern Scotland* **1**, 199–222.

Hunter, J. (1974). The emergence of the crofting community: the religious contribution 1798–1843. *Scottish Studies* **18**, 94–116.

Hunter, J. (1976). 'The making of the crofting community.' John Donald, Edinburgh.

Hutchinson, P. H. (1969). 'Rural growth centre policy: a case study of the Highlands and Islands of Scotland.' Unpublished B.Phil.Thesis, University of Glasgow.

Jones, D. T. *et al.* (1926). 'Rural Scotland during the War.' Oxford University Press, London.

Kermack, W. R. (1912). The making of Scotland: an essay in historical geography. *Scottish Geographical Magazine* **28**, 295–305.

Kermack, W. R. (1957). 'The Scottish Highlands: a Short History.' Johnstone-Bacon, Edinburgh.

Lea, K. J. (1961). Hydro-electricity in Scotland. *Transactions of the Institute of British Geographers* **46**, 155–65.

Lindsay, I. G. and Cosh, M. (1973). 'Inveraray and the Dukes of Argyll.' Edinburgh University Press, Edinburgh.

Lindsay, J. M. (1975a). Some aspects of timber supply in the Highlands 1700–1850. *Scottish Studies* **19**, 39–53.

Lindsay, J. M. (1975b). Charcoal iron smelting and its fuel supply: the example of Lorn furnace Argyllshire, *Journal of Historical Geography* **1**, 283–98.

Lindsay, J. M. (1976). The commercial use of Highland woodland 1750–1870. *Scottish Geographical Magazine* **92**, 30–40.

Lobban, R. D. (1969). 'Migration of Highlanders into Lowland Scotland 1750–1890.' Unpublished Ph.D. thesis, University of Edinburgh.

Lockhart, D. G. (1974). 'The evolution of the planned village of northeast Scotland *c*. 1700–*c*. 1900.' Unpublished Ph.D. thesis, 2 vols. University of Dundee.

Lockhart, D. G. (1980). The planned villages. *In* 'The Making of the Scottish Countryside.' (M. L. Parry and T. R. Slater, ed.), 249–70. Croom Helm, London.

MacCuish, D. J. (1976–8). Ninety years of crofting legislation. *Transactions of the Gaelic Society of Inverness* **50**, 296–326.

Macdermott, S. H. (1976). Industrial Development and Planning in Rural Areas.' Unpublished M.Sc. thesis, University of Strathclyde.

McEwan, J. (n.d.). 'Who owns Scotland?' Edinburgh University Student Publications Board, Edinburgh.

MacGregor, B. D. (1978). 'The Highland Problem: the difficulties of development in a remote rural area.' Unpublished M.Sc. thesis, Heriot-Watt University.

Marshall, M. (1975). 'Planning in a Highland region.' Unpublished M.Sc. thesis, University of Strathclyde.

Mathieson, J. (1924). General Wade and his military roads in the Highlands. *Scottish Geographical Magazine* **40**, 193–213.

Mather, A. S. (1971). Problems of afforestation in North Scotland. *Transactions of the British Institute of Geographers* **54**, 19–32.

Mather, A. S. (1972). Red deer land use in the Northern Highlands. *Scottish Geographical Magazine* **88**, 36–47; 86–99.

Mather, A. S. (1978a). The alleged deterioration of hill grazings in the Scottish Highlands. *Biological Conservation* **4**, 181–95.

Mather, A. S. (1978b). 'State-Aided Land Settlement in Scotland.' Aberdeen University Geography Department, Aberdeen.

Mather, A. S. (1979). Land use changes in the Highlands and Islands 1946–1975: a statistical review, *Scottish Geographical Magazine* **95**, 114–22.

Mitchison, R. (1970). The government in the Highlands. *In* 'Scotland in the age of improvement' (N. T. Philippson and N. Mitchison, ed.), 24–46. Edinburgh University Press, Edinburgh.

Moisley, H. A. (1961). Harris Tweed: a growing Highland industry, *Economic Geography* **37**, 353–70.

Moisley, H. A. (1962). The Highlands and Islands: a crofting region? *Transactions of the Institute of British Geographers* **31**, 83–95.

Moisley, H. A. (1966). The deserted Hebrides. *Scottish Studies* **10**, 44–68.

Muir, R. (1975). The development of sheriffdoms. *In* 'Historical Atlas of Scotland 400–1600.' (P. MacNeill and R. Nicholson, ed.), 30. Conference of Scottish Medievalists, St Andrews.

Munro, R. W. and Munro, J. M. (1975). The Lordship of the Isles. *In* 'Historical Atlas of Scotland 400–1600.' (P. MacNeill and R. Nicholson ed.), 65–7. Conference of Scottish Medievalists, St Andrews.

Nicholson, J. R. (1975). 'Shetland and oil.' William Luscombe, London.

Nicolson, N. (1960). 'Lord of the Isles.' Weidenfeld and Nicolson, London.

Nimlin, J. and Barry, J. (1979). Military aspects of St Kilda. *In* 'A St Kilda Handbook.' (A. Small, ed.), 90–2 National Trust for Scotland, Dundee.

O'Dell, A. C. (1939). 'Historical Geography of the Shetland Islands.' T. & J. Manson, Lerwick.

O'Sullivan, P. E. (1973). Land use changes in the forest of Abernethy. *Scottish Geographical Magazine* **89**, 95–106.

Prattis, J. I. (1977). 'Economic structures in the Highlands of Scotland.' Fraser of Allander Institute, Speculative Paper, 7.

Richards, E. (1970). The prospects of economic growth in Sutherland at the time of the clearances. *Scottish Historical Review* **49**, 154–170.

Richards, E. (1973a). 'Leviathan of wealth: the Sutherland fortune in the Industrial Revolution.' Routledge and Kegan Paul, London.

Richards, E. (1973b). Problems on the Cromartie estate 1851–3. *Scottish Historical Review* 52, 149–64.

Richards, E. (1974). Problems of Highland discontent 1790–1860. *In* 'Popular Protest and Public Order.' (R. Quinault and J. Stevenson, ed.), 75–114. Allen and Unwin, London.

Richmond, J. (1974). Ruthven in Badenoch. *Scots Magazine* 102, 302–8.

Ritchie, R. L. G. (1954). 'The Normans in Scotland.' Edinburgh University Press, Edinburgh.

Royal Commission (1884). 'Report of the Commission of Inquiry into the Condition of Crofters and Cottars in the Highlands of Scotland.' C. 3980. HMSO, London.

Royal Commission (1895). 'Report of the Royal Commission on the Highlands and Islands Appointed to Inquire into Land Occupied for the Purpose of Deer Forests.' C. 7681. HMSO, London.

Royal Commission (1964). 'Report of the Commission of Enquiry into Crofting Conditions.' Cmd. 9091. HMSO, Edinburgh.

Ruge, F. (1973). 'Scapa Flow 1919.' Ian Allan, London.

Salmond, J. B. (1934). 'Wade in Scotland.' Moray Press, Edinburgh.

Scottish Economic Committee (1938). 'Highlands and Islands of Scotland.' SEC, Edinburgh.

Scottish Home Department (1950). 'A Programme of Highland Development.' Cmd. 7976. HMSO, Edinburgh.

Scottish Office (1966). 'The Scottish Economy 1965–1970: a Plan for Expansion.' Cmnd. 2864. HMSO, Edinburgh.

Shaw, J. P. (1980). The new rural industries: water power and textiles. *In* 'The making of the Scottish countryside.' (M. L. Parry and T. R. Slater, ed.), 291–317. Croom Helm, London.

Small, A. (1968). Historical geography of the Norse Viking colonisation of the Scottish Highlands. *Norsk Geografisk Tidsskrift* 22, 1–16.

Smith, A. M. (1974). The forfeited annexed estates 1752–1784. *In* 'The Scottish Tradition: Essays in Honour of R. G. Cant.' (G. W. S. Barrow, ed.). 198–211. Scottish Academic Press, Edinburgh.

Smith, A. M. (1975). 'The Forfeited Annexed Estates.' Unpublished Ph.D. thesis, University of Dundee.

Smith, H. D. (1977). 'The Making of Modern Shetland.' Shetland Times, Lerwick.

Smout, T. C. (1970). The landowners and the planned village in Scotland 1730–1830. *In* 'Scotland in the Age of Improvement.' (N. T. Philippson and R. Mitchison, ed.), 73–106 Edinburgh University Press, Edinburgh.

Spaven, F. D. N. (1979). The work of the HIDB 1965–1978. *In* 'The Highlands and Islands: a contemporary account.' 10·0–10·6 HIDB, Inverness.

Stephen, J. R. (1936). 'The History of Roads in the Highlands of Scotland in the Eighteenth and Nineteenth Centuries.' Unpublished Ph.D. thesis, Aberdeen of University.

Storrie, M. C. (1961). Islay: a Hebridean Exception. *Geographical Review* 51, 87–108.

Storrie, M. C. (1965). Landholdings and settlement evolution in West Highland Scotland. *Geographical Review* **47B**, 138–61.

Thompson, F. (1979). 'The Highlands and Islands Advisory Panel: a review of its activities and influence.' Privately published, Stornoway.

Turner, W. H. K. (1972). Flax cultivation in Scotland. *Transactions of the Institute of British Geographers* **55**, 127–44.

Turnock, D. (1965). Hebridean car ferries. *Geography* **50**, 375–7.

Turnock, D. (1969). Regional development in the Crofting Counties. *Transactions of the Institute of British Geographers* **48**, 189–204.

Turnock, D. (1977a). 'The Lochaber area: a case study of changing rural land use in the West Highlands of Scotland.' Geographical Field Group, Nottingham.

Turnock, D. (1977b). Oil-related industry in North Scotland, *Geoforum* **8**, 183–200.

Vamplew, W. (1970). Railway investment in the Scottish Highlands. *Transport History* **3**, 141–53.

Watts, H. D. (1970). The location of aluminium reduction plant in the UK. *Tijschrift voor Economische en Sociale Geographie* **61**, 148–56.

Williams, A. (1973). 'The Highlands and Islands Development Board: Policy Making in an Administrative Setting.' Unpublished M.Litt. thesis, University of Glasgow.

Withrington, D. J. (1962). The SPCK and Highland schools in the mid-eighteenth century. *Scottish Historical Review* **41**, 89–99.

Woolmer, H. (1970). Grantown on Spey: an eighteenth century new town, *Town Planning Review* **41**, 237–49.

Youngson, A. J. (1973). 'After the 'Forty-Five: the Economic Impact on the Scottish Highlands.' Edinburgh University Press, Edinburgh.

10
Rural Land Use from *c.* 1870

G. Clark

The review of agriculture in Chapter 7 concluded that by 1870 'the scene was set for agricultural recession'. The forty years up to the First World War are often characterized as a period of depression in rural Scotland, 'forty bleak years' Symon (1959) called them in contrast to the preceding 'years of prosperity'. This was certainly a fair description of farming in eastern England at this time, but how true was it of Scotland? There were certainly years of poor weather, as in 1879, 1888 and 1907 when cereals would not ripen or lambs were killed by the cold, wet springs, and in the late 1870s cattle were severely affected by epidemics of pleuropneumonia. There was also a sustained increase in imports of cheap food—the value of food imports to Britain doubled between 1866 and 1877—the consequences of this have, however, often been exaggerated (Symon 1959).

The crop worst affected was wheat, but even at its peak it accounted for under 10% of the Scottish cereal crop. It was reduced in area by 75% between 1872 and 1895, completely disappearing from Aberdeenshire by 1886, although recovering a third of its decline by 1914. Wheat straw was useful for covering potato pits, and this helped to maintain production despite falling prices. The effect of falling prices can be exaggerated: a third of the decline in area occurred between 1872 and 1875 when prices were stable, and another third occurred in the single year of 1875–76 when prices fell from 57/- (£2.85) to 45/- (£2.25) a quarter (MAFF, 1968). Barley prices fared better, as demand from brewers and distillers was buoyant due to the steady rise in real industrial wages up to 1900 (Saul, 1969). The most important cereal, oats, maintained its area well into the 1890s and was still in demand for feeding horses. In contrast, the reduction in cereal prices was an advantage for cattle, pig and poultry farmers who bought grain for fodder. The diary sector continued its steady growth, as people could afford more fresh milk, while producers of high-quality beef still had a secure and expanding market in London. Some farmers were helped by small increases in yields of potatoes and oats. Hunter (1976) has noted that the 1870s and early 1880s were a period of unparalled prosperity for crofting families, with high stock prices and good wages from fishing being supplemented by the earnings of daughters in domestic service and sons working on sporting estates.

Although the universal and severe depression attributed to the later Victorian years has often been overestimated, there were undeniable difficulties for particular groups of farmers who had to adapt to the new conditions. Some were helped by landlords, like the Marquis of Aberdeen, who reduced rents or delayed their collection. Others emigrated or moved to England. After 1890, both wool and sheep prices were low, and many Highland estates were given over entirely to sport. The area of deer forest nearly doubled between 1883 and 1912 although the reduction in sheep production was less severe than this implies. By 1914, lowland farmers had made savings by reducing their cereal area, although only by half as much as in England, and also by increasing the area of permanent grass by about a quarter, although difficulties of definition make this figure unreliable. There is some evidence that farmers turned to a low-cost system of farming, accepting lower yields but more than compensating for this by savings on liming. Hay production, in place of turnips, became more popular in the lowlands, as did sheep farming; both needed less labour while mechanization continued, particularly for sowing, harvesting and threshing. Some farmers, however, found that they had to spend more on housing their workers, because the decline of the kitchen and bothy systems required them to build more tied cottages.

There were bankruptcies and lower standards of living for some farmers, but others who were more skilful, daring or affluent expanded rapidly. Families like the Dales in East Lothian bought land when it was at its cheapest and expanded their businesses. Thirty years later, when the Great Depression again reduced farm prices, the same variety of adaptations to adversity can be seen.

The forty years after 1870 not only witnessed short-term adaptations to changing prices and weather but also marked the start of three longer-term trends which were to alter profoundly the structure and functioning of the Scottish countryside. During the next hundred years these trends revolutionized the organization of landowning and farming and opened the way for the urbanization of the countryside and for its increasing control by government. These developments will be considered with particular reference to lowland Scotland; the Highlands and Islands are discussed separately in Chapter 9.

LANDOWNERS AND FARMERS

The observers of rural Scotland in 1870 could point to successful farmers and landowners who had risen in social position and wealth by effort and good fortune. He could see others reduced to bankruptcy or to the status of farm servant. A hundred years later such successes and failures can still be seen. However, one should step back from the individual to assess the broader changes over the period. The observer in 1870 would have described the normal method of organizing the countryside as one whereby extensive estates were rented to a large number of tenants most of whom farmed on a relatively small scale. Irrespective of the fortunes of particular individuals, the organization of the rural economy has altered considerably since then, both for the landowners and the occupiers of the farms.

THE LANDOWNERS

Scotland has long been distinguished from England by its marked concentration of landownership. In 1872 the Duke and Duchess of Sutherland owned 91% of their county and also sizeable parts of Ross and Cromarty and Staffordshire (House of Commons, 1874). One-third of Scotland was owned by the twenty-five largest landlords, whereas about 1200 people owned that proportion of England—a country only two-thirds larger than Scotland. By 1970 the twenty-five largest landowners held only 13% of Scotland (McEwen, 1977). How had this come about?

Data on the emotive subject of land ownership are notoriously sparse, but there is little reason to suppose there was any marked change in the concentration of landownership between 1870 and 1914 although individual estates waxed and waned. Conventional wisdom holds that a major cause of estate fragmentation was the need to meet the burden of estate duties. These were introduced in 1894 at a maximum rate of 8% on transfers of land and other property on death. Estates gifted over one year before death were effectively exempt from the tax. Even allowing for the additional burden of succession duty, this cannot be considered an onerous level of taxation. The rates of estate duty were raised in later years, but it is doubtful whether much land was sold before 1914 to meet this tax. Subsequently, deaths in the Great War and the collapse of farm incomes after 1920 meant that even the relief from the full burden of estate duty given in 1925 was insufficient. The index of agricultural prices fell by 46% between 1920 and 1923 (MAFF, 1968), land prices also fell, and many estates sold farms to sitting tenants at twenty-five times the annual rental (Northfield, 1979; Symon, 1959). In 1921 and 1922 one-quarter of all farm land in the United Kingdom changed hands, and the proportion of tenanted farms in Scotland, which had remained around 92% from 1870 to 1920, was reduced to 79% by 1930 (MAFF, 1968). The more skilful tenants and those with larger farms who had acquired savings during the war years, when profits were more easily made, bought land cheaply and enhanced their status in the community. Some of these new owners suffered later in the 1930s however, when commodity prices remained low and mortgage payments were more difficult to maintain.

After the Second World War estates again sold land, and by 1966 only 49% of holdings in Scotland were tenanted. The pressure to sell land was not now from falling prices, since subsidies had prevented that; rather the landowners' need for money had grown as agriculture had become more capital intensive. The increased construction of farm buildings, particularly after 1957, put considerable strain on landowners' resources, and land sales to tenants and for urban development helped them equip their remaining farms. The tenants were often eager to buy their farms: this gave them a capital gain in the long term and enhanced their status and borrowing potential in the short term. Furthermore, owner-occupied farms had an enhanced value, whereas security of tenure, enjoyed after 1948, and strict regulation of rents reduced the worth of tenanted farms.

Landowners also started farming more of their land themselves. Traditionally, an estate's home farm was a modest affair, but the increasing restriction on rents which landlords claimed successive governments had instituted led many estates to farm land themselves with the aid of a growing body of professional farm managers. Landowners also began employing outside professionals to manage the forested parts of their estates through arrangements with private forestry companies. There has therefore been a trend to owner-occupation and the fragmentation of estates over the last sixty years, but its progress has not been equally swift throughout Scotland: in Stirlingshire and Kirkcudbrightshire estate fragmentation has been thorough; in East Lothian and Sutherland it has occurred at the national rate; in Wigtownshire and Kincardineshire the ten largest estates were as extensive in 1970 as in 1872. The pattern of decline of large estates conforms to no obvious or simple spatial model (Clark, 1981a).

After about 1960 account must be taken of two other developments. First, the simple division into owned and rented land has become less accurate. Many partnerships, farming companies and false tenancies have been created for fiscal purposes, while the advent of lease-back forms of tenure provided a system which gave a farmer a capital gain by selling his farm while still allowing him to farm independently much as though he was still an owner-occupier.

Secondly, powerful new purchasers of land appeared, drawn from outside the ranks of the landed gentry and full-time farmers. The first were institutional owners of land. Some of these, such as the Sovereign, the Crown Estate

Commissioners and Oxford and Cambridge colleges, have owned land in rural Scotland for a long time, although some new purchases have occurred as with the Crown Estates Commissioners in the 1930s. In addition to these traditional institutional owners, there were financial institutions such as pension funds and insurance companies. Their motive was capital appreciation for their investors; this was achieved by putting a small part of their inflated revenues into buying good quality farmland as a long-term investment. By buying about 5% of the farmland sold in the 1970s, they have rapidly come to own about 0·5% of Scotland, mostly large estates on the eastern side of the country (Northfield Committee, 1979). Previously the best income for insurance companies came from lending money. As early as 1875 over two-thirds of the debts secured on landed estates were owed to insurance companies. Since 1960 it has been believed that farm rents and capital growth would out-perform lending, and with security of tenure having been strengthened in England in 1976, the institutions' previous reluctance to invest in Scotland has been removed.

The other powerful new force in the land market is the state. In 1872 local and national public bodies owned 0·3% of Scotland. Even when the land owned in 1872 by private gas, coal and railway companies and educational and medical institutions is included, the proportion of publicly owned land only rises to 0·7%. By 1979 public bodies and nationalized industries owned 13·9% of Scotland and leased a further 2·9% (Clark, 1981b). To some extent the increase was due to the transfer, either wholly or in part, of such activities as water supply and forestry from the private to the public sector. Two-thirds of the state-owned land is operated by the Forestry Commission, which although set up in 1919 did not buy the majority of its land until after 1945. Selling land to the Commission was often an elderly hill farmer's pension. Most of the public agricultural land was acquired between 1918 and 1938 as part of a programme to provide crofts in the Highlands and smallholdings in the Lowlands for the unemployed and ex-servicemen (Mather, 1978). Since 1957 these small farms have been amalgamated and some of the land has been sold. The other principal official bodies owning land are the Ministry of Defence, the National Coal Board, British Rail, and local authorities. Public land is characterized by rarely being sold—defence land after 1945 was an exception—and being dedicated to a single use. Despite experiments at Glenforsa since 1951 (Select Committee, 1972), the integration of land uses on public land has not proceeded as far as on the best privately managed estates. Currently, it is intended to sell some public land, particularly that of the Forestry Commission, as part of a programme of reducing costly or loss-making government activities.

THE FARMERS AND THEIR FARMS

Perhaps today the important group in rural Scotland is no longer the land-owners but the full-time working farmers. A majority of these also own their farms and some of the traditional landed gentry have joined their ranks by farming much more of their land themselves. Perhaps a fifth of the financial institutions also actively farm their land.

This dominant group of working farmers deserves closer study. They are still of predominantly rural stock, most being the sons of farmers or farm workers (Rettie, 1975). Indeed it can be argued that the hereditary character of the farming population is being reinforced by two trends. First, there are fewer tenanted farms available. As late as the 1930s an outsider with small savings had a fair chance of acquiring a tenancy and entering farming cheaply. Just enough farmers progressed to bigger farms to keep alive the illusion of a 'farming ladder'. In the 1880s and 1890s there was a steady migration of farmers not only from south-west Scotland to Essex but also from the south-west to the south-east, from the north-east to Angus, and from Caithness to Ross-shire (Symon, 1959). Today almost the only routes to a large farm are inheritance, careful marriage, or an agricultural degree leading to the mana-gership of a farm. Secondly, it is more difficult for non-farming people to afford farms, because farms not only continue to increase in size but also demand a greater intensity of capital investment for the provision of such items as buildings and machinery.

Farm enlargement can be detected throughout the period since 1870 as well as before but has intensified since the last war. Urquhart (1965), for example, noted small upland farms being amalgamated in considerable numbers in the glens of western Aberdeenshire in the 1870s. Periods of low prices in 1921–22, and after 1930 encouraged wealthier farmers to expand cheaply. In the early 1970s just under 1% of agricultural holdings were amalgamated with a neighbouring holding each year and, in addition, other widely separated farms were joining into more loosely integrated businesses (Clark, 1977). The need to expand or leave the industry has been a clear economic imperative since the last war. There has been a progressive squeeze on farmers' profit margins by successive governments since 1951, and Robson (1973) has shown that this has been greatest for the larger farmers. Expanding production is one way to maintain a farm's income, and enlarging the farm can contribute to the expansion.

On the other hand, amalgamation is the most expensive way to achieve an expansion of production. Land prices have outstripped farm income and general inflation since 1945, due partly to the incessant demand for land from farmers (Northfield, 1979). However, it is also widely perceived as the least risky method of expansion because it enhances flexibility of land use and usually provides a capital gain (Clark, 1977). It has been frequently observed to lead to changes in husbandry, as areas of low-intensity land use, such as pasture land, are allocated to distant parts of the expanded farm and livestock systems are modified. Where hill and lowland are united into an enlarged unit, cattle enterprises in particular become more self-contained and the traditional reliance on the store cattle market is dispensed with (Clark, 1977). About one-quarter of hill farms are no longer independent units but are part of multiple-unit businesses. Indeed, the basis of the 'hill farm problem' needs to be reassessed (Russell, 1970).

Farms are also becoming more expensive because they are more highly equipped than previously, and this is closely linked to an intensification of production. There are three ways in which a farmer can achieve this. One is by using strains of crops and breeds of livestock with potential yields superior to those of their counterparts of last century. This has not affected all enterprises equally, and the more pronounced improvement in the yields of barley than of oats is one of the reasons for the perennial decline in the cultivation of the latter since 1942. Another method of intensification is to change from an activity giving a low return per hectare, such as sheep-farming, to one giving a higher return, such as pig-breeding. Finally, intensification can be achieved by improved management to achieve lower mortality and disease loss, better weight gain and nutrition, and more efficient use of equipment and labour.

As farming has become more intensive it has also become more specialized. In 1870 it was normal for many farms to produce a range of products to give flexibility of output and more stable incomes in the face of changeable weather conditions and unregulated, volatile markets. Since the last war stability of farm prices has been guaranteed by government intervention in most agricultural markets, and a diversity of small-scale enterprises has become economically disadvantageous. In 1870 labour was plentiful and cheap relative to machinery, as witnessed by long rows of workers' cottages by Lothian farmsteads and the provision of bothies and chaumers in the north-east (Carter, 1979). Despite the establishment of minimum wages since 1937 (Symon, 1959; MAFF, 1968), farm workers today are still among those with the lowest average earnings. Newby (1974) notes that in England average agricultural wages were three-quarters of the average industrial wage in the late 1940s but only two-thirds in the mid 1970s. Nevertheless, farm workers are now expensive relative to machinery; the initial capital cost of machinery may be high but its marginal cost is much lower than a worker's. Some farm workers were dismissed to save money; others moved to better-paid jobs. The younger ones usually moved to urban employment immediately; the older ones with families initially found alternative employment in the countryside (Wagstaff, 1972). By 1891 every rural county in Scotland was losing population, and some had been experiencing a net outmigration for forty years. Wagstaff,

(1973) estimated that the proportion of the workforce employed in agriculture in the crofting counties, the south-west, and Borders decreased from 25% to half that between 1921 and 1951. Until about 1950 the decline was due mostly to farm workers rather than farmers leaving the land, but subsequently farmers also left. However, farming was not losing an unusually large number of workers compared with other industries; rather it was poor at recruiting outsiders into farming. The youngest farm workers are the least likely to stay: four-fifths of school leavers who enter farming leave it within ten years (Wagstaff, 1971).

As workers left and farms expanded and the cost-price squeeze on profits continued, the need to raise the productivity of the remaining employees was reinforced and mechanization was promoted by British and American engineering companies. Mobile steam engines for ploughing and theshing were used in the later nineteenth century and achieved particular popularity during the First World War when the government supplied them to counteract a shortage of labour. However, the diesel engine soon triumphed, and tractor numbers increased four-fold between 1942 and 1964; the number of horses on farms declined from over 150 000 in 1910 to under 10 000 in 1960 (MAFF, 1968).

The need for machinery has made farms more expensive to equip, but it has solved the problem of labour shortage while simultaneously prompting rural depopulation, particularly in the eastern arable areas where farm workers were most numerous. Mechanization also had another less obvious effect. When the first combine harvester appeared in Scotland at Whittingehame (East Lothian) in 1932, it was clear that this expensive piece of equipment would only be more profitable than employing people if the farmer expanded his cereal enterprise to the limit of the machine's capacity. Similarly the first British bulk-milk tank, installed in Kirkcudbright in 1955, signalled a general need to expand diary herds and removed other activities from the farm to make way for the extra cows. So mechanization encouraged further specialization, while specialization and intensification in the face of rural depopulation demanded further mechanization (Russell, 1970). If a farm was too small for a piece of equipment even after specialization, more land was needed, so mechanization and specialization also prompted farm enlargement. Today most farms specialize in only two or three saleable products, and the output of most enterprises is concentrated on a decreasing number of farms (MAFF, 1977). Nowhere has this gone further than in the poultry industry. In 1870 eggs from free-range hens were produced on most farms as pin money for the farmer's wife. In 1978, 64% of laying hens were kept on just 24 highly automated farms (DAFS, 1980). Specialized turkey production developed in the 1920s on farms such as Fenton Barns in East Lothian. Other enterprises, which have not attracted such advances in automation, like sheep and beef cattle production, have remained more widely distributed but still exhibit the same trend. Overall, the largest farm businesses, comprising only 10% of all farms, accounted for 52% of agricultural production in Scotland in 1970 (Russell, 1970). The trend to specialization of each farm's production has also affected the regional geography of Scottish agriculture. Each farmer had to decide on which sector to concentrate and sometimes the choice tended towards those which were best suited to the area's environmental conditions. So the arable areas of eastern Scotland have become more exclusively arable by the progressive removal of cattle and sheep. Conversely, upland areas have lost arable enterprises, while west-central and south-west Scotland have seen the dominance of dairying reinforced and, since 1900, extended to Galloway.

Other changes in regional specialization are less explicable in terms of the physical environment. Pig production has not only expanded greatly since 1870, it has shifted from south-west Scotland to the north-east with a continuing presence in suburban areas, particularly around Edinburgh (Coppock, 1976). Poultry production, which was widely dispersed in 1938, had become heavily concentrated west of Edinburgh by 1965 (Coppock, 1976). Beef production has moved from the arable areas where, in the 1920s, beasts were drafted in from Ireland and the lower uplands to use up the residues from arable farming. Since 1945, beef production has become faster and simpler than the breeding–rearing–fattening regime common between the wars (Clark, 1972). Beef cattle have become much commoner in the hills, where they displaced, sheep, and also in Orkney and around the Moray Firth. Oats have been replaced by barley since 1945 due to a relative decline in yields and in the number of horses to be fed. Lack of labour has reduced the popularity of turnips and swedes, continuously since 1875 and particularly after 1940. Production of vegetables has always been limited, partly reflecting their low consumption by the Scots. Areas traditionally growing field vegetable since before the 1870s, such as the coast east of Edinburgh, were augmented by production in the Carse of Gowrie and Strathmore after canning factories had opened in the 1920s. Vegetables have also been grown in a wider area of inland East Lothian and Berwickshire, as large-scale arable farmers found them a profitable substitute for sugar beet following the closure of the beet factory at Cupar, Fife in 1971 (Toulouse, 1977). Despite all these changes, the regional geography of Scottish farming has been more stable since 1870 than the economy of individual farms (Coppock, 1976).

The example of vegetable production in East Lothian demonstrates another method of achieving both expansion and specialization—cooperation. This can provide a way of obtaining some of the benefits of a large farm relatively cheaply while retaining much of that independence so important to farmers. Although the first Scottish agricultural cooperative was established in 1884 (Symon, 1959), the 1920s were the earliest period when they were formed in large numbers either to supply materials at discount prices or to market produce, particularly eggs and wool, at better prices than the small farmer could extract from large-scale buyers. Many cooperatives failed because their members were unwilling to pay enough for good management. Some farmers ruined their cooperative by selling outside it when prices were high and unloading produce on to it when prices fell. Each cooperative that failed made the task of maintaining members' loyalty harder in those which remained. The survivors, however, have often grown to a great size. The trend is for the cooperative to invest heavily to achieve vertical integration, particularly in processing and marketing, but it requires increasing discipline from its members, their independence being curtailed for the wider good, while it acquires a large central staff of managers and much equipment of its own. In short, it takes on the character of an industrial company.

The farms of Scotland have become fewer, larger, more specialized, more mechanized, and more productive. They have raised the productivity of their remaining employees by much more than the average of industry through heavy investment in equipment, buildings and chemicals, underpinned by subsidies of many kinds. Together these trends encapsulate the evolution of the organization of the Scottish countryside in the last century. It is difficult to think of any other way farmers' living standards and expectations could have been raised so high, given the political necessity before 1973 of cheap food in the shops and an expenditure on subsidies which was limited by European standards.

THE URBANIZATION OF THE COUNTRYSIDE

Farming

Where does the countryside stop and urban Scotland begin? In the late nineteenth century the answer was more obvious than today: rural areas then were more distinctive and self-sufficient. Many more of agriculture's inputs were produced in the countryside. Carts and tools were frequently made by the local blacksmiths, and fertilizer meant local lime or shell sand. Of course some farms after 1879 were using British and American reaper-binders made in the cities, some made butter in mass-produced churns, and guano fertilizer was imported from South America in considerable quantities in the late Victorian period. However, the dependence of the farmer on the products of industry was not nearly as great as it is today. Modern crops require more fertilizer to produce their higher yields, and the loss of farm labour for hoeing demands chemicals to control weeds and reduce crop diseases. Massey-Ferguson machinery has replaced the many small-scale farmers in the north-east who bred Clydesdales and the seasonal Donegal harvest workers (Johnson, 1967). Without the products of industry, it would be impossible to sustain high-yielding farms and forests covering hundreds of hectares yet employing under 3% of the labour force with fewer imports of food despite an expanded population.

Changes in food production have been matched by new methods of marketing. In 1870 most food was sold to the cities after minimal processing using a major urban 'Covent Garden-type' of market where many small suppliers confronted a lesser but still large number of wholesalers. The food was not always up to today's standards—the removal of dairies from Scottish cities was partly an effort to make milk more wholesome—and market prices were often very unstable. In the smaller markets it was easier for buyers to raise their profits by colluding to reduce prices, and this is still found today in the smaller store-sheep and cattle markets. However, for many commodities the model is obsolescent.

Today there are many fewer markets, the smaller ones having been closed as uneconomic or unhygenic. Also the whole character of the market has changed, as the independent retailer has given way to multiple stores and small shops interlinked in national organizations (e.g. Spar). As retailing has been concentrated into fewer units, so the number of buyers has shrunk and they can control prices more easily. The wholesale raspberry market is a good example. In the extreme case of the statutory marketing board for milk there is only one buyer; the boards for wool and potatoes can also influence or fix prices. Some major food processors have bypassed the market completely by entering directly into contracts with farmers who produce exclusively for one company. The full extent of contract farming in Scotland is not known, but anecdotal evidence from pig farmers indicated how this system can lead to tight control over many aspects of rearing and feeding in return for a guaranteed price for a specified quantity and quality of produce. Often the food-processing company has a factory in the local area, so that the effective market for produce is no longer the town. If that company closes, many farmers may find it very difficult to get another market. Indeed there are examples of even closer integration between farm and food-processing factory. Sainsbury farms land in north-east Scotland, Unilever operates fish farms, and the Imperial Tobacco Company controls one of the largest Scottish broiler chicken producers and processors. The monopoly enjoyed by Scottish farmers and the close correspondence between where food is grown and where it is sold to the public have been eroded by the reduced real cost of transport and evolution of the retail trade. However, these features have provided wider markets for farmers.

Farming has become more industrial and urban in character as its local linkages have been broken. It has traded increasingly with the industrial sector and has come under the tighter commercial discipline of urban retail managers.

It has also become more open to outside influences, as more formal methods of agricultural education at college and university have become available and as the results of systematic research into better husbandry have gradually been adopted.

The Wider Rural Community

One consequence of labour reduction on farms has been the increasing proportion of people in rural areas who are employed outside agriculture. The building and haulage trades are the commonest stepping stones out of agriculture for farm workers, while many small-scale farmers eased themselves out of the industry by taking another job which gradually replaced farming. However, some of those outside agriculture still rely on it for their livelihood. Wagstaff (1973) estimated that about 1·6 to 2 times the numbers employed in farming are indirectly dependent on it, and except in crofting areas the ratio has risen since the 1930s, particularly in areas with many creameries such as Ayrshire and Galloway.

Some of those completely outside agriculture work in industries which process local raw material, like the jam and canning works in Strathmore and the dairies in the south-west. Other rural industries, for example the border woollen mills and the remnants of the carpet industry, have discarded local suppliers in favour of imported materials more suited to the quality of their products.

Many other companies, unconnected with local raw materials, have been attracted to country towns by available labour, cheaper premises, lower wage rates, or a less unionized work force. Fraserburgh, Arbroath and Dumfries all have major engineering works which have flourished since becoming part of American multinational companies. Conversely, the withdrawal of such a major employer from a town can lead to high unemployment and migration. As the real cost of transport has declined, a rural location is no longer necessarily disadvantageous, and rural sites are evaluated more on the suitability and size of their labour supply than on their location (Gaskin, 1977).

The belief that rural Scotland's future was an industrial one originated well before 1870, but since then has been manifested in the remit of the North of Scotland Hydro-Electric Board (1943), the plans of Lord Leverhulme for Lewis between 1918 and 1925, and the terms of reference of the Congested Districts Board (1897). Certainly, industry has imposed its own regime on country people, giving the rural factory worker more in common with the citizens of any industrial town than with the farmers a mile away. However, the belief that manufacturing industry has succeeded agriculture, following its decline, is misleading. The dominant source of employment in rural areas, even more than in the cities, is the service sector. Employment in domestic service has been replaced by a job with the local authority. The hospital, the bus company, the railway, banks and shops all offered white-collar jobs and hence some status and security of employment even in the 1930s. More recently as small shops, schools and hospitals have closed, tourism has provided a fickle addition to service sector jobs. The optimism of the 1950s and 60s that the rapid growth of tourism would counteract its seasonality has evaporated, and the limited benefit to local people's incomes from several forms of tourism has become clearer (Brownrigg and Greig, 1974).

The other major source of employment for rural people is in the cities. The spread of suburban railways after 1880 around Glasgow and Edinburgh and of a dense network of motor bus services after 1918 allowed rural people to commute increasing distances to urban jobs, and many eventually migrated to the city. The expanding stock of council houses after 1919 facilitated urban migration in the face of the perennial decline of the privately rented sector and the limited development of council housing in rural areas (Adams, 1978).

Mobility brought the rural commuter urban employment and a wider range of services, although the cost of travelling meant forgoing other expenditure. Conversely, it allowed the urban dweller access to rural houses while he maintained his job in the city. By 1900 the expansion of the railways allowed urban people to commute to Edinburgh from North Berwick and south Fife and to Glasgow from Dunbartonshire and even from Rothesay on the Island of Bute. They had substantial houses built for they had to be affluent to afford the higher real cost of commuting at that time. Commuting increased as incomes and car ownership rose after 1945. Private builders catered for their housing needs, the village shopkeepers prospered, the standard of services was maintained or even increased while the possibly exaggerated, social cohesiveness of the villages was reduced (Pacione, 1980). In sharp contrast other villages further from the cities have witnessed a much reduced provision of services relative to those elsewhere, and this has severely affected those without a car. As the standard of living has risen, the contrast in the level achieved by the occupants of villages nearer cities as against that by people in remoter settlements and between car owners and non-car-owners has become increasingly noteworthy.

In time, some of the urban workers retired to the countryside. From the start of the twentieth century the Fife coastal towns and even Grangemouth, before the oil refinery was built, attracted retirement settlers. Often they bought a house before they retired, using it initially as a second home and getting the local builder to help them improve it gradually. In small numbers retirement settlers and second home owners have not been a problem. Sometimes they congregated in particularly scenic places, such as Plockton in Wester Ross, Lochranza (Arran), and Isle of Whithorn (Wigtownshire). The question arises as to whether so many houses occupied seasonally or by the retired and valued at high urban prices constitutes a problem (Dartington, 1977). Sometimes they may be perceived as a threat to a Gaelic-speaking culture as expressed in the term "White Highlands" applied by local people to parts of Wester Ross. Those in low-wage industries, like farming, forestry or tourism, might be unable to compete for housing with well-paid townspeople who have perhaps made a capital gain by selling their town house. Some local families have had to live in caravans, while the local authorities in several rural areas report long waiting lists for council houses and as high a proportion of substandard houses as in many urban areas. The official consensus is that the pressure on housing is not great enough to circumscribe the free market.

The last hundred years have seen the separateness and distinctiveness of rural areas reduced in various ways. Cultural homogeneity, encouraged by migration and the mass media, has compounded a growing economic similarity founded on stronger trading links and the dominance of both town and country by service and industrial employment. The cities, their people, values, and organizations have come to fashion the countryside increasingly. Town and country have always been mutually interdependent as buyer and seller of food, but to this has been added newer foci of dependence based on industry, recreational needs, commuting, and competition for housing. One of the most interesting fields in which this growing mutual dependence has been worked out is in the activities of government.

THE GOVERNMENT AND THE COUNTRYSIDE

Scottish local government was reorganized in 1889 on a three-tier basis and again in 1929 as a two-tier system with the abolition of parish councils. The principle was that most services in rural areas should be provided by the county council, their range being progressively extended by the increased provision of council houses after 1919, the growing range of personal social services, and the development of planning.

Effective planning in rural areas did not start until after the Town and County Planning (Scotland) Acts of 1943 to 1947, despite the exhortations of earlier statutes in 1909, 1925 and 1932. Indeed, the effectiveness of the 1947 Act is questionable. Certainly rural areas near cities were affected by the policy of green belts, thus sharpening the division between the built-up area and open land (Skinner, 1976). This provided a neater landscape, though perhaps a deceptive one since it gave the illusion of a sharp rural–urban dichotomy. The policy could also be misused, as when a green belt was inserted into the narrow passage of unattractive land between Falkirk and Grangemouth. Today, green belts are outmoded as a restriction on urban growth because car ownership allows so many to leap-frog them, although they are still valuable in protecting farm land from developers. However, some feel that green belts should provide, instead of their purely restrictive role, a positive contribution to land-use planning.

Beyond the green belts there was concern to protect the landscape from unsightly intrusions. This was expressed in the designation of Areas of Great Landscape Value, Areas of Special Planning Control, and the creation of National Park Direction Areas in 1948. These were the five areas unsuccessfully proposed for national park status by the Ramsay Committee in 1945. The last two of these special area designations entailed a greater degree of control over development by the Scottish Office or the Countryside Commission for Scotland, whereas elsewhere the local authority decided on most planning applications. Such a multiplicity of designations had its more absurd moments: the Pentland Hills south of Edinburgh were simultaneously a Green Belt area, an Area of Great Landscape Value, and an Area of Special Planning Control while still being used by the Army for rifle practice.

However, it is generally true that rural areas were subject to less planning control than urban areas. This was partly because there was less pressure for development and partly because many forms of rural development were approved automatically under the 1947 Act's General Development Order. Most changes in agriculture and forestry and the activities of government departments were exempt from local control, although since 1971 local authorities have been able to ask the Scottish Office to set up an enquiry into proposals submitted by government departments. Consequently, in rural areas more than elsewhere, control requires landownership or voluntary agreement with the landowner to achieve an outside body's objectives. In this way the National Trust for Scotland (founded in 1931) and the Royal Society for the Protection of Birds have successfully met their aims, whereas the system of designating Sites of Special Scientific Interest has often been imposed on unwilling people and so has been less successful in protecting land.

The process of reforming local governmemt, including the changes in 1975, tended to concentrate power in the hands of the upper tier of local government (the county council, region or islands authority). However, since the Second World War, the growing extent to which local conditions are determined by central government, particularly the Scottish Office, has reduced the power of all local councils. This situation developed during the Second World War and has been consolidated by the more or less interventionist policies of most Labour and Conservative Governments since 1945. Whether for reasons of equity or controlling public expenditure, central government perceived a clear need to erode local autonomy. This is shown clearly by the Rate Support Grant. This system, which attained approximately its modern form in 1929, has allowed central government to distribute nationally generated tax revenue to local authorities to ensure that a roughly comparable standard of services is provided in all areas. Along with the social security system and uniform national prices for some services and goods, this has raised the standard of living in rural Scotland more than all the explicitly regional policies. In 1888 grants from central government formed only 14% of local revenue (Prest, 1963); now they account for two-thirds and in the Western Isles 90% and have become a means whereby central government can control in detail how money is used by local authorities.

Increasing central control is also evident in planning. Not only does the Scottish Office have to approve all developments and structure plans, but it has also produced a set of National Planning Guidelines to control local planning still further (Scottish Development Department, 1977). These guidelines developed from the self-evident need to plan on a Scottish scale for North Sea oil developments and to mediate between local authorities over out-of-town shopping developments. The guidelines now include advice on landscape assessment, forestry, mining and conservation (Diamond et al., 1979). In similar vein, the apparent acceptance by the Scottish Office of a system designating National Scenic Areas and a hierarchy of urban, country, regional and special parks is a further step towards a central control of planning not found so clearly in England (Countryside Commission for Scotland, 1978 and 1974).

Central government has also sought to extend its influence in other directions by legislation. After 1866 it ran an agricultural census and a veterinary service, legislated on land tenure repeatedly, and has provided minor funds for land drainage since the 1840s. Since then it has continued to legislate in these areas, particularly with regard to land tenure and, in 1930 and 1941, land drainage. In 1886 the Crofters Holdings (Scotland) Act created a new form of secure, heritable tenancy at fixed rent for very small Highland farms, and between 1911 and 1948 this was extended to small farms elsewhere by the creation of land-holder tenure. In 1976 crofters were allowed to buy their tiny in-bye holdings, but by this time crofting had long ceased to be an agricultural way of life for most crofters. It was either an active form of retirement for the many elderly crofters or a minor adjunct to employment in weaving, fishing or the service sector (Mewett, 1977). (Crofting is dealt with more fully in Chapter 9.) For other farms, legislation charts the shifting balance of opinion over the fair distribution of power between landowner and tenant. The Ground Game Acts of 1880 and 1906 benefited the tenants, who could now protect their crops from rabbits, while the Agricultural Holdings Acts of 1875 to 1906 established fair compensation to outgoing tenants for unexhausted improvements. The abolition of the exploitative truck system in Shetland and Lewis was of great value to the crofters since it reduced the power of landlords and fish curers. Sometimes the determination of rents and tenancies benefited the landowner;

at other times the tenant benefited more from low rents and secure, heritable tenancies.

Central government has also sought to extend its influence in new areas, e.g. farm incomes, by operating systems of farm subsidy. Their importance during the First World War was self-evident because the price of farm products was closely linked to the country's total food supply. After 1918 their peace-time role was not immediately accepted and free trade was re-established, but from 1925 onwards more and more products were subsidized in one way or another. In 1938 the level of protection from cheap imports was still limited, especially given the range of products from Scottish farms, and it was only after the Agriculture Act of 1947 that a policy of major and sustained price support for most farm products was instituted in peace-time. This support has included, at various times, deficiency payments, reduced liability to taxation, statutory marketing boards, market-sharing agreements, intervention buying and import taxes—the last two being particularly common after 1973 when the United Kingdom joined the European Economic Community (EEC).

Different groups of farmers have been affected in different ways by this subsidy of their incomes. Small-scale farmers received the least support in monetary terms, but its marginal utility was arguably greater for them than for large-scale farmers and probably fewer have left farming than would have without the support. Large-scale farmers have benefited most in monetary terms from price support and also from the capital and production grants which they have always taken up more rapidly (Clark, 1977; Bowler, 1979); some may even have been over-subsidized, particularly for cereals. Hill farmers have gained greatly because their special subsidies since 1946 have formed a high proportion of their net incomes, and this has helped to counteract the price fluctuations in store livestock markets and the limited benefit they received from other subsidies. The sectors gaining least have been those of horticulture, pig- and poultry-farming, and their survival has relied more heavily on increased efficiency, a weak pound sterling as protection against imports, buoyant demand, and the alteration of their produces to suit changing tastes and income levels. The potato sector has received some limited support but has become something of a gamblers' crop with large-scale farmers taking big profits in dry years when yields are low (Dunn, 1977).

The paradox is clear. Farmers are a decreasing sector of the British voting population yet their political influence remains strong despite the conflicting interests of many groups within farming. Their influence is partly a legacy of the war years and it can be over-rated (Mackintosh, 1970); nevertheless it still draws strength from current conditions. It is a power based not on a squire-archy as formerly, nor on farmers as Members of Parliament (Larner, 1968), but rather on skilful lobbying and the cultivation of an exaggerated public belief in their efficiency during a period of rising real incomes and repeated concern over the balance of payments both before and after the entry to the EEC (Centre for Agricultural Strategy, 1980). One feels that the recommendations of the National Farmers Union are often accepted by governments less on their agricultural merits than on the likelihood that they will help meet broader economic and political objectives.

The farmers' influence is, of course, partisan and so fits neatly into the generally sectional character of government rural policy. Since the re-establishment of a Board of Agriculture in 1889 many government departments and quangos (quasi-autonomous national governmental organizations) as well as numerous pressure groups have been concerned with promoting some sector of rural life. As these interested parties have proliferated, there have been calls for the establishment of a body to coordinate the activities of government in rural areas and to achieve an optimum balance of land uses (Select Committee on Scottish Affairs, 1972). Three responses have been made to these calls. One reaction lies in the regional reports and structure planning undertaken by local authorities since 1969 to designate priority areas for farming, forestry, conservation or tourism. The former free-for-all in rural areas is being replaced by a broad zoning akin to that practised in towns since 1947. Slowly, rural development is being edged into the planning system. A second reaction has been the establishment of a Standing Committee within the Scottish Office to bring together the major departments and official bodies with rural interests. The Standing Committee's work on rural information systems may yet achieve some of the integration and optimization of land use and consistency of decision-making which the Select Committee on Scottish Affairs recommended in 1972. The Standing Committee was wound up in 1980.

Third and less directly, the creation of the Highlands and Islands Development Board (HIDB) in 1965 potentially opened the way for a more broadly based view of rural development. The Board has assisted many projects concerned with livestock marketing, fishing, tourism and community cooperatives, and since 1976 it has operated industrial estates. The Board's approach has been pragmatic rather than integrated, seizing any windfall that might be beneficial instead of pursuing a coherent strategy. The fortuitous similarity between the Holmes plan for Easter Ross and the subsequent progress there of oil-related development is a case in point (Jack Holmes Planning Group, 1968). There is no real equivalent of the HIDB in Lowland Scotland, although the Development Commission used to operate there. Its role has been taken over by the Scottish Development Agency as have the functions of the Scottish Industrial Estates Corporation and the Small Industries Council for Rural Areas of Scotland. The desire for a unitary approach to rural development is not a new one, having been started by the Congested Districts Board in 1897, but a truly integrated approach to development by public agencies is still a long way off. Indeed it may never be achieved until a consensus is reached on the development goals, the role of the state in achieving them and the proper balance between investment in infrastructure, private industry and social provision. If this consensus is not forthcoming—and it may never be—the HIDB's approach may be the most practical one in a world less convinced that in the 1960s of the superiority of integrated, centralized planning.

The government has also found itself influencing rural areas indirectly as a consequence of measures it had introduced for other reasons. For example, taxes have been levied since 1894 on the inheritance of estates, and the amount of tax payable may be so large that productive investment may be delayed and even some land sold. This may conflict with the government's more recent objectives of increasing the size of farms and promoting capital investment. Similarly, the subsidies on farm products, the progressive removal of rates on farmland since 1896, and the reliefs on estate duty after 1925 have all tended to be capitalized into higher land prices. This makes farm expansion more difficult and the acquisition of land for forestry more expensive. The subsidies may also make farmers less conscious of the need to cut costs, yet the production of food at minimum cost is another aim of policy. Similarly, one reason for promoting forestry is the employment it creates, but the imposition of cash limits on the Forestry Commission has caused it to raise labour productivity and so employ fewer people. Governments have discovered some of the interdependencies of rural life and how the pursuit of one policy objective can make it harder to achieve another. Since the original objectives were conflicting and have also changed with time, the task has become even harder.

Since 1973 the highest tier of government has been the European Economic Community (EEC), and it can be argued that its effect on rural areas so far has been relatively limited. The United Kingdom's agricultural policy was modified before entry to ease our transition and the system of green currencies has allowed the function of fixing prices for farm products to be exercised in London as well as Brussels. This will not necessarily continue but it focuses attention on the extent to which the EEC is still an *Europe des patries*. National self-interest and the bargaining to maintain it give the UK Government some say in the formulation of European policies. The Less Favoured Areas Directive (EEC 75/268) was instigated by the UK virtually to ratify the existing system of hill subsidies and the European Regional Development Fund was a similar case of national self-interest being indulged as a *quid pro quo* for concessions by the UK in other areas.

CONCLUSION

As rural areas have become more open to the influence of governments and urban areas, the ranks of farmers and fishermen have become more closed to outsiders. The industrial and urban character of farming and the rest of the countryside is reinforced with every capital-intensive technical innovation and every amalgamation. The distinction between urban and rural, *Gesellschaft* and *Gemeinschaft*, is no longer particularly valid or productive. The rural areas have lost population yet their political influence has been maintained at every level of government. The Scottish countryside is now accessible to everyone yet misunderstood by most. The stereotypes of rural life, and particularly Highland life, are powerful, and most townspeople cling tenaciously to them, perhaps because they want the countryside to appear archaic, simple, pictures-que and, above all, different. The fallacies may not matter; they help rural communities and tourism. Yet they also mould agricultural policy and deter-mine which groups benefit most from public expenditure. The country may now be wealthy enough and the rural population small enough for it to be indulged with subsidies and bolstered against the inherent costliness of the countryside on grounds of equity. It is still important enough as a producer of food for government to justify the indulgence and attractive enough for townspeople not to object.

REFERENCES

Adams, I. H. (1978). 'The Making of Urban Scotland.' Croom Helm, London.

Bowler, I. R. (1979). 'Government and Agriculture.' Longman, London.

Brownrigg, M. and Greig, M. A. (1974). 'The Economic Impact of Tourist Spending in Skye.' Highlands and Islands Development Board Special Report 13, Inverness.

Carter, I. (1979). 'Farm life in Northeast Scotland, 1840–1914.' John Donald, Edinburgh.

Centre for Agricultural Strategy (CAS) (1980). 'The Efficiency of British Agriculture.' CAS, Reading.

Clark, G. (1972). "Geographical Aspects of Beef Production in East Lothian and Nothern Berwickshire." Unpublished MA dissertation, University of Edinburgh.

Clark, G. (1977). 'The Amalgamation of Agricultural Holdings in Scotland, 1968–1973.' Unpublished Ph.D. thesis, University of Edinburgh.

Clark, G. (1981a). Some secular changes in landownership in Scotland. *Scottish Geographical Magazine* 97(1), 27–36.

Clark, G. (1981b). Public ownership of land in Scotland. *Scottish Geographical Magazine* 97(3), 140–146.

Coppock, J. T. (1976) 'An Agricultural Atlas of Scotland.' John Donald, Edinburgh.

Countryside Commission for Scotland (CCS) (1974). 'A Park System for Scotland.' CCS, Perth.

Countryside Commission for Scotland (CCS) (1978). 'Scotland's Scenic Heritage.' CCS, Perth.

Dartington Amenity Research Trust (1977). 'Second Homes in Scotland.' Dartington (Devon).

Department of Agriculture and Fisheries for Scotland (DAFS) (1980). 'Agricultural Statistics, 1978.' HMSO, Edinburgh.

Diamond, D. *et al.* (1979). The uses of strategic planning: the example of national planning guidelines in Scotland. *Town Planning Review* 50, 18–35.

Dunn, J. M. (1977). The changing structure of Scottish potato production. *Scottish Agricultural Economics* 27, 98–100.

Gaskin, M. (1971). 'Freight Rates and Prices in the Islands.' Published for Highlands and Islands Development Board, Inverness.

House of Commons (1874). 'Owners of Lands and Heritages, 1872–73 (Scotland).' House of Commons Accounts and Papers 1874, 72(3).

Hunter, J. (1976). 'The Making of the Crofting Community.' John Donald, Edinburgh.

Jack Holmes Planning Group (1968). 'The Moray Firth.' Report to Highlands and Islands Development Board, Inverness.

Johnson, J. H. (1967). Harvest migration from nineteenth-century Ireland.' *Transactions of the Institute of British Geographers* 41, 97–112.

Larner, C. (1968). 'The Scottish MP Since 1910.' reported in *The Scotsman*, 20 October 1979.

McEwen, J. (1977). 'Who owns Scotland?' Edinburgh University Student Publications Board, Edinburgh.

Mackintosh, J. P. (1970). The problems of agricultural politics. *Journal of Agricultural Economics* 21, 23–35.

Mather, A. S. (1978). 'State-Aided Land Settlement in Scotland.' O'Dell Memorial Monograph No. 6, Department of Geography, University of Aberdeen.

Mewett, P. G. (1977). Occupational pluralism in crofting. *Scottish Journal of Sociology* 2, 31–49.

Ministry of Agriculture, Fisheries and Food (MAFF) and Department of Agriculture and Fisheries for Scotland (1968). 'A Century of Agricultural Statistics, Great Britain 1866–1966.' HMSO, London.

Ministry of Agriculture, Fisheries and Food (MAFF), Department of Agriculture and Fisheries for Scotland and Department of Agriculture for Northern Ireland (1977). 'The Changing Structure of Agriculture, 1968–1975.' HMSO, London.

Newby, H. (1979) 'Green and Pleasant Land?' Heinemann, London.

Northfield Committee (1979). 'Report of the Committee of Inquiry into the Acquisition and Occupancy of Agricultural Land.' Cmnd. 7599, HMSO, London.

Pacione, M. (1980). Differential quality of life in a metropolitan village. *Transactions of the Institute of British Geographers* 5 (2), 185–206.

Prest, A. R. (1963). 'Public Finance in Theory and Practice.' Weidenfeld and Nicolson, London.

Ramsey Committee (1945). 'Report of the Scottish National Parks Survey Committee.' Cmd. 6631, HMSO, London.

Rettie, W. J. (1975). Scotland's farm occupiers. *Scottish Agricultural Economics* **25**, 387–393.

Robson, N. (1973). 'The Problems of Small Scale Farms.' Unpublished Ph.D. thesis, University of Aberdeen.

Russell, T. P. (1970). The size structure of Scottish agriculture.' *Scottish Agricultural Economics* **20**, 299–325.

Saul, S. B. (1969). 'The Myth of the Great Depression. 1873–1896.' Macmillan, London.

Scottish Development Department (SDD) (1977). 'National Planning Guidelines.' Circular 19/1977, Edinburgh.

Select Committee on Scottish Affairs (1972). 'Land Resource Use in Scotland.' House of Commons Papers, 511 i-v, HMSO, London.

Skinner, D. N. (1976). 'A Situation Report on Green Belts in Scotland.' Countryside Commission for Scotland Occasional Paper 8, Perth.

Symon, J. A. (1959). 'Scottish Farming—Past and Present.' Oliver and Boyd, Edinburgh.

Toulouse, N. F. (1977). Some aspects of land use changes in relation to sugar beet and peas 1971–1975. *Scottish Agricultural Economics* **27**, 92–97.

Urquhart, G. A. (1965). The amalgamation of agricultural holdings: a study of two parishes in western Aberdeenshire. *Journal of Agricultural Economics* **16**, 405–412.

Wagstaff, H. R. (1970). Scotland's farm occupiers. *Scottish Agricultural Economics* **20**, 277–285.

Wagstaff, H. R. (1971). Recruitment and losses of farm workers. *Scottish Agricultural Economics* **21**, 7–16.

Wagstaff, H. R. (1972). Recruitment, labour turnover and losses of full-time male workers in Scottish agriculture, 1967–1970. *Scottish Agricultural Economics* **22**, 103–112.

Wagstaff, H. R. (1973). Employment multipliers in rural Scotland. *Scottish Journal of Political Economy* **20**, 239–261.

11

Urbanization, Capital Accumulation, and Class Struggle in Scotland, 1750–1914

J. Doherty

In assessing the outcome of a conference held by the Past and Present Society in 1975, Philip Abrams judged that among urban historians a fundamental reinterpretation of the concept of town had emerged in which

> the tendency was to move away from any attempt to treat towns as variables in themselves—whether dependent, independent or merely intervening—and also from the attempt to regard the town as a generic social reality, and to see cities and towns instead as fields of action integral to some larger world and within which the interactions and contradictions of that larger world are displayed with special clarity (Abrams, 1978, 3).

To the extent that this stress on the historical specificity of the significance of urbanism is a discernible trend it represents a welcome advance on earlier conceptions of the town in that it explicitly rejects any assumed necessary and invariant association between urbanization and economic growth, challenges the universalistic application of the concept of rural–urban antithesis and, perhaps most importantly, counters the notion of urban autonomy.

However, in attempting to distance himself from the fetishistic notion of the town having a separate ontological existence, Abrams goes on to propose that cities and towns be treated merely as a 'resource for the understanding of the structure and processes of a more inclusive reality' (Abrams, 1978, 3). Abrams thus appears to reduce the town to a mere location, or to use his term a 'site', a passive unimportant spatial characteristic of wider social activities; for Abrams the town ceases to be 'an intrinsically problematic social object at all' (p. 13).

In espousing this kind of perspective Abrams lends support intentionally or otherwise to much of the work of econmic historians, including recent contributions from those of varying political perspectives working on nineteenth-century Scotland (see, for example, Smout, 1969; Lenman, 1977; Dickson, 1980). Here the analysis of economic development is preceded by a brief and abstracted presentation of statistics on urban growth to be followed by a detailed *aspatial* examination of agricultural and industrial change; aspatial in that reference to urban centres merely serves to define the locational coordinates of economic development. Thus in place of 'fetishism' in which urban centres are regarded as having an autonomous social and spatial existence, operating according to their own 'laws of internal transformation' (Harvey, 1973, 304), we have the avoidance of any consideration of space or at best its relegation to virtual insignificance.

A case could be made for the preferability of an aspatial as opposed to an ahistorical analysis, but superior to both is an approach which integrates space and history in the concrete investigation of social activity. Historical geographers would presumably claim to be doing just that, and they certainly try. Yet the implications of this deceptively straightforward statement are manifold, and the pursuit of its logical conclusion would take historical geography beyond the confines of its traditional boundaries.

Historical geography as a subdiscipline takes its idea of space from its parent science, and geography as a whole lacks an adequate theoretical conceputalization of space. From the excessive formalism of 'locational analysis' through to the more satisfactory but still flawed 'structuralist' perspective which attempts to relate spatial structure to social structure, space is viewed as having a real, and not just an analytically, separate existence; it is viewed as an object of scientific study in its own right. This perspective of space tends to restrict the level of investigation, at best, to a mechanical justaposition of spatial pattern and social process and helps confine the definition of process to the indentification of superficial, surface features of social existence.

The strictures which Abrams applied to the concept of town employed in much urban history are equally applicable to the concept of space adopted in geography, historical or otherwise. There is clearly a need to reconstitute the study of urbanization and urbanism by slipping the harness of restrictive spatial categories while avoiding a headlong gallop into the abyss of spacelessness.

The perspective afforded by the adoption of a political economy approach to the study of urbanism would seem to offer the best way forward. In this approach it is recognized that space is created by social activity and that as such it has no separate existence apart from that activity. Space is seen not merely as a 'reflection' or 'effect' of social process, but as an integral part of a social whole, of a totality which is at once social and economic and political. The corallary of this commitment to and focus on the totality is the rejection of any notion of the ontological primacy of space. Unrestrained by such notions, a freedom is gained to shift the balance of investigation to social activity, to burrow beneath the surface of social existence, without losing sight of the potential importance of space. Such a view allows, for example, space to be readily incorporated as an 'effecting' agent, interacting and evolving with other aspects of the totality rather than as a mere passive receptor of social imperatives.

The adoption of this view of space leaves the way clear for the rehabilitation of the town in historical and present-day studies. A rehabilitation which crucially starts from a rejection of the concept of urban autonomy. Urbanism, like space generally, has to be seen as an integral part of the totality, created by social activity and, once formed, interrelating and evolving with that social activity as part of the development of society.

In the political economy perspective urbanism is manifest as the built environment—literally the physical infrastructure which facilitates the process of production, circulation, exchange and consumption in society. Using Anderson's (1975, 7) revealing analogy, it is the man-made 'pitch', the condition of which can influence the outcome of the game. The built environment is the result of capital investment and capital consumption, often of a conspicuous nature, and is thus centrally related to the whole process of capital accumulation. As Harvey suggests, it represents the 'geographical concentration of the socially designated surplus product' (1973, 240). The built environment also has a social manifestation which, extending Anderson's analogy, is equivalent to the players on the pitch constantly changing position and fighting for control; the study of urbanism thus implies and necessitates the examination of class conflict.

For political economy then the town as a spatial and social entity can only be understood as part of the wider issues of 'social development, economic growth and political control' (Anderson, 1977, 36); it cannot be understood apart from the process of the development of capitalist society. It is around the two themes of capital accumulation and class struggle that the present investigation of urban development in Scotland from the late eighteenth to the beginning of the twentieth century is structured.

URBANIZATION AND CAPITAL ACCUMULATION

In Scotland after 1780 there was no sudden take-off into an industrial revolution, but rather a more rapid penetration of capitalist relations into the economy. The base for capital accumulation had already been laid. . . . What happened after 1780 was more a development of this base, and the acceleration of capital accumulation on more mature capitalist principles, rather than a new beginning (Dickson, 1980, 137).

Background

The preconditions for nineteenth-century urban expansion and industrial development in Scotland were established in the middle and later years of the eighteenth century. During this period the Scottish economy demonstrated an increased ability to sustain the production of surplus, particularly an agricultural surplus despite localized harvest failures, and was characterized by an accelerating rate of change in the forms of social and economic organization, particularly in rural districts (see Chapter 8).

The absence of subsistence crises and the limited effects of famine and disease, at least in comparison with seventeenth-century experience, helped to reduce the high death rates and stimulated population increases. This growing population itself stimulated productivity for an expanding market, encouraged land use and organizational changes, and provided the basis for an enlarged and increasingly mobile labour force. Although the reorganization of rural activity required a considerable number of workers, it probably resulted in an eventual relative decline in agricultural employment and consequently increased the number of landless labourers who were, in part, absorbed by the reconstituted and expanding industrial sector. In this context the role that the government-sponsored agencies, such as the Board of Trustees for the Encouragement of Manufactures and Fisheries (established in 1727) and the Commission on Forfeited Estates (established after 1745), played in the development of industry is disputed (see Smout, 1980). Of undoubted importance were the activities of the 'improving' landlords as expressed, for instance, in the planned village movement (see Lockhart, 1980). It was from some of these settlements, especially those that were developed in the last quarter of the eighteenth and early part of the nineteenth centuries, that according to Adams (1978, 87) the 'embryo industrial town emerged'.

The increasing buoyancy of the Scottish economy is further indicated by the expansion of trade both at home (e.g. cattle) and overseas (e.g. tobacco and cotton) and by the gradual establishment of Scottish banking, credit and legal systems. By the last quarter of the eighteenth century capital accumulation in Scotland, associated with commercialization and the penetration of market relations to all sectors of the economy, was taking place at an accelerating rate. However, the regional manifestation of this accumulation process demonstrated a considerable unevenness. During the eighteenth century certain regional specializations associated with increasing wealth and expanding production, became apparent (e.g. pastoralism in the North-East and cereal growing in the Lothians), but other areas, notably sections of the Highlands, disturbed the general patterns of development and progress. Uneven regional development was to be as characteristic of Scottish capitalism as it was of capitalist expansion elsewhere (see Mandel, 1975).

Urbanization, Industrialization and Uneven Development

In the context of an expanding economy Scotland experienced a rapid population growth and an accelerated rate of urbanization. In 1755 Scotland's population was 1·25 million, by 1801 it exceeded 1·5 million and it continued to expand through the nineteenth century, reaching nearly 3 million by 1851 and over 4·5 million in 1901. During this period there was also a substantial increase in the proportion of the population concentrated in urban centres, and within this emerging urban system a greater proportion was centralized in the larger towns and cities, particularly Glasgow, Edinburgh, Aberdeen and Dundee.

In 1755 there were 4 towns with over 10 000 inhabitants comprising some 9% of the total population. In 1821 these figures had increased to 13 towns and 25% of the population. At this time 7 out of 10 Scots could still be regarded as rural dwellers (Smout, 1969, 242), but by 1851 32·2% of the country's population lived in towns of 10 000 or more and by 1891 the proportion was 49·9%.

These trends towards urban concentration were a direct result of a combination of legislative (boundary extensions) and demographic (natural increase and migration) changes. More fundamentally, however, they must be seen as an integral part of the whole process of economic growth and expansion associated with the transition of Scotland during the course of the nineteenth century from an essentially agricultural society to a predominantly industrial society (see Chapter 8). As Kemp (1978, 9) says:

> The central characteristic of industrialisation is machine production, the basis for an enormous growth in productivity and thus for economic specialisation in all directions. It created a new environment for work, with its own demands and laws—the factory. It brought about the concentration of workers in big industrial units and the growth of towns to house the working population, creating a new urban environment for social living. The new type of town growing mushroomlike with industrialisation, was not an adjunct to a predominantly agrarian society but a new dynamic force for change, the home of the majority of the population in a predominantly industrial society.

Textiles predominated in the early part of Scotland's 'industrial revolution' as they did elsewhere. The spinning of linen yarn and cotton was mechanized from the 1780s, but before the adoption of steam, textile manufacture was locationally bound by the need for suitable water-power sites for spinning and also by the persistence of residual patterns of work organization in the form of domestic handloom weaving. As late as 1838 there were an estimated 84 000 handloom weavers operating in Scotland (Smout, 1969, 401).

Many of the sites for the early spinning factories expanded little beyond their initial settlements, for example, New Lanark, Catrine, Deanston and Stanley;

others, such as Barrhead and Hawick, grew into substantial towns (Adams, 1978, chapter 5; Cook, 1977). Weaving, originally a rural pursuit, rapidly became an urban activity as the trade moved from a supplementary to a full-time occupation in response to the increase in demand reflected in the expanding yard output of the spinning factories. Many weaving villages did of course survive after 1820, but it was the larger towns such as Paisley that came to dominate even in the handloom phase. As late as 1831, for instance, among the third of Glasgow's population engaged in cotton textiles the domestic handloom weavers still outnumbered the factory-based powerloom operators (Smout, 1969, 369).

During the early phases of industrialization the spinning and weaving stages of textile production maintained a precarious balance despite the increasing divergence in their methods of production. The greater productive potential of a mechanized and factory-based spinning was partly offset in the early years of its use by the continuation of substantial, though declining, hand-spinning operations and by the inefficiency of the early water-powered mills. The preference of the emerging proletariat for weaving and its domestic routines and in particular their dislike for the imposed discipline of the spinning factories, together with the need, in many instances, for employers to build a suitable living environment for the spinning workforce further constrained the early expansion of factory spinning. It was not until after 1815, when demobilization at the end of the Napoleonic Wars and immigration from Ireland began to have an effect, that textiles generally and spinning in particular could call upon a reserve army of labour. Yet in the case of weaving the privileged position of the handloom operators was being threatened much earlier by the influx of surplus rural labour. In 1812 weavers throughout Scotland struck in an unsuccessful attempt to restrict entry to the trade and to enforce a minimum price for cloth (Smout, 1969, 398). However, despite these developments the discrepancy between the productive capacities of spinning and weaving became more evident during the first decades of the nineteenth century and was to be heightened and then largely solved as steam power was introduced first to spinning and subsequently to weaving.

Under the stimulus of expanding domestic and external markets the application of steam power to spinning and weaving introduced a new phase of capital accumulation, a phase closely associated with the concentration of industrial activity in Scotland's urban centres. As steam power freed spinning from the locational constraints imposed by its energy requirements and took weaving out of its domestic setting, textile production became increasingly factory-based and urban-oriented. The factory organization of production encouraged the concentration of textile-manufacturing activities; concentration in larger units of production as well as in central places in order that such activities could benefit from scale and agglomeration economies. Town locations thus proved attractive to the early industrialists. Here it was easier to tap a surplus labour force of workers needed for the arduous, and low-paid routines of early factories; here individual employers could have the housing and other social reproduction needs of their work force catered for by speculative builders and entrepreneurs; here, also, the increasing interlinkages between manufacturing activities, for example between the Glasgow chemical and textile industries (Lenman, 1977, 127), could best be facilitated (see Chapter 8). Towns generally occupied favoured locations on the emerging communications system. From 1770 the construction of turnpikes and canals had established a rudimentary transport network which was filled out by the building of a substantial railway system in the 1840s and 50s. A town location thus facilitated both the distribution of finished commodities to a wider market and access to raw materials. Indeed until the advent of cheap rail transport the prohibitive costs of the overland movement of coal tended to favour coastal or near-coalfield sites for steam-powered enterprises. The larger urban centres, benefited, of course, from industrial concentration, but many middle-order and smaller centres also grew in consequence.

In relation to these lower-order settlements Saunders (1950) has identified three broad groupings. The first is illustrated by such towns as Perth, Ayr, Dumfries, Stirling, Inverness, Elgin and Haddington, which were active local centres occupying historic sites and attracting local commerce and a mix of smaller industries. In some instances they also operated as important regional centres for professional and cultural services. Their growth was marked, but not exceptional, and although they retained their local importance, their position in the urban hierarchy declined as the century progressed (see Gordon, 1977). They were replaced in the hierarchy by the second group indentified by Saunders, the rapidly expanding industrial centres, of which the textile towns of Paisley, Kilmarnock, Dunfermline and Hawick were most prominent. In this group also Saunders includes Greenock and Alloa as examples of ports serving industrial hinterlands, while Falkirk, Hamilton, Coatbridge and Motherwell grew as coal-mining and iron-smelting centres.

Between these two extremes Saunders notes a series of disparate local developments from the village burghs of Galloway to the market towns of the Highland margins, the fishing ports of the east and Ayrshire coasts, the small spinning and weaving towns along the base of the Grampians (e.g. Blairgowrie, Brechin, Forfar, Montrose), in the Ochils and in the Borders, and the spa and tourist resorts such as Peebles, Rothesay and Oban.

Taking the percentage in centres of 2000 or more inhabitants as a measure of urbanization, Scotland had passed the 50% mark by 1851. Indeed in that year Scotland's urban population (51·8%) marginally exceeded that of England (50·1%); this situation was reversed shortly afterwards and by 1891 Scotland had 65·4% in towns of 2000 or more compared with England's 72·1% (Weber,

Table 11.1 Urban and rural population 1861–1901 (%)

	1861	1871	1881	1891	1901
Town[a]	52·78	57·10	61·75	65·37	69·77
Village[b]	11·09	13·03	11·99	11·57	10·42
Rural	36·13	29·87	26·26	23·06	19·81

[a] settlements of 2000 and over
[b] settlements between 300 and 2000
Source: Census of Scotland 1861–1901

1899, 59), a figure which Scotland could not match even in 1901 (see Table 11.1).

The concentration of population in urban centres continued through the nineteenth and into the twentieth century. In 1911, when a new census definition of urban as centres of 1000 or more was introduced, 75% of the country's population could claim to be urbanized. This represents an increase of nearly 20% over the 1861 figure. The bulk of this increase took place in the last 40 years of the nineteenth century at a rate of about 4% per decade.

Together with these increases in population size and levels of urbanization, the nineteenth century also saw a discernible change in the regional pattern of population and urban growth. Indeed, according to Turnock (1979, 13), the basis for this change was apparent as early as the seventeenth century, when the central region emerged as a favoured area for economic development, particularly in association with glass making, the extraction of coal and salt and the production of fine woollens. Despite these developments, in 1755 over 50% of Scotland's population still lived north of the Clyde–Tay line. However, during the next 50 years the regional concentration of population showed a marked shift towards the central area, a shift which gathered momentum through the nineteenth century and continued during the twentieth. In 1851 over half of

Table 11.2 Distribution of Scotland's population by region (%)

Year	Central Region	Southern Region	Northern Region
1755	37	11	51
1801	43	11	46
1821	47	11	42
1851	53	—————— 47 ——————	
1861	58	9	33
1871	61	8	31
1891	66	7	27
1901	67	—————— 33 ——————	
1911	72	5	23

Sources: Smout (1964, 242); Lythe and Butt (1976, 94); Turnock (1979, 18); Census of Scotland (1951, Table I, Vol. 3).

the country's population was located in the central belt, comprising the counties of Ayr, Dunbarton, Lanark, Renfrew, Clackmannan, Stirling and Fife, plus the Lothians and the city of Dundee; by 1911 this proportion had risen to 72% (Table 11.2).

By the middle of the nineteenth century the central belt had clearly emerged as the most populous and most extensively urbanized region in Scotland. In 1861 only four counties had over 50% of their populations living in burghs of 10 000 or more inhabitans—Renfrew, Lanark, Midlothian and Angus (Fig. 11.1). By 1911, notwithstanding increases in Aberdeen and Selkirk, the pattern had been reinforced with the addition of Dunbarton to the above four and with lower-level increases observable in other central counties (Fig. 11.2).*

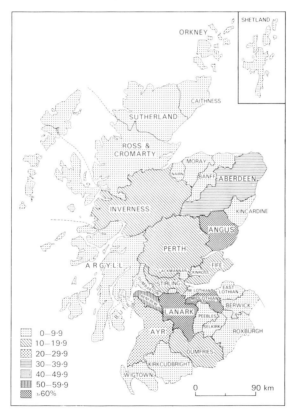

Fig. 11.1   Proportion of county populations in Burghs of 10,000 or more, 1861

* I am grateful to Ronald Brown, former Geography research student at Edinburgh for providing the figure on which his analysis is based.

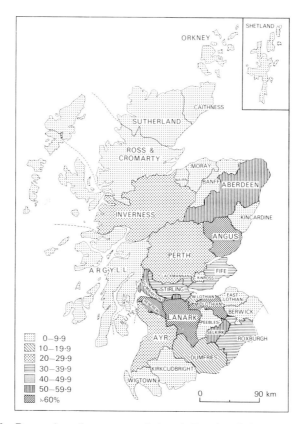

Fig. 11.2   Proportion of county populations in Burghs of 10,000 or more, 1911

An examination of the lower index of urbanization (urban equals a population of 1000 or more) confirms this pattern of central area dominance with the
additional identification of important urban concentrations in the north-east.
On this index Renfrew, Lanark, Midlothian and Angus again emerge as the
most urbanized counties in mid-century with over 70% of their populations
living in centres of 1000 or more (Fig. 11.3). By 1911 these four counties had
been joined by Dunbarton, Stirling, Clackmannan, Fife and Selkirk (Fig.
11.4). A closer look at this index demonstrated that apart from Perth and
Kinross all counties associated with the central and north-eastern lowlands had
passed the 50% urban mark by 1861.[*] At a regional level also it is clear that the
central area in 1911 had maintained the dominant urban position it had

---

[*] Gordon's analysis (1977, 204) of the distribution of burghs with 5000 or more inhabitants
confirms the pattern of central region dominance (see also Flinn, 1977, 313).

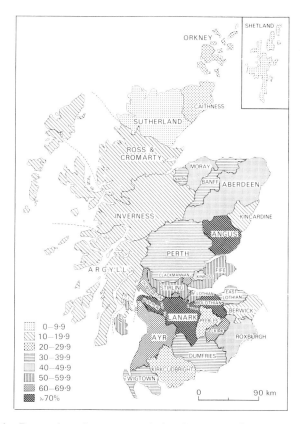

Fig. 11.3 Proportion of county populations in centres of 1000 or more, 1861

achieved by mid-century (Table 11.3). However, it is also apparent from Table 11.3 that within the central region itself the difference between the eastern and western halves was gradually being reduced: in 1861 the west was nearly 10% more urbanized than the east; in 1911 the difference was only 6·5%.

The configuration of urban settlements that emerged in the later years of the eighteenth and first half of the nineteenth centuries was largely consolidated and expanded in the decades after 1850. If the earlier period was characterized by the spectacular creation of new settlements and by the rapid expansion of some existing towns after long periods of relative stagnation, the later period saw steady and cumulative increases in the size of the now established industrial centres and particularly in the size of the largest (Fig. 11.5). The nineteenth-century history of Scotland's leading settlements vividly illustrates the nature of the urban-industrial economy that emerged during this period and demonstrated many of its strengths and weaknesses. Its strengths

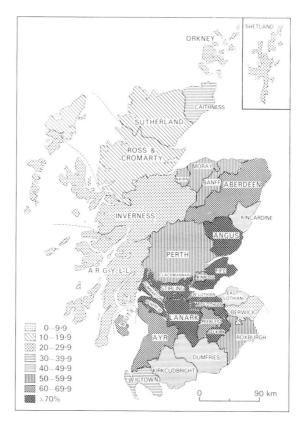

Fig. 11.4   Proportion of county populations in centres of 1000 or more, 1911

Table 11.3 Urban[a] and rural population by region (%)

	1861		1891		1911	
	Urban	Rural	Urban	Rural	Urban	Rural
Northern Region	32·6	67·4	43·7	56·3	49·1	50·9
Southern Region	33·5	66·5	44·1	55·9	47·8	52·2
Central Region	75·9	24·1	84·1	15·9	85·8	14.2
East	70·1	29·9	79·4	20·6	81·7	18·3
West	79·8	20·2	87·0	13·0	88·2	11·3

[a] settlements of 1000 or more
Source: Census of Scotland, 1951.

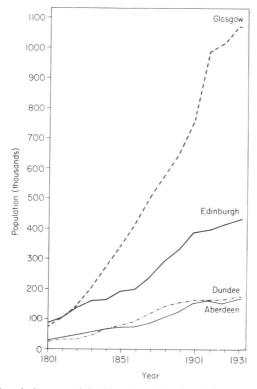

Fig. 11.5 Population growth in Aberdeen, Dundee, Edinburgh and Glasgow, 1801–1931

sustained urban growth throughout the nineteenth century and early decades of the twentieth. Thereafter its weaknesses became more clearly apparent and the course of urban development was consequently changed.

Edinburgh with Leith was the largest town in Scotland in 1801, and its population almost doubled in the first quarter of the nineteenth century from around 80 000 to approximately 150 000. The town's growth from the latter half of the eighteenth century was based on its roles as the cultural capital of the country and the major regional centre of the fertile and productive Lothians. Edinburgh bankers and lawyers served the grain and stock farmers of the surrounding district and offered specialist legal and financial services to a wider market. Edinburgh grew as the foremost ecclesiastical, medical and legal centre in the country, and in 1831 its social structure was dominated by 'bankers, professional men and capitalists' who comprised some 5% of the town's population (Saunders, 1950, 388).

Leith became a focus for industrial activity and emerged as an important centre for ship repairing, sugar refining, and soap and glass making. Other industrial activities, such as printing, furniture making and brewing, were more widely scattered and organized predominantly in small units. These, perhaps because of low capitalization, were disproportionately affected by the 1825 recession, and although Edinburgh continued to grow, it was quickly outstripped by Glasgow whose industrial base was more firmly established.

Edinburgh's growth in the second half of the nineteenth century was in some part associated with the development of new industries—rubber manufacture, whisky blending and engineering—but was predominantly due to the expansion of already established cultural and financial activities. The ascendancy of Edinburgh in banking and insurance being finally established after the collapse of the City of Glasgow Bank in 1878.

Glasgow's expansion (from its position as regional centre) was assured after the Act of Union with the development of substantial entrepot activities. The tobacco trade provided the first fillip to the town's growth. Towards the end of the eighteenth century, cotton textiles benefiting from the residual skills of a significant but declining linen trade, created the manufacturing base for the subsequent burgeoning of the city. The 1830s also saw important developments in coal, iron, chemical and engineering activities which were to be in the forefront of Glasgow's growth when cotton production faltered after 1847. Slaven (1975, 10) has identified the key features of the regional basis of Glasgow's growth during this period:

> North and east of Glasgow coal and iron held north Lanarkshire and the Clyde basin under their sway, while south and west of the city textiles were still dominant. Glasgow united the two parts as the commercial capital and the river Clyde, emerging as a great port and shipbuilding centre, linked the thriving industries to the outside world. This commercial and industrial core was surrounded by a more rural fringe, supporting industrial salients in north Ayrshire, but characterised by highly commercial mixed farming geared to the needs of the urban-industrial towns which now sheltered over 80 per cent of the region's people.

The cumulative effects of the development of textiles, coal and steel, shipbuilding and heavy engineering activities were starkly demonstrated in the sustained increase in Glasgow's population throughout the nineteenth century and its emergence as the 'Second City of the Empire' (see Fig. 11.5).

Saunders (1950, 130) describes Aberdeen as 'a true regional capital' supported by and serving a varied hinterland. Although linen, cotton and wool manufactures contributed substantially to the town's prosperity in the early part of the nineteenth century, Aberdeen was never just a textile town and developed a variety of other industries in the middle and later years of the century. The most spectacular was perhaps the extension of fishing from inshore herring to sea trawling after 1870 when the development of an inland railway system assured ready access to markets as far away as London. In 1911, with some 200 trawlers operating out of its harbour, Aberdeen was Britain's third largest fishing port. But in line with its regional focus Aberdeen's prosperity was also based on the use of local resources in granite polishing, paper making and, for a while, shipbuilding.

In the Scottish context Dundee was to emerge as the classic mono-industrial manufacturing town in the late nineteenth century. The basis for this development was laid in the period before 1850, when linen manufacture was concentrated in the town, dwarfing in importance the existing port and whaling activities. Dundee's economic base, perhaps more than any other centre in Scotland was externally oriented, with the town's linen and, from the 1830s, jute industries dependent on imported raw materials and overseas markets.

Dundee's growth in the second half of the nineteenth century reflected the enormous expansion from 1860 in the town's textile base. Jute production dominated in this period, but linen manufacture continued into the twentieth century. Although Dundee was excessively reliant on textiles for local income (48 000 were employed in jute at the turn of the century), several ancillary industries expanded in the later years of the nineteenth century, of which perhaps the most significant were shipbuilding and textile engineering; for every three jobs in jute, two were created elsewhere (McDowell, 1978).

When booming, bourgeois Britain of the Victorian era was the 'workshop of the world', the focus of Scottish industry on capital goods and textile production contributed to the economic prosperity of the country's urban centres. In the heyday of free trade, with British industry expanding to the four corners of the world, the dependence of the leading sectors of Scotland's industry on external markets and external sources of raw materials, and the absence of domestically oriented consumer goods industry were of little concern. However, as Britain's position of world dominance was challenged by new twentieth-century competitors and calls for protectionism began to be heard, the precarious position of Scotland's industrial base was exposed. The very strengths of Scottish industry in the nineteenth century were to be its undoing in the twentieth (see Chapter 8).

Capital Accumulation and the Built Environment

In nineteenth-century Scotland industrialization and urbanization evolved together as mutually interacting parts of an expanding capitalist society. Workplace and residence, separated by rural reorganization and the advent of the factory system, were reunited in the urban concentration of industry and its workforce. Expanding urban populations created a potential market and available source of labour for further industrial concentration and capital accumulation. However, urbanization in the nineteenth century was more than a demographic manifestation of economic and social processes: it entailed the production of a built environment (factories, roads, houses, ports etc.) on an unprecedented scale, the creation of a physical infrastructure which facilitated the expansion of industrial capitalism.

At least two distinct but related roles can be identified for the built environment in the context of nineteenth-century Scotland, as in other emerging capitalist societies of the time. First, from the perspective of those capitalists such as builders, contractors and property speculators directly involved with the creation of its various elements, the built environment can be seen as composed of individual 'exchange values': investment in buildings, roads, railways and houses was regarded as a potential source of profit which could only be obtained by the realization of the exchange values of these various elements in the market. Secondly, and in a wider perspective, the built environment can be regarded as a set of 'use values', which served a social purpose for capital in that their availability facilitated the general as well as the specific process of accumulation. Each of these roles can now be considered, albeit briefly because of the sparseness of work on these issues, in relation to the history of urbanization in nineteenth-century Scotland.

The production of the built environment by individual members of the construction industry was part of a more general process, conceived in its widest sense, of fixed capital formation. It is apparent from general observation as well as from more detailed analysis that there were considerable fluctuations in fixed capital formation in Scotland from the end of the eighteenth to the beginning of the twentieth century. The variation in investment associated with the relatively minor canal boom beginning towards the end of the eighteenth century and the altogether more impressive booms in railway investment and housing construction around the middle and end of the nineteenth century can be cited as examples. Satisfactory explanations of these fluctuations have, however, proved elusive.

In the context of Britain as a whole no overall direct and uniform correspondence between fixed capital formation and economic growth has been identified. At best, if there was an association, it reflected the quality and variety rather than the quantity of the fixed capital involved (see Deane, 1967; Pollard, 1964; Crouzet, 1972). In the absence of separate analysis it must be assumed that the Scottish experience conformed to this wider pattern.

Clearly, in examining the nature of fixed capital investment disaggregation is necessary: as Harvey (1978, 115) has observed, each element of the built environment is 'produced under different conditions and according to quite different rules'. In this context the trend noted by Whitehand (1977, 405) towards an inverse relationship between investment in Glasgow's institutional structures and investment in Glasgow's housing during the construction boom of the 1870s and the slump of the 1910s is illustrative.

In the Scottish context most work on the built environment appears to have focused on housing construction, particularly housing construction in late-nineteenth century Glasgow, Cairncross's (1953) analysis of residential building activity in Glasgow from mid nineteenth century to the outbreak of the First World War being a pioneer study. He argued that investment in building responded to a combination of supply and demand factors; population increases on the one hand with credit availability on the other—in sum effective demand—slumps in building activity being explained by overstocking and/or withdrawal of credit. This explanation has been largely supported by more comprehensive studies of building activity in Britain and elsewhere (Lewis, 1965; Thomas, 1974; Gotlieb, 1976). Among the additional features of these later studies, however, was the identification of regular cycles of building activity—the 15 to 25 year Knuznets cycles. The fluctuations identified by Cairncross (1953), Butt (1971) and Whitehand (1972) in Glasgow's post-1850 housing construction, with booms in the periods 1859–77 and 1894–1908 and slumps between 1878–93 and 1909–23, provide at least circumstantial support for the presence of similar cycles in nineteenth and early twentieth century Scotland.

In a series of articles Harvey (1975, 1978, 1978a) has reopened the question of building cycle behaviour by proposing that investment in the built environment generally reflects crises of 'overaccumulation' which periodically occur when, for various reasons, more directly productive avenues for capital investment in what he calls 'the primary circuit of capital' are closed. Capital then seeks investment opportunities in 'the secondary circuit', the built environment, until such time as the crisis is alleviated and investment in the primary circuit again becomes attractive. If these broad notions concerning the behaviour of building cycles are to be useful in explaining urbanization in nineteenth-century Scotland, they must be matched with the detail of historical experience; the evidence available from Scottish cities on the organization of investment in the residential sector of the built environment is somewhat equivocal, although it generally supports Harvey's thesis. Elliot and McCrone, for instance, in their study of residential construction activity in Edinburgh at the end of the nineteenth century show that 'investment in housing, and working class housing in particular, was attractive to small savers, often middle and small bourgeois families who saw a relatively safe and secure form of investment in "stone and lime"' (Elliot and McCrone, 1980, 10). The small savings of these individuals were not sufficient to finance complete developments and were organized into larger portfolios and investment funds by property companies and local lawyers for use in the housing market. Indeed Simpson (1977, 59), with reference to Glasgow, has suggested that the 'largest single source of development capital and mortgages were the trust funds', of individual families, 'orgainsed and managed by accountants and lawyers'. Supporting evidence for the prevalence of this kind of capital investment in Scottish housing is given by Gauldie (1974, part 3). Yet as Elliot and McCrone indicate in their case studies, reasonably large sums from businessmen were also invested in working class housing through the agency of local lawyers and, in the case of Marchmont, a middle-class housing area in the south of Edinburgh, investments of a considerable size organized by the local landlord were forthcoming from insurance companies and banks (Elliot and McCrone, 1980, 11–13).

The history of housing construction in Dundee in the late nineteenth century indicates a similar mix of sources for capital, with 'almost every class of person' speculating in housing (Lenman et al., 1969, 85). However, by far the most important were individuals looking for some return on small outlays. Between 1850 and 1914 these small investors were responsible for the construction of three times as many houses in Dundee as the large speculative building contractors.

Clearly, substantial sums of capital could be mobilized for the housing market given appropriate circumstances, namely the availability of surplus capital. The nature of these circumstances is illustrated by the fact that once alternative and more lucrative outlets could be identified, the organizing agents of the capital market had no qualms about diverting construction capital. Thus in 1900 when overseas investment began to pay a higher interest than housing investment Edinburgh lawyers diverted their clients' funds into the burgeoning investment trusts, with the result that many builders went bankrupt and housing construction tailed off (McCrone and Elliot, 1980, 10–12).

Although investment in Scottish housing was clearly related to effective demand and overaccumulation trends, other factors need to be taken into consideration. In Dundee, for instance, the 20 year delay in housing provision from 1850, when severe overcrowding demonstrated the immediate need for additional accommodation, can be explained by the availability of more attractive investment opportunities in jute textiles and by the absence of effective demand, (wages were low among the working population). Any full explanation of this delay would also need to take account, first, of the possibility, as perceived by builders and investors, of large-scale emigration at this time to North America, which would critically reduce demand and, second, of the severe shortage of locally available building materials which imposed a major constraint on building activity (Lenman et al., 1969, 88). National, indeed international, as well as local factors must be considered in any complete examination of building cycle activity.

Additionally when specific contexts are under examination the possibility of differential effects on housing construction and built environment creation resulting from the same factors has to be recognized. Overseas investment opportunities clearly contributed to a decline in working-class housing construction at the turn of the century, but the high returns from these investments would have helped stimulate demand for higher-quality dwellings among some sections of town populations. The first decades of the twentieth century saw substantial suburban developments in many Scottish cities, for example, east Clepington and parts of Broughty Ferry in Dundee, Kelvinside and Langside in Glasgow. These developments were linked with a more general movement of town populations at this time associated with the depopulation of inner city areas and a general increase in the populations of the outer parishes (Census of Scotland, 1911, Vol. I).

In turning to a consideration of the second and wider role of the built environment in capitalist society, which was identified above, Lojkine (1976, 127) has provided a succinct summary:

> The city thus appeared as the direct effect of the need to reduce the indirect costs of production and costs of circulation and consumption in order to *speed up the rate of rotation of capital* and thus increase the period during which capital was used productively [Italics added]

In pursuing their search for profits and responding to the accumulation imperatives of the capitalist mode of production, capitalists require the assistance of fixed capital investments, directly in the form of machinery and machine-tools and indirectly in the form of the built environment. In elucidating the nature of the various components involved, Harvey (1978) draws a distinction between the built environment for production and the built environment for consumption.* The built environment for production includes those elements indirectly involved in the production process—factories, warehouses, canals, railways and the like; the built environment for consumption refers to those elements aiding and abetting the consumption process—market facilities, shops, trading systems etc. The categories are not mutually exclusive; transport facilities, for example, appear in both. To perform effectively these elements must retain their use values over time through several production and consumption cycles, and so the quality and maintenance of these individual elements are important in contributing to their overall efficiency. Equally important is their mix, the way the individual

---

* In considering these issues Harvey, following Marx, uses a more precise definition of fixed capital, reserving its use for those structures that yield 'value' in the process of production: those elements of the built environment, such as shops and houses, that are not involved in the production process are regarded as part of the consumption fund (see Marx, 1971 edit., chapter 10; Harvey, 1978, 106).

elements, produced as they are under different stimuli, converge to create a particular spatial configuration of the built environment. Here, in this configuration, the two roles of the built environment, identified above, combine; the individual elements converge to act as commodities embodying exchange value and use value. The 'social' consequences of the construction decisions of builders, contractors and property speculators are reflected in the spatial configuration of the built environment as it is manifest both in the internal morphology of individual cities and in the organization of city-systems.

The effectiveness of the built environment in contributing to the reduction in the rotation time of capital in nineteenth-century Scottish cities and city systems is unclear, since little or no work on Scotland has adopted this particular perspective. Indeed published work generally on nineteenth-century urban morphology and city systems in Scotland, other than fairly straightforward but nevertheless useful historical descriptions, is sparse; Whitehand's (1972) study of building cycles and urban growth in Glasgow is one of the few. However, some of these themes can be taken up in the context of an examination of the internal structure of Scottish cities in the nineteenth century; this is the subject of the final section of this chapter.

URBANIZATION AND CLASS STRUGGLE

One side of the picture exhibits the elements of prosperity in unprecedented vigour amongst us, the other points not less clearly to a still more alarming augmentation of misery, pauperism and crime. This has long been familiar to all persons practically acquainted with the condition of the working class, especially in our great manufacturing towns, or seats of commercial industry (Sir Archibald Alison, 1841).

Poverty, crime and misery were probably no less prevalent in mid eighteenth century Scotland than in the mid nineteentch century, but perhaps they were less immediately apparent in the smaller, more compact cities and the scattered, isolated rural communities of those earlier years. Certainly they were of a type and order which had characterized the country during numerous preceding decades and despite a gradually expanding economy were not yet heightened by contrast with new and conspicuous manifestations of economic prosperity. The intervening century, however, witnessed a burgeoning of cities and towns associated with industrial growth and population increases and thus for many rural poverty was exchanged for urban poverty, and the cumulative effects were seen in the emergence of the festering urban slums.

The concern of the author of the *Blackwood's Magazine* article quoted above was fired ostensibly by moral and religious sentiments, but the apparent contradiction to which he referred, and subsequently examined in the context of mid nineteenth century Glasgow, was also of immediate and growing revelance to capitalists intent on maintaining the momentum of accumulation. Indeed legislation designed to deal with its consequences was not even devised until the material interests of the bourgeoisie, threatened by uncontrolled slum growth and proletarian militancy coalesced with this moral concern.

Until at least the 1820s the prevalent attitudes of the ruling classes towards slum formation, as the most obvious manifestation of the undesirable consequences of industrial capitalism, varied from one of 'sentimental philanthropy' (Saunders, 1950, 163) to one of disdain and neglect. These attitudes, for the most part, were founded on a belief that the victims to a large extent were the cause of their own circumstances and that the 'hidden hand' of *laissez-faire* would eventually provide a cure-all, given a degree of self-improvement motivation from the slum dwellers themselves. The transition from these individualistic, moral and essentially optimistic views to the more interventionist and pessimistic stance of mid-century was brought about by a succession of epidemics, economic recession, unemployment, and the real threat of public disorder. Legislatively the potential of the interventionist position was not consolidated until the Reform Acts of the 1830s effectively removed the old town oligarchies from power and replaced them with elected councils. This battle, a reflection of related conflicts at national level between the rising bourgeoisie and the landed aristocracy, was enjoined quite early in the century. In 1816, for example, in an unsuccessful attempt to rid Dundee of the deadening hand of the incumbent oligarchy personified in Alexander Riddoch's 40-year rule, several of the town's emerging industrialists, Baxter, Low, Edwards and Gilroy, signed a parliamentary petition for better representation on the town council (Lythe, 1979, 72). Saunders (1980, 170) further illustrates this point with examples of how the interventionist potential of the Dean of Guild's Court was effectively shackled by a very literal interpretation of the law.

In examining the post-1830s urban reform legislation and activity, an immediate contrast appears between the relative success of those measures designed to deal with sanitation and public health and those directed at housing conditions. The Burgh Acts of 1833 and 1834 established in Scotland a standardized constitution which provided for a £10 property franchise and the election of town councils without, however, extending the council's jurisdiction. They also allowed for the creation in Royal and Barony Burghs of police commissions and hence extended a situation which had been established by local acts in several individual towns over the past decades—as early as 1773 in Greenock, from 1800 in Glasgow, 1820 in Peterhead, and 1829 in Aberdeen (McKichan, 1978, 75). In 1847 commissions were extended to parliamentary burghs, in 1850 to settlements of over 1200 and over 700 in 1862 (Adams, 1978,

131). It was largely through the agency of these police commissions, which had the right to levy rates for the purpose, that sewage, drainage and paving operations were completed in Scottish urban centres. Perhaps the best indication of these developments was the provision of a regular and clean supply of water, first to Glasgow via Loch Katrine in 1859 and belatedly to Dundee from the Sidlaws in 1875. However, the implementation of the various types of legislation and the provision of these various elements of the built environment were extremely variable. Thus Stirling, because of the reluctance of the town's wealthier inhabitants to accept assessment for the levy, refused to establish a police commission until the town was threatened with compulsory annexation by the County Commission following the 1875 Police Act (McKichan, 1978).

Although it was to take until after the First World War for dramatic improvements to become apparent, the level of success of the sanitation measures of the second half of the nineteenth century in Scotland was indicated by the general drop in the death rate from the 1870s, especially in relation to communicable diseases (Flinn, 1977, 402). However urban death rates still exceeded rural death rates, largely because of the persistence of tuberculosis and respiratory diseases in the large industrial cities, which according to Flinn (1977, 412) could be attributed to 'overcrowding and the poisoned, smoke-laden atmosphere' (see also Lennox, 1928).

The persistence of high mortality in the urban centres of late nineteenth and early twentieth century Scotland is indicative of the relative ineffectiveness of the post-1850 legislation in dealing adequately with the problem of slum formation, particularly as it was manifest in airless, damp and overcrowded dwellings. Although some overall improvement is evident, for example the reduction in the proportion of the country's population living in one- and two-room dwellings from around 70% in 1861 to 50% in 1911, it is clear from the report of the Royal Commission on Housing in Scotland (1917) that many of the appalling conditions of working-class housing and its attendant problems identified by Chadwick some 70 years earlier persisted. In 1911, 56% of all one-room dwellings had more than two persons in each room; for two- and three-room dwellings the respective figures were 47% and 24%, proportions which were much the same as 50 years earlier (Lenman, 1977, 204; Campbell, 1968, 223).

National legislation motivated by 'a passion for sanitary purity' (Adams, 1978, 159) progressed from the Dwelling Houses and Nuisances Removal Acts of 1855 which encouraged local authorities to become involved in environmental improvement, through the 1875 Artisans and Labourers Dwellings Improvement Act, whereby municipalities assumed the right to demolish nuisance areas, to the 1890 Housing of The Working Classes Act, which encouraged public housing construction. All Scotland's major urban centres initiated 'improvement' schemes under their own local acts or under the umbrella of this national legislation. Glasgow with its 1866 Improvement Trust anticipated national events by several years; Edinburgh soon followed with a similar if less ambitious scheme in 1867, Dundee in 1871, Greenock in 1877 and Aberdeen in 1884. The focus of all these schemes was demolition, and relatively little rebuilding took place even after the 1890 Act and its extensions in 1903 and 1909. By 1913 Glasgow had built just over 2000 houses, Edinburgh about 600 and Aberdeen 130; Dundee had yet to contribute.

The bulk of the housing infrastructure in Scottish cities prior to the First World War was produced by the private enterprise of the construction industry. The provision of worker accommodation by employers, a feature of the early period of industrialization, had largely ceased by the 1840s (Gauldie, 1979, 21) and in any case contributed very little to the residential built environment of Scottish cities. In Dundee, for example, there is only one instance of large-scale building by a textile firm for its workers, that of Malcolm Ogilvie during the 1890s (Lenman *et al.*, 1969, 86). Similarly, the additions to the housing stock in the second half of the nineteenth century from the various 'self-help' housing and building societies, which operated largely under middle class patronage, were relatively small (Tarn, 1969).

The waning interest of companies in the direct provision of workers' housing from mid-century reflected their decreasing need to attract labour with housing incentives as factory disciplines became more widely accepted and tolerated. It also reflected the creation of a substantial reserve army of labour in the industrial towns as Highland and Irish immigration supplemented a labour force hitherto dependent on natural increase and localized rural–urban migration. In these circumstances industrialists were happy to surrender working class housing to the free market: it relieved them of a costly burden and helped lower the social reproduction costs of labour as workers crowded together in substandard dwellings. In addition this transference of workers' housing to the market aided the mobility of labour over time and allowed an 'optimum' location of residence by families whose members had different employers. Further, as Walker (1978, 190) and Gauldie (1979, 21) both stress, the process served an ideological purpose by interposing an intermediary, the landlord, between capital and labour.

The living conditions of the working class could never be left entirely to the vagaries of market forces. The interventionist sanitation measures of the second half of the nineteenth century were, notwithstanding a degree of genuine philanthropy, motivated by self-interest and the necessity to ensure the reproduction of an individually efficient but socially quiescent labour force. The cholera epidemics that raged through Britain and every Scottish city from the 1830s to the 1860s, epidemics which did not respect class boundaries, and the rumblings of social discontent associated with the Chartist and Anti-Corn Law agitation of the 1830s and 1840s were the immediate incentives for intervention. The perceived potential for 'sedition' in the crime-ridden slums, heightened by the 1848 rebellions in Europe, together with growing workplace militancy in the following decades (see Young, 1979) provided further encouragement for intervention. The implementation of the sanitation legislation in Scotland under the auspices of Police Acts is illustrative of these twin concerns of the capitalist class.

The limitation of direct intervention in the housing market of late nineteenth century Scotland to demolition and 'ticketing' of tenements with the legal number of occupants is also explicable in these terms when it is seen as motivated principally by a desire to eliminate potential or actual pockets of crime and disease (MacLaren, 1979, 5). The low levels of municipal house building in late nineteenth century Scotland* certainly reflected financial constraints and had much to do with the persistence of attitudes associated with the 'principle of community' and 'self-help' first publicized from the pulpit of Thomas Chalmers in the early decades of the century (Lenman, 1977, 158; Harvey, 1978, 128). Additionally, however, and perhaps most importantly in circumstances where the revolutionary threat of the working class so poignantly perceived in mid-century seemed to have abated (Gauldie, 1974, 1979), the maintenance of the conditions for capital accumulation did not yet necessitate a high level of intervention in this area. Indeed to a large extent the free operation of the market served these purposes admirably: it produced a spatial pattern of residential differentiation which, on the one hand, allowed the bourgeoisie and the middle classes to distance themselves from the nastiness of the slums and, on the other, facilitated a division of the working class between the relatively affluent and the poverty stricken. If the first trend tended to heighten class consciousness, the second dissipated it, at least among the working class.

These tendencies towards residential segregation on class lines were apparent from as early as the middle and later years of the eighteenth century and most conspicuously in the creation of Edinburgh's New Town and the initial emergence of Glasgow's West End in the Blythswood estate development. The decentralization of the wealthier groups gained momentum through the course of the nineteenth century, aided and abetted by various transport developments, especially that of the railways. Richardson, for example, notes the incorporation of the outlying suburbs of Corstorphine, Slateford, Joppa and Barnton following the mid-century development of railways in Edinburgh (Richardson et al., 1975, chapter 1). The later provision of cut price 'villa tickets' on both the Glasgow and Edinburgh railways actively encouraged suburban construction on railway land (Checkland, 1964; Simpson, 1977).

---

* By 1876, after 10 years of operation, Glasgow's Improvement Trust had displaced some 25 375 people, but had built only 1646 replacement houses (Gauldie, 1974, 86).

These kinds of movement, apparent in all of Scotland's larger towns (see Walker, 1979; McKenzie, 1953), which Harvey (1978, 113) dismisses as 'icing on top of a cake' certainly had elements of conspicuous consumption about them, but they were also extremely important in determining the pattern of town growth and in freeing the central area of towns for use by increasingly concentrated and growing industries and their workforces. In these locations, at least in the early industrial cities, backward and forward linkages between different industries and between industry generally and markets, raw materials, labour and transport were facilitated, the agglomeration economies contributing to an overall reduction in the rotation time of capital.

The adjustment of the built environment inherited from pre-industrial periods to the need of the industrial era was characterized by costly failures, numerous bankruptcies and for many, of course, the creation of appalling living environments. The failure, towards the end of the eighteenth century, of David Laurie's Gorbals estate in Glasgow as a high-class residential area, due to the penetration of incompatible industrial activities, is an early illustration of these features (Kellett, 1961; Best, 1973), but the creation of the industrial slum was to be the most enduring example of uneven development in this context.

The competition in the central area of industrializing cities between working class residential needs and the land use needs of industry and transport, together with the feuing system of land tenure (Saunders, 1950, 164–8) contributed to the prevalence of high land values and encouraged the construction of high-density backland tenements which formed the basis of urban slums in Scottish cities. The building of explicitly working class tenements in the 'surplus capital' construction booms of the late nineteenth century provided some relief for the more affluent workers (Gray, 1979; Melling, 1980, chapter 1), but these decades were also characterized by many shoddily built structures that did little to relieve the problems of slum life. The presence towards the end of the century of large numbers of unoccupied housing in most Scottish cities (Adams, 1978, chapter 8) was seen by contemporaries as justification for the pursual of the 'self-improvement' approach to the housing problem and has even been taken by some present-day commentators as an indication of an emerging solution (Walker, 1979). However, as Gauldie (1974) more realistically indicates, these unoccupied dwellings were symptomatic of the overall problem in that their rents were too high and they were often wrongly located to benefit those in real need.

In the economic conditions of the nineteenth century, Scotland's housing market was structurally incapable of providing a solution to the slum problem. In the provision of other elements in the built environment the exchange value interests of the construction industry could be realized in the provision of 'social' use values. Investment in working-class housing, however, was at best risky and at worst just not profitable. In circumstances of muted working class consciousness the pressures on capital to relieve the stresses of slum life were minimal and were readily absorbed in token public housing schemes and in the patronage of 'self-help' and cooperative ventures such as the Dundee Workingmen's Houses Association and the Edinburgh Workingmen's Building Association.

The closing years of the nineteenth and the early part of the twentieth centuries saw a growing working class militancy in relation to the housing question with, for example, the founding of the Workingmen's National Housing Conference in 1898, the agitation of the Scottish Miners' Federation in 1909, and most dramatically the 1915 Glasgow rent strike (Damer, 1980). The permissive legislation of the 1890, 1903 and 1909 Housing Acts was the initial response to these pressures, but it was not until central government subsidies were made available to local authorities in the changed circumstances of the interwar years that state intervention in the housing market was assured. The 1919 Addison Act initiated this process, and its implementation was to bring about a profound transformation of the internal structures of Scottish cities.

CONCLUSION

The legacy of the nineteenth century remains with Scottish cities to the present day, but there have also been profound changes in these cities—in their economic base and in their spatial structures. The externally orientated manufacturing industries, the bastion of nineteenth century expansion, have experienced significant contraction. Light engineering, service industries, and oil, particularly since World War Two, have come to dominate the Scottish economy (see Chapter 8). The effects on the configuration of the urban system have been small, with the stagnation of the larger centres, the expansion of some middle-order settlements and the creation of New Towns, through state intervention, being the most notable. The internal structures of towns and cities—especially of the largest—have been more profoundly altered; again the intervention of the state played a significant part. Decentralization of industry and its work force has been paralleled by the renewal of inner areas and the burgeoning of retail and commercial facilities. The nineteenth-century *laissez-faire* economy, eroded in the first decades of the twentieth century, has slowly yielded to state regulation and control. But while this intervention was designed to cushion the effects of economic change and deal with the legacy—especially the social legacy—of the nineteenth century, the structures it has created have themselves become part of a new problem, manifest in soaring unemployment, de-industrialization and new slum creation.

REFERENCES

Abrams, P. (1978). Towns and economic growth: some theories and problems. *In* 'Towns and Economic Growth.' (P. Abrams and W. A. Wrigley, ed.) pp. 1–46. Cambridge University Press, Cambridge.

Adams, I. (1978). 'The Making of Urban Scotland.' Croom Helm, London.

Alison, Sir Alexander (1841). Social and moral condition of the manufacturing districts in Scotland. *Blackwood's Magazine* 50, 659–673.

Anderson, J. (1975). 'The Political Economy of Urbanism.' Unpublished paper, Architectural Association, London.

Anderson, J. (1977). Geography, political economy and the State. *Journal of St Andrews Geographers Spec. Pub.* 2, 34–46.

Best, G. F. A. (1973). Another part of the island, *In* 'Victorian Cities.' (H. J. Dyos and M. Wolff, ed.) Vol. II, pp. 388–411. Routledge and Kegan Paul, London.

Butt, J. (1971). Working class housing in Glasgow, 1851–1914. *In* 'The History of Working Class Housing.' (S. D. Chapman, ed.) pp. 57–92. David and Charles, Newton Abbot.

Campbell, R. H. and Dow, J. B. A. (1968). 'Source Book of Scottish Economic and Social History.' Basil Blackwell, Oxford.

Cairncross, A. K. (1953). 'Home and Foreign Investment, 1870–1913.' Cambridge University Press, Cambridge.

Checkland, S. G. (1964). The British industrial city as history: the Glasgow case. *Urban Studies* 1 (1), 34–53.

Cook, A. (ed.) (1977). 'Stanley.' Department of Extra-Mural Education, University of Dundee.

Crouzet, F. (1972). 'Capital Formation in the Industrial Revolution.' Methuen, London.

Damer, S. (1980). State, class and housing: Glasgow 1885–1919. *In* 'Housing, Social Policy and the State.' (J. Melling, ed.) pp. 73–111. Croom Helm, London.

Deane, P. and Cole, W. A. (1967). 'British Economic Growth, 1688–1959: Trends and Structure.' Cambridge University Press, Cambridge.

Dickson, T. (1980). The making of a class society. *In* 'Scottish Capitalism.' (T. Dickson, ed.) pp. 151–286. Lawrence and Wishart, London.

Elliot, B. and McCrone, D. (1980). Urban development in Edinburgh: in contribution to the political economy of place. *Scottish Journal of Sociology* 4 (1), 1–26.

Flinn, M. (1977). 'Scottish Population History.' Cambridge University Press, Cambridge.

Gauldie, E. (1974). 'Cruel Habitations.' Allen and Unwin, London.

Gauldie, E. (1979). The middle class and working class housing in the nineteenth century. *In* 'Social Class in Scotland: Past and Present.' (A. A. MacLaren, ed.) pp. 12–35. John Donald, Edinburgh.

Gordon, G. (1977). Urban Scotland. *In* 'A Geography of Scotland.' (K. J. Lea, G. Gordon, I. R. Bowler, ed.) pp. 199–238. David and Charles, Newton Abbott.

Gotlieb, M. (1976). 'Long Swings in Urban Development.' National Bureau for Economic Resources, New York.

Gray, R. Q. (1979). Thrift and working class mobility in Victorian Edinburgh. *In* 'Social Class in Scotland: Past and Present.' (A. A. MacLaren, ed.) pp. 104–135. John Donald, Edinburgh.

Harvey, D. (1975). The political economy of urbanisation in advanced capitalist societies: the case of the United States. *In* 'The Social Economy of Cities.' (G. Gappett and H. Rose, eds.) pp. 119–163. Sage, London.

Harvey, D. (1978). The urban process under capitalism. *International Journal of Urban and Regional Research* **2** (10), 101–130.

Harvey, D. (1978a). Labor, capital, and class struggle around the built environment in advanced capitalist societies. *In* 'Urbanization and Conflict in Market Societies.' (K. Cox, ed.) pp. 9–37. Methuen, London.

Kellet, J. R. (1961). Property speculators and the building of Glasgow, 1730–1830. *Scottish Journal of Political Economy* **8**, 211–232.

Kemp, T. (1978). 'Historical Patterns of Industrialization.' Longman, London.

Lea, K. J. (1977). Introduction. *In* 'A Geography of Scotland.' (K. J. Lea, G. Gordon, and I. R. Bowler, ed.) pp. 28–49. David and Charles, London.

Lenman, B. (1977). 'An Economic History of Modern Scotland.' Batsford, London.

Lennox, D. (1928). 'Working Class Life in Dundee: 1878–1903.' Unpublished MS. St. Andrews University.

Lewis, J. Parry (1965). 'Building Cycles and Britain's Growth.' Macmillan, London.

Lockhart, D. (1980). The planned village. *In* 'The Making of the Scottish Countryside.' (M. L. Parry and T. R. Slater, ed.) pp. 249–270. Croom Helm, London.

Lojkine, J. (1976). Contribution to a Marxist theory of capitalist urbanisation. *In* 'Urban Sociology: Critical Essays.' (C. G. Pickvance, ed.) pp. 119–146. Methuen, London.

Lythe, S. G. E. (1979). The historical background. *In* 'The City of Dundee.' (J. M. Jackson, ed.) pp. 69–89. Herald Press, Arbroath.

Lythe, S. G. E. and Butt, J. (1976). 'An Economic History of Scotland, 1100–1939.' Blackie, Edinburgh.

MacDowell, S. (1978). 'Trade Adjustment and the British Jute Industry: a Case Study.' The Fraser of Allender Institute, University of Strathclyde, Glasgow.

MacKenzie, H. (1953). History. *In* 'The City of Aberdeen.' (H. MacKenzie, ed.) pp. 35–90. Oliver and Boyd, Glasgow.

McKichan, F. (1978). A burgh's response to the problems of urban growth: Stirling, 1780–1880. *Scottish History Review* **57**, 163, 68–86.

MacLaren, A. A. (1979). Introduction: an open society. *In* 'Social Class in Scotland: Past and Present.' (A. A. MacLaren, ed.) pp. 1–11. John Donald, Edinburgh.

Mandel, E. (1975). 'Late Capitalism.' Verso, London.

Marx, K. (1971, edit.). 'Capital.' Progress Publishers, Moscow.

Melling, J. (1980). Introduction. *In* 'Housing, Social Policy and the State.' (J. Melling, ed.) pp. 9–38. Croom Helm, London.

Pollard, S. (1964). Fixed capital in the industrial revolution in Britain. *Journal of Economic History* **24** (3). Reprinted in Crouzet (1972), pp. 143–161.

Richardson, H. W., Vipond, J., and Furbey, R. (1975). 'Housing and Urban Spatial Structure.' Saxon House, London.

Royal Commission on Housing in Scotland (1917). 'Report on the housing of the industrial population of Scotland, rural and urban.' HMSO, London.

Saunders, L. J. (1950). 'Scottish Democracy.' Oliver and Boyd, London.

Simpson, M. A. (1977). The West End of Glasgow, 1830–1914. *In* 'Middle Class Housing in Britain.' (M. A. Simpson and T. H. Lloyd, ed.) pp. 44–85. David and Charles, London.

Slaven, A. (1975). "The Development of the West of Scotland, 1750–1960". Routledge and Kegan Paul, London.

Smout, T. C. (1969). 'A History of the Scottish People, 1560–1830.' Collins, London.

Smout, T. C. (1980). Centre and periphery in history with some thoughts on Scotland as a case study. *Journal of Common Market Studies* **18** (3), 256–271.

Tarn, J. N. (1969). 'Working Class Housing in 19th Century Britain.' Architectural Association, London.

Thomas, B. (1974). 'Migration and Economic Growth.' Cambridge University Press, Cambridge (2nd edit.).

Turnock, D. (1979). 'The New Scotland.' David and Charles, London.

Walker, D. (1979). The manmade landscape. *In* 'The City of Dundee.' (J. M. Jackson, ed.) pp. 36–49. Herald Press, Arbroath.

Walker, R. (1978). The transformation of urban structure in the nineteenth century and the beginnings of urbanisation. *In* 'Urbanization and Conflict in Market Societies.' (K. Cox, ed.) pp. 165–212. Methuen, London.

Weber, A. (1899). 'The Growth of Cities in the Nineteenth Century.' Columbia University, New York.

Whitehand, J. W. R. (1972). Building cycles and the spatial pattern of urban growth. *Transactions of the Institute of British Geographers* **56**, 39–56.

Whitehand, J. W. R. (1977). The basis for a historico-geographical theory of urban form. *Transactions of the Institute of British Geographers* N.S. **2** (3), 400–416.

Young, J. (1979). 'The Rousing of the Scottish Working Class.' Croom Helm, London.

Subject Index

269

Index of Places

135, 136, 137, 167, 174, 179, 217, 218, 219, 221, 222, 223, 232, 245
Esk, River, 129, 173
Eskdale, 51
Eskdalemuir (Borders), 52
Essex, 222
Ettrick Forest, 52

Falkirk (Central), 178, 230, 245
Fife, 32, 60, 63, 67, 74, 81, 113, 127, 130, 145, 156, 160, 175, 179, 225, 229, 247, 248
Flanders, 79
Forfar (Tayside), 245
Forres (Grampian), 81
Fort Augustus (Highland), 196
Fort William (Highland), 196, 203
Forteviot (Tayside), 32
Forth, Firth of, 5, 10, 25, 26, 30, 77, 78, 79, 89, 111, 122, 124, 126, 129, 130, 147, 151, 168, 169
Forth, River, 7
Foyers (Highland), 206
France, 93, 135
Fraserburgh (Grampian), 105, 132, 228

Galashiels (Borders), 167, 171, 176
Galloway, 27, 28, 29, 38, 79, 81, 122, 126, 129, 135, 171, 225, 228, 245
Garioch (Grampian), 129
Germany, 178, 179
Glasgow, 76, 84, 85, 87, 88, 89, 99, 100, 106, 108, 122, 129, 130, 131, 132, 159, 167, 168, 169, 171, 172, 173, 175, 176, 177, 178, 185, 229, 242, 244, 245, 252, 255, 256, 257, 258, 259, 260, 261, 262, 263, 264
Glencoe, 195, 198
Glen Dessary (Highland), 198
Glen Falloch (Strathclyde), 52
Glenforsa (Strathclyde), 221
Glengarnock (Strathclyde), 178, 183
Glen Livet (Highland), 114
Glen Moriston (Highland), 169

Glen Orchy (Strathclyde), 50
Glenrothes (Fife), 185
Golspie (Highland), 203
Grampian Region, 191, 196, 200, 208
Grangemouth (Central), 187, 229, 230
Grangepans (Central), 132
Great Cumbrae, 113
Great Glen, 194, 205
Greenland, 105
Greenock (Strathclyde), 106, 130, 132, 173, 185, 245, 259, 261

Haddington (Lothian), 87, 136, 245
Hamilton (Strathclyde), 245
Harris, 206
Hawick (Borders), 171, 176, 191, 244, 245
Hebrides, 8, 49, 125, 201, 203, 204
Helmsdale (Highland), 203
Highlands, 9, 29, 55, 58, 59, 63, 64, 66, 93, 95, 96, 97, 98, 99, 101, 102, 105, 106, 111, 113, 121, 122, 125, 127, 132, 134, 135, 159, 168, 178, 191–211, 221, 234, 236, 242, 245
Holyrood Abbey (Lothian), 77
Hownam (Borders), 26
Hunterston (Strathclyde), 183

Iceland, 46
Inchinnan (Strathclyde), 183
Innerleithen (Borders), 171
Inveresk (Lothian), 16
Inverness, 39, 76, 87, 99, 192, 203, 204, 205, 206, 245
Inverness-shire, 32, 57, 194, 197, 205
Iona, 30, 195
Ireland, 14, 27, 28, 30, 38, 39, 101, 102, 126, 159, 225, 244
Irvine (Strathclyde), 83, 129
Islay, 38, 53, 113, 194, 200
Isle of Man, 38

Jarlshof (Shetland), 39, 40, 42